DATA INFORMATION LITERACY

Librarians, Data, and the Education of a New Generation of Researchers

Purdue Information Literacy Handbooks

Sharon Weiner, Series Editor

DATA INFORMATION LITERACY

Librarians, Data, and the Education of a New Generation of Researchers

edited by Jake Carlson and Lisa R. Johnston

Purdue University Press, West Lafayette, Indiana

Library of Congress Cataloging-in-Publication Data

Data information literacy : librarians, data, and the education of a new generation of researchers / edited by Jake Carlson and Lisa R. Johnston.
    pages cm. — (Purdue information literacy handbooks)
  Includes bibliographical references and index.
  ISBN 978-1-55753-696-9 (pbk.) — ISBN 978-1-61249-351-0 (epdf) — ISBN 978-1-61249-352-7 (epub) 1. Academic libraries—Services to graduate students. 2. Academic libraries—Relations with faculty and curriculum—United States—Case studies. 3. Academic librarians—Effect of technological innovations on. 4. Information literacy—Study and teaching (Higher) 5. Electronic information resource literacy—Study and teaching (Higher) 6. Science—Data processing—Management. 7. Research—Data processing—Management. 8. Database management. 9. Cyberinfrastructure. 10. Digital preservation. I. Carlson, Jake, 1970– editor. II. Johnston, Lisa (Lisa R.), editor.
  Z711.92.G73D38 2015
  028.7071'1—dc23
                        2014030428

CONTENTS

FOREWORD

This book is the second in the Purdue Information Literacy Handbooks series. The book fulfills the purpose of the series, which is to promote evidence-based practice in teaching information literacy competencies through the lens of different academic disciplines. Information literacy implies the ability to find, manage, and use information in any format, and editors Carlson and Johnston apply it to the format of raw data. They coined the term *data information literacy* as an application of information literacy in the context of research.

Since much data is accessible on the Web now and federal agencies are encouraging reuse of data, rather than re-creating data sets, librarians have embraced the opportunity to apply the organization and management principles of library and information science to data.

Data Information Literacy: Librarians, Data, and the Education of a New Generation of Researchers is a timely work based on research funded by the Institute of Museum and Library Services. Carlson and Johnston included librarians who worked with different scientific disciplines in the Data Information Literacy (DIL) project to write for this publication. Through interviews, the voices of faculty and graduate students revealed the need for a more effective way to learn DIL competencies and integrate them into their practice. The DIL project revealed specific skill gaps that graduate students in the sciences and engineering have related to managing, publishing, and preserving data sets for research. Librarians developed and assessed tailored educational strategies for addressing these gaps in five settings.

Carlson and Johnston make a strong case for the role of librarians in teaching graduate students to manage, publish, and preserve data. They and the chapter authors give advice based on their experience for academic librarians to establish DIL programs at their institutions.

This handbook will have value for librarians and library administrators in colleges and universities in which students participate in faculty research projects. With it, they can develop and implement plans to address an important, unmet educational need. Although this book focuses on some of the science and engineering disciplines, those in the humanities and social sciences may be able to apply the methods used for identifying and addressing educational issues in their areas. This book will support library administrators who want their libraries to participate in the educational and research mission of their institutions. It will give practitioners guidance for developing such an effort.

Sharon Weiner, EdD, MLS
Series Editor
Professor and W. Wayne Booker Chair in Information Literacy, Purdue University Libraries
Vice President, National Forum on Information Literacy
August 2014

PREFACE

We did not set out to write a book on the subject of data information literacy. Our initial intent was to explore the educational needs of graduate students in working with data and to report our findings to the research library community. When we started our investigations in 2010, there was a dawning recognition among academic librarians that the rising expectations for researchers to manage, document, organize, disseminate, and preserve their data in ways that would contribute to the advancement of their fields would require novel educational initiatives and programs. More importantly, we recognized that this was an area where librarians could potentially make important contributions. At the time, there were only a few examples of educational programs that addressed issues relating to data management and curation and very little practical guidance on what content should be taught.

Our early investigation into articulating "data information literacy," or DIL as we came to call it, was tremendously helpful for us in better understanding the needs of faculty and students in this space. However, as the needs surrounding educational programming on data issues became more apparent, the more questions we had. Based on prior research by a Purdue University team the 12 DIL competencies helped us to see possibilities for developing educational programming, but what would our programming actually include, what pedagogies could be applied, and what would we as librarians be qualified to teach to researchers? In short, how could we apply the theoretical competencies for DIL in ways that would have a real-world impact on students? Thanks to the generous support of the Institute of Museum and Library Services, we had the opportunity to seek answers to these questions through developing the Data Information Literacy project.

This book contains descriptions of our work in carrying out the DIL project, but our goal in sharing our findings in this way goes far beyond simply reporting our experiences. We believe that DIL represents an opportunity to leverage the expertise, knowledge, and skill sets of librarians and apply them to an area of growing need. Fulfilling this need represents a potentially significant advancement for librarians in engaging in both the teaching and research missions of the academy. To further this goal, we share our findings and our experiences from a practical approach, in ways that will enable librarians and other information professionals to build on our work and to incorporate what we have learned into their own DIL programs as appropriate. It is our sincere hope that this book will serve not only as a resource to those who seek to develop DIL initiatives and programs at their institutions, but as a means to further a discussion on the direction of DIL and how it could take shape as a component of services offered by the library.

ACKNOWLEDGMENTS

The editors of this volume would like to recognize the commitment, hard work, and dedication of every DIL team member who participated on this project. Without the creativity and passion of these individuals in shaping and implementing the DIL project, as well as in writing up their experiences with their respective programs, this book would not be at all possible. Thank you Camille Andrews, Marianne Bracke, Michael Fosmire, Jon Jeffryes, Christopher C. Miller, Megan Sapp Nelson, Dean Walton, Brian Westra, and Sarah Wright for making this book and the DIL project a success. We also wish to thank the Institute of Museum and Library Services for their generous support in funding this project, Dr. Sharon Weiner for her thorough review and helpful suggestions, and the staff at the Purdue University Press, who have been a joy to work with in putting this book together. Finally, a special thank you to our trusted graduate assistant, Mason Nichols, who diligently tweeted our praises, caught and corrected our mistakes, and kept us on track through documenting our progress.

Jake Carlson
Lisa R. Johnston
August 2014

INTRODUCTION

Jake Carlson, University of Michigan
Lisa R. Johnston, University of Minnesota

> *"The data management skills that students need are many and they don't necessarily have them and they don't necessarily acquire them in the time of the project."*
>
> —Faculty member interviewed in the Data Information Literacy project

> *"Finally, I'm finding that by taking this class and doing these readings I'm becoming more aware of different data management services in my own field."*
>
> —Graduate student's evaluation of a Data Information Literacy course

We developed the Data Information Literacy (DIL) project to answer two overarching questions. First, what data management and curation skills are needed by future scientists to fulfill their professional responsibilities and take advantage of collaborative research opportunities in e-science and technology-driven research environments? Second, how can academic librarians apply their expertise in information retrieval, organization, dissemination, and preservation to teaching these competencies to students? By answering these questions our goals were to build a foundation in the library community for teaching DIL competencies, to teach students DIL competencies appropriate to their discipline, and to develop a robust process for librarians to develop DIL curricula and programming. We accomplished these goals through designing, constructing, implementing, and assessing programs to teach a selection of the DIL competencies to graduate students to bolster productivity in their current work and foster success in their eventual careers. In many ways, we successfully accomplished what we set out to do. Students and faculty who participated in our programs are better able to identify and articulate their data needs (for example, in constructing a National Science Foundation [NSF] data management plan [DMP]), and are now better equipped to address these needs. However, there is much more work to be done. In addition to increasing our collective capacity to develop and offer effective DIL programs, we need to raise awareness of larger issues and enable participants in our programs to contribute to their disciplines' efforts to address data management and curation issues at a community level. It is our hope that this next important step will be facilitated by the experiences, examples, and informative guide, included in this volume, so that academic librarians may continue this work at their own institutions.

to better share research data (Holdren, 2013), the lack of data curation services tailored for the "small sciences," the single investigators or small labs that typically comprise science practice at universities, has been identified as a barrier in making research data more widely available (Cragin, Palmer, Carlson, & Witt, 2010).

Academic libraries, which support the research and teaching activities of their home institutions, are recognizing the need to develop services and resources in support of the evolving demands of the information age. The curation of research data is an area that librarians are well suited to address, and a number of academic libraries are taking action to build capacity in this area (Soehner, Steeves, & Ward, 2010).

NEW ROLES FOR LIBRARIANS: DATA MANAGEMENT AND CURATION

Computationally intensive research, also known as *cyberinfrastructure* or *e-science*, depends on ready access to high-quality, well-described data sets. However, the capacity to manage and curate research data has not kept pace with the ability to produce them (Hey & Hey, 2006). In recognition of this gap, the NSF and other funding agencies are now mandating that every grant proposal must include a DMP (NSF, 2010). These mandates highlight the benefits of producing well-described data that can be shared, understood, and reused by others, but they generally offer little in the way of guidance or instruction on how to address the inherent issues and challenges researchers face in complying. Even with increasing expectations from funding agencies and research communities, such as the announcement by the White House for all federal funding agencies

AN UNMET NEED: EDUCATIONAL PROGRAMMING ON DATA

The NSF's (2007) *Cyberinfrastructure Vision for 21st Century Discovery* advocated that

> curricula must also be reinvented to exploit emerging cyberinfrastructure capabilities. The full engagement of students is vitally important since they are in a special position to inspire future students with the excitement and understanding of cyberinfrastructure-enabled scientific inquiry and learning. Ongoing attention must be paid to the education of the professionals who will support, deploy, develop, and design current and emerging cyberinfrastructure. (p. 38)

Despite the articulated need for educational initiatives focused on e-science, there has been little attention to ensuring that graduate students learn the skills required for the management, organization, access, reuse, and preservation of research data as a component of their educational program. Several institutions, including Indiana University and Rensselaer Polytechnic Institute, have introduced stand-alone courses to provide such an education (Indiana University Pervasive Technology Institute, 2010; TWC, n.d.). However, students may hesitate to enroll in courses listed outside of their discipline and may not gain a full understanding of the expectations, norms, and best practices of their discipline from such general courses.

A few information schools, including the University of North Carolina at Chapel Hill and the University of Illinois at Urbana-Champaign, developed programs to teach concepts and issues in data curation (GSLIS, 2010, 2011; Tibbo & Lee, 2010). These programs and workshops illuminate the potential roles of librarians in data curation and management and have done a lot to advance the field of librarianship. However, these courses are isolated from scientific activities and are generally intended to train not disciplinary specialists, but information professionals. Our approach in the DIL project has been to forge strong relationships with the disciplines through partnerships with science faculty and graduate students through in-depth interactions to develop a rich understanding of their disciplinary and real-world needs. Thus, the main difference between the programming done by information schools and the DIL project is our focus on the frontline researcher and student, making sure that our content is relevant, useful to their work, and delivered successfully. Data curation curricula at information schools center on production of information while the Association of College and Research Libraries' (ACRL's) 2000 information literacy standards focus on the consumption of information. But science research faculty and students need a curriculum that balances both perspectives and concentrates on specific, practical skills needed for working with data.

REIMAGINING AN EXISTING ROLE OF LIBRARIANS: TEACHING INFORMATION LITERACY SKILLS

Many academic librarians have embraced their role as educators through information literacy programs at their institutions. Information literacy centers on teaching students "the ability to recognize when information is needed and have the ability to locate, evaluate and use effectively the needed information" (ACRL, 2000, p. 2), with the ultimate goal of enabling lifelong learning. Ideally information literacy programs are targeted to the specific context of the intended audience, are in-depth in their coverage, and are integrated within courses and curricula.

The DIL project was structured on a belief that there is great potential to match existing librarians' expertise in information literacy with support for e-science. By combining the use-based standards of information literacy with skill development across the whole data life cycle, we sought to support the practices of science by developing a DIL curriculum and providing training for higher education students and researchers. We increased capacity and enabled comparative work by involving several institutions in developing

Our approach in the DIL project has been to forge strong relationships with the disciplines through partnerships with science faculty and graduate students through in-depth interactions to develop a rich understanding of their disciplinary and real-world needs.

instruction in DIL. Finally, we grounded the instruction in the real-world needs as articulated by active researchers and their students from a variety of fields.

THE FRAMEWORK FOR THIS BOOK

This book is divided into three parts. Part I, "Making the Case for Data Information Literacy," follows the history and evolution of this emerging field in academic librarianship and in the DIL project specifically. Part II, "Data Information Literacy Disciplinary Case Studies" describes five DIL disciplinary case studies that cover a range of student and faculty needs with distinct approaches to library-based education in DIL. Part III, "Moving Forward," includes a robust guide for practicing librarians seeking to build DIL programs and an exploration of how DIL may develop in the future.

Part I: Making the Case for Data Information Literacy

We begin by looking closely at the research that led to the development of DIL as a concept. In Chapter 1, we reprint an article that first articulated the 12 DIL competencies (Carlson, Fosmire, Miller, & Sapp Nelson, 2011). The research behind the development of the 12 DIL competencies is explained, and a brief comparison is performed between DIL and information literacy, as defined by the 2000 ACRL standards.

Chapter 2 provides a description of the Institute of Museum and Library Services–funded DIL project, which ran from 2011 to 2014, and applies the 12 DIL competencies in practice. This chapter includes our thinking and approaches toward engaging researchers and students with the 12 competencies, a review of the literature on a variety of educational approaches to teaching data management and

curation to students, and an articulation of our key assumptions in forming the DIL project.

Chapter 3 contains an in-depth analysis of each of the 12 DIL competencies from the perspective of our faculty partners in the DIL project and some of their graduate students. Here we compared and analyzed the qualitative aspects of the interviews we conducted to gain a better overall understanding of their needs. We compared the responses from faculty and graduate students for each of the competencies and discuss the differences between them. As with this introduction, portions of Chapters 2 and 3 originally appeared in a 2013 issue of the *International Journal of Digital Curation*.

Part II: Data Information Literacy Disciplinary Case Studies

This section of the book includes the DIL case studies that resulted from the work of the five faculty-librarian partnerships in the DIL project. The method of case studies was chosen to provide a disciplinary look at the needs of students and faculty in the DIL competencies. We selected case studies as our research approach as they emphasize gathering individual perceptions through personal interactions for analysis (Blatter, 2008). Each of the five teams defined learning outcomes and developed pedagogies for teaching and evaluating their students' learning on the basis of the particular needs identified in the interviews. The five approaches explored DIL training in a variety of settings while remaining grounded in disciplinary and local needs. In these case studies, each team detailed how they developed their DIL program, the educational interventions they employed, the results of the assessments they conducted, and their recommendations for future iterations of their program.

Chapter 4 reports on the experiences of Cornell University in developing a 6-week, for-credit course for graduate students in the Department of Natural Resources. This case study involves a research lab that collects a variety of different data pertaining to fishing and water quality over a number of years, emphasizing the crucial need for data curation and maintenance over the extended life span of the data. Because these longitudinal data cannot be reproduced, acquiring the skills necessary to work with databases and to handle data entry was described as essential. Interventions took place in a classroom setting through a spring 2013 semester one-credit course entitled Managing Data to Facilitate Your Research taught by this DIL team.

Chapter 5 presents how the Carlson and Sapp Nelson DIL team from Purdue University worked with an engineering service-learning center to develop an approach to teach students how to document software code and project work. This team formed a collaboration with the Engineering Projects in Community Service (EPICS) center that provided undergraduate students practical experience through applying their engineering skills to assist local community organizations. Many of the service projects involved developing and delivering software code as a component of the completed project. This chapter details the DIL team's embedded librarian approach of working with the teaching assistants (TAs) to develop tools and resources to teach undergraduate students data management skills as a part of their EPICS experience. And it reveals significant concerns about students' organization and documentation skills. Lack of organization and documentation presents a barrier to (a) successfully transferring code to new students who will continue its development, (b) delivering code and other project outputs to the community client, and (c) the center administration's ability to understand and evaluate the impact on student learning. By integrating themselves into existing structures to enable close collaborations, the team developed short

skill sessions to deliver instruction to team leaders, crafted a rubric for measuring the quality of documenting code and other data, served as critics in student design reviews, and attended student lab sessions to observe and consult on student work.

Chapter 6 describes the work done by the Bracke and Fosmire DIL team at Purdue to teach metadata and other DIL competencies to graduate students in an agricultural and biological engineering lab through a series of workshops. An important aspect of the research process for the students is comparing observed data collected in the field to simulation data generated by an array of hydrologic models. Although the faculty researcher had created formal policies on data management practices for his lab, this case study demonstrated that students' adherence to these guidelines was limited at best. Similar patterns arose in discussions concerning the quality of metadata. This case study addressed a situation in which students are at least somewhat aware of the need to manage their data; however, they did not address this need effectively in practice. This DIL team worked with the faculty to implement the lab policies in a more structured fashion. Their educational program centered on creating a checklist to serve as a means of comparing individual practice against the recommended procedures and to promote a smooth transition of the data from student to faculty upon the student's graduation. In support of propagating the checklist, this DIL team offered three workshops addressing core skills in data management, metadata and data continuity, and reuse.

Chapter 7 describes the work from the University of Minnesota team to design and implement a hybrid course to teach DIL competencies to graduate students in civil engineering. Students collected various types of data—primarily from sensors placed on active bridges—to study factors which may lead to bridges being classified as unsound. The faculty researcher expressed concern over his students' abilities to understand and track issues affecting the quality of the data, the transfer of data from their custody to the custody of the lab upon graduation, and the steps necessary to maintain the value and utility of the data over time. To respond to these needs, the DIL team developed an online e-learning course composed of seven modules with additional readings and links. The course was self-paced, allowing students to complete it outside of their formal course work and research activity, and included an in-person workshop session. After completing the course, student outcomes included a written DMP for creating, documenting, sharing, and preserving their data.

Chapter 8 focuses on the work of the University of Oregon DIL team and how they made the most of a limited window of opportunity for teaching crucial data management skills. The DIL team in this case study developed a one-shot session to address the needs of graduate students who were wrapping up a grant-funded project. While the research team shared field equipment manuals and some standard operating procedures via their internal project website, they did not have written data management guidelines. Their practices were promulgated through the experiences team members brought to the project, or, through team discussions and other informal methods. This DIL team assigned independent readings followed by a discussion-based instruction session during a regularly scheduled research team meeting. The topics of the session included lab notebooks and note taking, data backup and storage, file management, data repositories, metadata, and links to tools and further information.

Part III: Moving Forward

The third portion of the book leverages the experiences, efforts, and findings of the DIL project toward advancing the capacity of librarians to design and implement their own programs and describe an agenda for further research and exploration in DIL.

Chapter 9 provides a guide for developing DIL programs based on a distillation of the experiences of the five project teams. To develop this guide, each of the project teams read and critiqued the case study reports produced by the other project teams. These case studies collectively present patterns and commonalities across the five DIL programs which were used as the basis for the guide.

Chapter 10 revisits our findings on the 12 DIL competencies and suggests areas for further research in developing each of them. Sapp Nelson analyzed the eight faculty interviews conducted for the DIL project, with a particular focus on the skills or components of a DIL competency that were identified by the researcher beyond the descriptions that we presented to them. Her findings provide additional insight into faculty perspectives on educating graduate students about data management and curation issues. This is a reminder that our understanding of DIL competencies is evolving.

Finally, Chapter 11 examines the questions and areas of exploration for furthering the development of DIL as a role for librarians. Carlson draws from two sources of information in charting a course for the growth of DIL programs and communities of practice. The first is the revision of ACRL's information literacy standards. ACRL is signaling a need to move beyond the checklist-of-skills approach that characterized the application of the 2000 standards (ACRL, 2012). There are indications that the new framework will center on an understanding of the environment and context in which learning takes place, including the experiences of the students themselves, and in understanding information-related concepts that students must acquire before they can develop expertise in their field of study. Many of the ideas and approaches articulated in the framework drafts echo the key assumptions of the DIL project and inform new directions for developing DIL.

The second source of information for charting future directions in DIL was our Data Information Literacy Symposium. The DIL teams held a 2-day symposium in 2013 at Purdue University. The intent of the symposium was to explore roles for practicing librarians in teaching competencies in data management and curation and to plant seeds of a community of practice on this topic. More than 80 librarians registered for this event, and we reached capacity within 2 days after opening registration. We disseminated our findings to attendees for their review, and this provoked a great deal of thoughtful discussion. Each of the DIL teams presented their work and shared their experiences through presentations, discussions, and hands-on exercises. The symposium concluded with an articulation of ideas for future directions for further developing roles for librarians in delivering DIL programs. These articulations inform a community-driven map for future research and directions in DIL. Video and materials from the DIL Symposium are available at http://docs.lib.purdue.edu/dilsymposium.

CONCLUSION

This book articulates an emerging area of opportunity for librarians and other information professionals developing programs that introduce students in higher education to the knowledge and skills needed to work with research data. By viewing information literacy and data services as synergistic activities, we seek to connect the progress made and the lessons learned in each service area in order to forge strong approaches and strategies. The intent of presenting this information in one publication is to help librarians develop practical strategies and approaches for developing customized DIL programs using the work done in the DIL project as real-world case studies. We invite others to build from our experiences—both from these case studies and through the lens of current understandings of information literacy—to make recommendations for future directions and growth of DIL. More information about the DIL project can be found on the project's website (http://datainfolit.org).

NOTE

Portions of this chapter are reprinted from Carlson, J., Johnston, L., Westra, B., & Nichols, M. (2013). Developing an approach for data management education: A report from the Data Information Literacy project. *International Journal of Digital Curation, 8*(1), 204–217. http://dx.doi.org/10.2218/ijdc.v8i1.254

REFERENCES

Association of College and Research Libraries (ACRL). (2000). *Information literacy competency standards for higher education.* Retrieved from http://www.ala.org/acrl/files/standards/standards.pdf

Association of College and Research Libraries (ACRL). (2012). *ACRL AC12 doc 13.1* [Memorandum to ACRL Information Literacy Standards Committee regarding task force

recommendations]. Retrieved from http://www
.ala.org/acrl/sites/ala.org.acrl/files/content
/standards/ils_recomm.pdf

Blatter, J. (2008). Case study. In L. M. Given
(Ed.), *The SAGE encyclopedia of qualitative
research methods* (pp. 68–72). http://dx.doi
.org/10.4135/9781412963909.n39

Cragin, M. H., Palmer, C., Carlson, J., & Witt, M.
(2010). Data sharing, small science and institutional repositories. *Philosophical Transactions
of the Royal Society A, 368*(1926), 4023–4038.
http://dx.doi.org/10.1098/rsta.2010.0165

Graduate School of Library and Information Science. (2010). GSLIS to host 2010 summer
institute on data curation. *LIS Newsroom.* Retrieved from University of Illinois at Urbana-
Champaign Graduate School of Library and Information Science website: http://www.lis.illinois
.edu/articles/2010/05/gslis-host-2010-summer
-institute-data-curation

Graduate School of Library and Information Science.
(2011). Masters of science: Specialization in data
curation. *LIS Newsroom.* Retrieved from University of Illinois at Urbana-Champaign Graduate School of Library and Information Science
website: http://www.lis.illinois.edu/academics
/degrees/specializations/data_curation

Hey, T., & Hey, J. (2006). E-science and its implications for the library community. *Library Hi Tech, 24*(4), 515–528. http://dx.doi
.org/10.1108/07378830610715383

Holdren, J. P. (2013). *Increasing access to the results of
federally funded scientific research* [Memorandum

for the heads of executive departments and
agencies from the Office of Science and Technology Policy, Executive Office of the Presi-
dent]. Retrieved from http://www.whitehouse
.gov/sites/default/files/microsites/ostp/ostp
_public_access_memo_2013.pdf

Indiana University Pervasive Technology Institute.
(2010). D2I introduces two courses in managing
and archiving data. Retrieved from http://d2i
.indiana.edu/news/course-offerings-2011
-taught-d2i-faculty

National Science Foundation (NSF). (2007). *Cyberinfrastructure vision for 21st century discovery.*
Retrieved from http://www.nsf.gov/pubs/2007
/nsf0728/nsf0728.pdf

National Science Foundation (NSF). (2010). Dissemination and sharing of research results. Retrieved from http://www.nsf.gov/bfa/dias/policy
/dmp.jsp

Soehner, C., Steeves, C., & Ward, J. (2010). *E-
science and data support services: A study of ARL
member institutions.* Retrieved from Association
of Research Libraries website: http://www.arl
.org/storage/documents/publications/escience
-report-2010.pdf

Tetherless World Constellation (TWC). (n.d.).
Data science course. Retrieved from Rensselaer
Polytechnic Institute website: http://tw.rpi.edu
/web/Courses/DataScience

Tibbo, H. R., & Lee, C. (2010). DigCCurr. Retrieved from University of North Carolina website: http://ils.unc.edu/digccurr/

PART I

Making the Case for
Data Information Literacy

CHAPTER **1**

DETERMINING DATA INFORMATION LITERACY NEEDS

A Study of Students and Research Faculty

Jake Carlson, University of Michigan

Michael Fosmire, Purdue University

C. C. Miller, Purdue University

Megan Sapp Nelson, Purdue University

INTRODUCTION

The nature and practice of research and scholarship is undergoing dramatic change with the advent of ready access to high-bandwidth networks, the capacity to store massive amounts of data, and a robust and growing suite of advanced informational and computational data analysis and visualization tools. The practice of technology-driven research, known as *e-science,* or more broadly as *e-research,* has had a transformative effect in the science and engineering fields. E-research applications are growing within the humanities and social science disciplines as well, where e-research is poised to have similar effects on the nature and practice of research.

The complexity and scale of e-research in turn requires an evolution of traditional models of scholarly communication, library services, and the role of librarians themselves. In response, librarians are initiating discussions and projects to situate themselves in those areas of e-research most in need of library science expertise (Jones, Lougee, Rambo, & Celeste, 2008). In light of the federal expectation that grant proposals have a data management plan (DMP; NSF, 2011), libraries are starting conversations in their universities to negotiate a role in the management of research outputs.

Data management skills also provide the opportunity for an evolution of instruction in libraries. Academic libraries offer information literacy courses and programs as part of the educational mission of the institution. Extending information literacy to include programs on data management and curation provides a logical entry point into increasing the role of libraries in supporting e-research. A successful education program, however, must be based on a firm understanding of current practice and standards as well as the needs of the target audience. There is a lack of research on the needs of both the researchers and the students grappling with these issues in the classroom and in the laboratory. The authors attempted to address this knowledge gap by gathering data from interviews with faculty researchers and from the authors' own Geoinformatics course. With this information, the authors proposed a model set of outcomes for data information literacy (DIL).

BACKGROUND

E-Research and Implications for Libraries

E-research has had a tremendous impact on a number of fields, increasing the capabilities of researchers to ask new questions and reduce the barriers of time and geography to form new collaborations. In astronomy for example, the National Virtual Observatory (NVO) makes it possible for anyone from professional astronomers to the general public to find, retrieve, and analyze vast quantities of data collected from telescopes all over the world (Gray, Szalay, Thakar, Stoughton, & vandenBerg, 2002; National Virtual Observatory, 2010). For scholars of literature, the HathiTrust Digital Library not only provides a tremendous collection of scanned and digitized texts, but also its Research Center provides tools and computational access to scholars seeking to apply data mining, visualization, and other techniques toward the discovery of new patterns and insights (HathiTrust Research Center, n.d.). It should be no surprise, of course, that such projects simultaneously produce and feed upon large amounts of data. The capture, dissemination, stewardship, and preservation of digital data are critical issues in the development and sustainability of e-research.

Funding organizations and professional societies identified a need for educational initiatives to support a workforce capable of e-research initiatives. The National Science Foundation (NSF) first described the connection between e-research and education. The 2003 Atkins Report highlighted the need for coordinated, large-scale investments in several areas, including developing skilled personnel and facilities to provide operational support and services (Atkins et al., 2003). In 2005 the National Science Board produced a report that articulated existing and needed roles and responsibilities required for stewarding data collections, followed by a series of recommendations for technical, financial, and policy strategies to guide the continued development and use of data collections (National Science Board, 2005). The American Council of Learned Societies issued a report in 2006 calling for similar attention and investments in developing infrastructure and services for e-research in the humanities fields (Welshons, 2006). More recently, the National Academy of Sciences issued a report advocating the stewardship of research data in ways that ensured research integrity and data accessibility. The recommendations issued in the report included the creation of systems for the documentation and peer review of data, data management training for all researchers, and the development of standards and policies regarding the dissemination and management of data (National Research Council, 2009).

While the rich, collaborative, and challenging paradigm of e-research promises to produce important, even priceless, cultural and scientific data, librarians are determining their role in the curation, preservation, and dissemination of these assets. In examining how e-research may affect libraries, Hey and Hey argued that e-research "is intended to empower scientists to do their research in faster, better and different ways," (Hey & Hey, 2006, para. 10). They particularly emphasized that information and social technologies made e-research a more communal and participatory exercise, one that will see scientists, information technology (IT) staff, and librarians working more closely together. A particular challenge looming with the rise of e-research is the "data deluge"—that is, the need to store, describe, organize, track, preserve, and interoperate data generated by a multitude of researchers to make the data accessible and usable by others for the long term. The sheer quantity of data being generated and our current lack of tools, infrastructure, standardized processes, shared workflows, and personnel who are skilled in managing and curating these data pose a real threat to the continued development of e-research.

Gold (2007) provided an outline of the issues and opportunities for librarians in e-science. Starting from the familiar ground of GIS (geographic information systems), bioinformatics, and social science data, Gold argued that librarians working in e-science will develop relationships—both upstream and downstream of data generation—and the effort may be "both revitalizing and transformative for librarianship" (Sec. 2.2, para. 6). Similarly, the *Agenda for Developing E-Science in Research Libraries* outlined five main outcomes that focused on capacity building and service development in libraries for supporting e-science (Lougee et al., 2007). Walters (2009) further asserted that libraries taking "entrepreneurial steps" toward becoming data curation centers are on the right track, reasoning that "a profound role for the university research library in research data curation is possible. If the role is not developed, then a significant opportunity and responsibility to care for unique research information is being lost" (p. 85). In other words, the academic library community seems reasonably sure that supporting e-research is not so novel that it falls outside of the mission and founding principles under which libraries operate.

Educational Preparation for E-Research

Ogburn (2010) predicted that e-science will quite certainly fail if future generations of scholars are not savvy with *both* the consumption and production of data and tools. "To prepare the next generation of scholars the knowledge and skills for managing data should become part of an education process that includes opportunities for students to contribute to the creation and the preservation of research in their fields" (p. 244). It is not enough to teach students about handling incoming data, they must also know, and practice, how to develop and manage their own data with an eye toward the next scientist down the line. The Association of Research Libraries reported to the NSF in 2006 that because

> many scientists continue to use traditional approaches to data, i.e., developing custom datasets for their own use with little attention to long-term reuse, dissemination, and curation, a change of behavior is in order. . . . [This change] will require a range of efforts, including . . . perhaps most important of all, concerted efforts to educate current and future scientists to adopt better practices. (Friedlander & Adler, 2006, p. 122)

The inspiration for the authors' own work on instructional components to e-science comes from the NSF's *Cyberinfrastructure Vision for 21st Century Discovery,* in which the dramatic rhetoric of revolution and recreation does indeed trickle down to education:

> Curricula must also be reinvented to exploit emerging cyberinfrastructure capabilities. The full engagement of students is vitally important since they are in a special position to inspire future students with the excitement and understanding of cyberinfrastructure-enabled scientific inquiry and learning. Ongoing attention must be paid to the education of the professionals who will support, deploy, develop, and design current and emerging cyberinfrastructure. (National Science Foundation Cyberinfrastructure Council, 2007, p. 38)

Although many articulated the need for educating a workforce that understands the importance of managing and curating data in ways that support broad dissemination, use by others, and preservation beyond the life of its original research project, there has been very little examination of what such a program would contain. We believe that librarians have a role in developing these education programs and will need to actively engage in these discussions.

Gabridge (2009) notes that institutions experience

> a constantly revolving community of students who arrive with . . . uneven skills in data management. . . . Librarian subject liaisons already teach students how to be self-sufficient, independent information consumers. This role can be easily extended to include instruction on data management and planning. (p. 17)

With the respectful elision of "easily," we argue in the remainder of this chapter that there are indeed gaps in the knowledge of current e-researching faculty and students (both as producers and consumers of data) that librarians may address by developing DIL curricula.

Environmental Scan of Related Literacies

For the sake of clarity, it is important to distinguish DIL from other literacies such as data literacy, statistical literacy, and information literacy. Typically, data literacy involves understanding what data mean, including how to read graphs and charts appropriately, draw correct conclusions from data, and recognize when data are being used in misleading or inappropriate ways (Hunt, 2004). Statistical literacy is "the ability to read and interpret summary statistics in the everyday media: in graphs, tables, statements, surveys and studies," (Schield, 2010, p. 135). Schield finds common ground in data, statistical, and information literacy, stating that information literate students must be able to "think critically about concepts, claims, and arguments: to read, interpret and evaluate information." Furthermore, statistically literate students must be able to "think critically about basic descriptive statistics, analyzing, interpreting and evaluating statistics as evidence." Data literate students must "be able to access, assess, manipulate, summarize, and present data." In this way, Schield (2004, p. 8) creates a hierarchy of critical thinking skills: data literacy is a requisite for statistical literacy, and, in turn, statistical literacy is required for information literacy. Stephenson and Caravello (2007) extol the importance of data and statistical literacies as components of information literacy in the social sciences, arguing that the ability to evaluate information essentially requires that one understand the data and statistics used in an information resource.

Qin and D'Ignazio (2010) developed a model, Science Data Literacy, to address the production aspect of data management. SDL refers to "the ability to understand, use, and manage science data" (p. 2) and an SDL education

> serves two different, though related, purposes: one is for students to become e-science data literate so that they can be effective science workers, and the other is for students to become e-science data management professionals. Although there are similarities in information literacy and digital literacy, science data literacy specifically focuses less on literature-based attributes and more on functional ability in data collection, processing, management, evaluation, and use. (p. 3)

Whereas definitions of *data, statistical,* and *information literacy* focus on the consumption and analysis of information, the production of information is often overlooked in literacy instruction. E-research is, by definition, a social process, and contributing to—not just extracting from—the community's knowledge base is crucial. DIL, then, merges the concepts of researcher-as-producer and researcher-as-consumer of data products. It builds upon and reintegrates statistical, information, and science data literacy into an emerging skill set.

Prior Instructional Efforts in Data Information Literacy

Several libraries have developed programs or prototypes to address those needs. The Massachusetts Institute of Technology Libraries created a robust "Manage Your Data" subject guide/tutorial, supplemented by seminars such as Managing Research Data 101 (Graham, McNeill, & Stout, 2011). Both resources include data planning checklists that include the following topics:

- Documentation and metadata
- Security and backups
- Directory structures and naming conventions
- Data sharing and citation
- Data integration
- Good file formats for long-term access
- Best practices for data retention and archiving

The University of Virginia Library created the Scholars' Lab and Research Computing Lab. These projects, collaborative ventures between IT and library departments, created a new service model that included traditional roles for IT (software support and training) and librarians (subject knowledge and departmental interactions), as well as services that bridged those disciplines such as data management and analysis, computational software support, and knowledge of emerging technologies. Librarians from the University of Virginia explained: "We chose to promote the service areas of software support, current awareness, data, collaboration, and research communication. . . . Collectively, we view these as being supportive pieces to the entire research lifecycle, rather than just a single point" (Hunter, Lake, Lee, & Sallans, 2010, p. 341). While the University of Virginia model focused primarily on reference and project-based services, the Scholars' Lab also provided workshops and seminars on special topics in data management such as GIS, Web application development, and text digitization.

The Science Data Literacy project at Syracuse University developed a program "to train students with the knowledge and skills in collecting, processing, managing, evaluating, and using data for scientific inquiry" (Qin & D'Ignazio, 2010, p. 2). As part of the project, Qin developed a credit-bearing course, Science

Data Management, covering the fundamentals of scientific data and its description, manipulation, visualization, and curation. Project SDL made its syllabus for the course, with lecture notes, available online (Science Data Literacy Project, 2010).

The Purdue University Libraries are active in this area as well. Two of the authors of this chapter developed a Geoinformatics course with a faculty member in the Department of Earth, Atmospheric, and Planetary Sciences (Miller & Fosmire, 2008). The instructors designed Geoinformatics for beginning graduate and advanced undergraduate students. The course provided a holistic approach to GIS and spatial data, encompassing the full cycle of data, from discovery and acquisition to conversion and manipulation, analysis, and finally visualization, metadata, and re-sharing. The syllabi are online (Miller, 2010).

ASSESSMENTS OF FACULTY AND STUDENT NEEDS IN DATA INFORMATION LITERACY

Like e-research, DIL is not new, but rather compiles expertise and portions of existing research methods, information and other literacies, and computing curricula to offer more holistic, communal, and participatory perspectives and techniques for e-researchers. Just as e-research encourages researchers from a variety of disciplines to collaborate to advance scientific knowledge, disciplinary and library faculty must work together to determine the skill sets that a data literate student should demonstrate and to develop best practices for imparting those skills to the students. Both faculty members and students have perspectives on the necessary data management skill sets in their fields. Grounded in these perspectives are their real-world perceptions and practices and a first-hand knowledge of how one conducts research in his or her respective discipline. Any attempt to define a DIL program must be aligned with current disciplinary practices and cultures if it is to be relevant to and accepted by its intended audience(s). The authors compiled the perspectives of both faculty and students from two different research projects, one based on interviews with faculty members and the other on surveys of students and an analysis of their course work. In the next two sections, the authors report on the DIL priorities articulated by both faculty and students as discovered through our assessments.

Assessment of Faculty Needs: A Reexamination of the Data Curation Profiles Project

In the fall of 2007, the Purdue University Libraries and the Graduate School of Library and Information Science at the University of Illinois at Urbana-Champaign (UIUC) received funding from the Institute of Museum and Library Services (IMLS) to carry out the Data Curation Profiles (DCP) project. The goals of the DCP project were to better understand the willingness of research faculty to share their data with others—including the conditions necessary for data sharing to take place—and to investigate possible roles for librarians in facilitating data sharing and curation activities.

The investigators interviewed participating faculty at Purdue and UIUC, focusing on three broad areas: the nature and life cycle of one of the data sets generated by researchers; their data management practices; and their needs for making their data available to others and curating their data for long-term access. These interviews resulted in the creation of "data curation

profiles," each of which summarized the information gathered from the interview under a common framework that enabled comparisons to be made among the researchers' responses (Witt, Carlson, Brandt, and Cragin, 2009).

The first round of interviews for the DCP project took place at Purdue and UIUC in the summer and early fall of 2008. A convenience sample of faculty participants was recruited from a broad selection of departments in the sciences and engineering on the basis of prior relationships with project personnel or liaison librarians. The semi-structured interviews asked broad, open-ended questions to allow participants to control the direction of the discussion and identify the most important issues related to sharing and curating their data. The investigators then extracted common themes from the transcripts using grounded theory.

The DIL project was predicated in part by the Data Curation Profiles project, which explored the willingness of research faculty to share their data with others—including the conditions necessary for data sharing to take place—and to investigate possible roles for librarians in facilitating data sharing and curation activities.

One of the common themes emerging from the interviews concerned the skills, knowledge, and training needed by graduate students to effectively manage and curate research data. Graduate students actively generated and curated data in support of their own research. Many also oversaw the management of data generated by the entire research group. A few of the faculty noted that their graduate students had been asked to share their data with individuals not affiliated with the research and therefore had to consider similar issues of whether or not to share and what conditions to place on sharing. Typically, faculty reported that graduate students were unprepared to manage or curate the data effectively. While acknowledging that this was an area of concern, they often could not provide adequate guidance or instruction because it was not an area that they knew well or fully understood.

The investigators conducted a second round of interviews in the spring of 2009 to gather additional details from faculty and address gaps from the first interview. Investigators asked the faculty participants at Purdue whether there was a need for a data management and curation training program for graduate students, and what such an educational program should contain. Responses from these second interviews were coded and analyzed with the information from the first interviews. A total of 19 faculty from both schools completed both interviews.

The overwhelming majority of researchers in this study felt that their students needed some form of DIL education.

Faculty Assessment: Results

Generally, faculty in this study expected their graduate students to carry out data management and handling activities. However, the extent of data management responsibilities varied among the faculty interviewed. Some took an active, hands-on role in managing their data with minimal student involvement, while others delegated most data management tasks to their students. Typical responsibilities of graduate students included processing or cleaning the data to enable use or analysis, assuring the quality of the data, compiling data from different sources, and organizing the data for access and use by project personnel.

In addition, faculty often considered data management duties as distinct from other research responsibilities.

Analysis of the interviews revealed that the training graduate students received and the training methods varied widely. Some of the researchers taught their graduate students data management tasks, such as how to develop and assign metadata to the data files. Other researchers reported that their graduate students had not received much, if any, formal training in data management and were left to figure things out on their own.

Given the variance in the range of responsibilities and training in data management received by graduate students, it is not surprising that faculty presented a mixed picture in assessing the work of their students in this area. Several faculty expressed frustration with their inability to understand or make use of the data their students had been working on, especially after they graduated. Other comments provided a positive statement of individual students' skills, which they generally acquired without formal training.

The overwhelming majority of researchers in this study felt that their students needed some form of DIL education. However, even in stating a need for such a program, several respondents expressed an uncertainty or a reluctance to teach data management skills to their students themselves. Some faculty expressed a concern about getting too involved in telling students what to do in what should be the students' own work, or in making their work more difficult by introducing new software or formats to work with. Furthermore, although faculty identified the lack of data management skills in their graduate students as a strong concern and described broad themes that should be addressed, they often could not articulate precisely what skills should be taught to remedy the situation.

>Interviewer: Is there a need for education in data management or curation for graduate students?
>
>Faculty: Absolutely, God yes . . . I mean we're . . . We have the ability to accumulate huge datasets now[,] especially with the new tools that we have.
>
>Interviewer: So, what would that education program look like, what would it consist of? What kind of things would be taught?
>
>Faculty: Um, I would say, um, and I don't really know actually, just how do you manage data? I mean, where do you put it? Um, how secret does it need to be? Or you know, confidentiality things, ethics, probably um . . . I'm just throwing things out because I hadn't really thought that out very well. (Soil Scientist)

After coding and analysis, several major themes emerged from the faculty's observations of graduate students' deficiencies in data management. These themes are metadata, standardizing documentation processes, maintaining relationships among data, ethics, quality assurance, basic database skills, and preservation.

Metadata

An understanding of metadata and how to apply it were frequently mentioned as areas of need, although the term *metadata* was not used often. More often, researchers said their students needed to know how to annotate and describe data. In most cases, references to "annotations" included both a need to provide information about a data file as well as information about individual components of the data (such as a cell in a spreadsheet). The main reasons for providing metadata include

assuring that data can be understood by others (both within the lab and by external audiences), enabling its continued usability over time, and fostering use of the data beyond its original purpose.

Researchers also expressed the need to apply and conform to metadata standards. One researcher stated that not only must students be taught "how to approach the idea of metadata," but also they must develop an awareness of standardized disciplinary ontologies and how to apply them to their own work.

Standardizing Documentation Processes

Standardizing documentation processes is a rather broad theme that applies to both high-level organization as well as to specific, local needs. Researchers frequently reported a need for students to be able to organize data by documenting it in a systematic and logical fashion. Explanations given for the need for rich documentation often extended beyond the immediate needs of the researcher's lab and included such high-level needs as enabling the sharing of data outside the research team, submission to repositories, reuse by external audiences, and preservation beyond the research life cycle. At the local level, this category addresses folder and file naming conventions, data sharing among the lab/project team(s), and assigning staff responsibilities for managing data, communication, and workflow.

Several major themes emerged from the faculty's observations of graduate students' deficiencies in data management: metadata, standardizing documentation processes, maintaining relationships among data, ethics, quality assurance, basic database skills, and preservation.

Researchers expected their graduate students to share responsibility for documenting the lab or project's data, as well as the student's own interactions with it. Documenting data focuses on what needs to be recorded and provided while generating, processing, analyzing, and/or publishing the data to later validate and verify it. This includes such tasks as generating and maintaining data dictionaries, glossaries, or definitions of variables; maintaining lab notebooks or their equivalent; and capturing the provenance of the data. Overall, researchers expressed that students' documentation needs to stand the test of time.

Researchers in this study acknowledged the problem of data documentation, not only for their students but for themselves as well. Difficulties in documenting data contributed to a larger concern: the lack of standardization and consistency in how the data are organized. Faculty repeatedly mentioned that every student employs different methods of documenting his or her data. The lack of standardized and shared data management protocols and practices across a research group often led to a "tower of Babel" situation, where it is difficult to understand what was done, by whom, and for what reason. This further led to difficulties in correlating and relating one data file with another or with the data collection as a whole. The inevitable turnover of students exacerbated this problem. Although most of the researchers in this study required their students to document their work with the data, actual documentation practices followed by the students varied from one to the next. Moreover, they often did not provide complete or detailed enough documentation to enable others to understand their work.

Several researchers suggested creating a standard operating procedure for data formatting and management. One faculty member noted that he created standard operating procedures

for most equipment and procedures in the lab and proposed that a similar standard operating procedure be developed for handling and managing his data. When asked to describe an ideal situation for organizing data, several of the faculty members noted the need for students to develop and use a standardized set of best practices.

Maintaining Relationships Among Data: Master Files and Versioning

Many interviewees described the challenge of relating data files to each other. This includes issues related to taking data generated at a particular time or for a particular purpose and enabling its integration with other data to create a new data set. This category also includes the converse action, generating a subset of the data from a larger data set or file.

Several researchers specifically mentioned the need for the creation of an official record of the data (a "master file") to ensure the authority and integrity of this record compared to the working copies of data sets or files created and used for specific purposes by subsets of lab or project personnel.

Many researchers desired that the master file bring a number of disparate files together into a searchable database that engenders question development and helps assure quality control for research. A lack of standardization in data management practices, a high learning curve, and a perceived lack of support for the advanced database utilities and programs required to create such files hindered the ability of researchers to achieve these goals.

Researchers expressed the need to balance the requirements for a particular research project with those for making the data accessible and useful to the larger research community.

This focus on the specific research needs of the student (or the faculty sponsor in some cases) often led to situations in which the faculty member could not retrace the steps taken in processing the data and relate the graduate student's work back to the larger data set to which it belonged.

Akin to these issues of compiling or merging data, researchers frequently brought up versioning as an often neglected but very important concept for students to learn. In this study, researchers clearly reported the importance of maintaining documentation of different versions of their data. They wanted to know which data files were used for what analysis, what file contained the current version being used by the research group, and how these versions differed from each other. However, several faculty members admitted that they themselves had a difficult time in maintaining adequate documentation and struggled to consistently generate the needed documentation in a timely manner.

Ethics

Faculty members in this study identified "data ethics" as another area where most students need assistance. Data ethics includes intellectual property rights and ownership of data, issues of confidentiality/privacy and human subjects, implications and obligations of sharing (or not sharing) data with others (including open access), and assigning attribution and gaining recognition of one's work. Although faculty clearly stated ethics as a needed area of instruction, they generally did not provide much description as to what the curriculum of such an ethics program would include. In one case, the professor tied ethics to an understanding of ownership of data.

Basic Database Skills

Several researchers expressed the expectation that students be able to understand and develop relational databases and use database tools effectively. Frequently, students' lack of basic understanding of database development and usage frustrated the interviewees. However, the expectations of student skills differed among the researchers. A civil engineering professor acknowledged that students needed some basic understanding of relational databases, normalization of data, database tools, and documentation techniques.

Quality Assurance

Researchers expected their graduate students to review or check their data and evaluate its quality. Interviewees mentioned the difficulty of knowing exactly what their students had done to compile and analyze the data. Thus the provenance of the data was unknown. One professor stated that she could not understand the work done by her students.

Quality assurance is in some ways a blend of technical skills (familiarity with equipment), disciplinary knowledge (whether the result is even theoretically possible), and a metacognitive process that requires synthesis on the part of the students. Primarily, quality assurance is the ability to recognize a pattern or consistency in the data. Quality assurance may also facili-

Faculty repeatedly mentioned that every student employs different methods of documenting his or her data.

tate or impede the quality of documentation (annotation/metadata) produced, and the organizational schema, of a given data set.

Preservation

Researchers expect their students to know how to preserve their data and document the processing of the data. Much like the discussion of metadata, faculty members generally understood the term *preservation* in a broad and loose sense of the word, often conflating it with the simple backing up of files. They were unaware of or unacculturated to preservation from a library perspective, instead focusing much more on the immediate issues and procedures surrounding backing up their data.

Although researchers recognized the need for backups, the methods and timing of performing backups differed considerably among research groups. Some, having learned the hard way through lab disasters, kept geographically dispersed backups. Others relied largely on graduate students to create backups on departmental servers. Still others had no real-time backup system in place. A common problem expressed with backups was tracking versioning.

Faculty Assessment: Lessons Learned

The design of any DIL program requires an understanding of the real-world needs of research groups, where research either progresses or is impeded by their ability to handle data in the ways described here. The faculty supervisors are no doubt acutely aware of the deficiencies in their students' abilities to properly care for their research input and output. The interviews analyzed for this study provide a window into the ground-level interaction with data and in fact become a magnifying glass through which we can spot the deficiencies and gaps in knowledge that a DIL curriculum might target.

Although faculty clearly stated ethics as a needed area of instruction, they generally did not provide much description as to what the curriculum of such an ethics program would include.

We would be remiss, however, not to account for the gaps in faculty responses on data practices, as these interviews also expose faculty interaction with data. Many faculty admitted or otherwise revealed that they themselves lacked expertise or experience with data management, even as they critiqued their students' abilities. We must assume their critiques of their students' (and their own) facility with any or all aspects of data management may be somewhat shallow. In other words, they may not know what they don't know about data management and curation. Therefore, a program based entirely on faculty self-report risks incompleteness, and other viewpoints on what should constitute the objectives for DIL must be taken into account.

As a complement, then, the next section will draw conclusions that help to complete our DIL core objectives from a direct source, a course taught at Purdue University that broached some of these exact topics, including data source evaluation, metadata, databases, preservation, and sharing.

This course allowed us to examine the DIL of students directly and learn from firsthand observation. Because we gained insight into what the students do not know, our own evaluation of student performance in a (classroom-simulated) research environment can serve as an important second front in developing a richer and more comprehensive list of core DIL objectives.

ASSESSMENT OF STUDENT NEEDS

Enrollees in the 2008 and 2010 offerings of the course Geoinformatics provided the sample population for our student assessment. The combined number of students enrolled totaled 27: 12 in 2008 and 15 in 2010. Most of these were students majoring in earth, atmospheric, and planetary sciences, but other majors represented in this course included civil engineering, agricultural and biological engineering, and forestry and natural resources. In 2008, the core course content revolved around a "who-dunit" concept. Students were asked to track down, over the course of several laboratory exercises, the location of a fictitious chemical spill by gathering data (both spill data and underlying geology) and using various geospatial analysis and visualization techniques. Student projects provided the rest of the context for learning DIL skills. The 2010 course dropped the "whodunit" mechanism to shift more attention toward a longer, more involved semester project.

To improve and tailor the course, the authors used several methods to probe students' interests, their perceived needs, and their abilities to carry out data management tasks. Among these were a pre-course assessment to inventory the students' technology and information skills and a post-course survey to determine their perceptions of how important different topics were to their research. The instructors also analyzed student semester projects to determine how well they demonstrated mastery of DIL skills.

We administered the pre-course survey in both offerings of Geoinformatics. It contained short-answer questions, mainly probing the students' background in databases, GIS, and programming, such as "What computer programming languages do you know (for example, Fortran, C)?" and "What geospatial software do you use?" The instructors then tailored the course content to address the ability levels of the students. The post-course survey was given only to students in 2008. For each course topic, students rated, on a 5-point Likert scale, the lectures, the lab, and the importance of the topic to the course and to their own research. They also recommended improvements to the course labs.

These instruments probed students' attitudes toward various topics related to DIL. However, there were disconnects between student perceptions and their performance. As Grimes and Boening (2001), among others, have observed, novices tend to overstate their expertise, in large part because they don't know what they don't know. To provide a check of the degree to which the students actually demonstrated DIL skills, the instructors analyzed the students' projects. The project required students to identify a problem or research question with geospatial components and use the skills and techniques discussed in class to advance that research and present the results of their work. It required both the acquisition of original data and the use of external, "published" data. And it involved analysis and visualization and required a summary of how the research answered or at least clarified the question or problem. It should be noted that this course did not teach research methods or disciplinary content knowledge: the students needed to get content assistance from their own research group.

Student Assessment: Results

Although in both course offerings several students indicated they had a rudimentary understanding of the technologies identified in the pre-course survey, none indicated that they felt able to command the tools to accomplish their own ideas and solutions. The survey, in fact, revealed low levels of exposure to most of the course content. Students reported little experience with GIS at all, and the experience they had was limited to a handful of data types and rather turnkey operations. Both offerings of the course required the instructors to cover fundamental concepts before moving on to a higher order agenda. These lessons included an introduction to databases and data formats, basic use of GIS and GPS tools, rudimentary visualization and analysis techniques, and metadata and presentation skills. The instructors decided

TABLE 1.1 *Results of the 2008 Post-Course Survey, on a 5-Point Likert Scale, of the Importance of Different Topics to the Course and to the Students' Research (n = 5)*

Topic	Importance to Course	Importance to Research
Databases	4.8	5.0
Data formats	5.0	4.8
Data gateways/portals	4.6	4.6
Introduction to GIS	4.8	4.8
GIS analysis	5.0	5.0
GIS data conversion	5.0	5.0
Workflow management	4.6	4.6
Metadata	5.0	5.0
Statistics	4.6	4.4
GPS	4.6	4.2
Data visualization	5.0	5.0
Ontologies	4.0	3.6
Data preservation	4.2	4.2

against using some technologies because, for example, students had no experience working in Unix/Linux systems or using low-level programming languages.

Students indicated a high level of interest in all the topics covered in the class and had an appreciation for DIL skills. In the standard end-of-course evaluations to which all students (n = 12) responded, the course received an overall rating of 4.8 out of 5.0, and several students remarked that after taking the course they finally understood what they were doing and now could contribute new procedures for analyzing data to their research groups. Of the 12 enrolled students, 5 completed the 2008 post-course survey, with the results summarized in Table 1.1.

The high level of interest in basic topics such as data formats and an introduction to

databases indicate the relative lack of preparation in the core technology skills necessary to work in an e-research environment. All but one topic (ontologies) received a rating of at least 4.0 (very important) as important to research.

In addition to extracting information from course surveys, the instructors also carefully examined students' completed course work to determine which concepts, skills, or ideas students still lacked. For example, the authors found that most students had ready access to the primary data used by their research groups and that these data often formed the basis for their semester project analysis. A focus of the course was on students' abilities to identify and synthesize supplementary data, such topographic, political, or land-use data to overlay on the data collected by the research group. Analysis of the student semester projects indicated that students indeed could find, identify, and incorporate external data sources into their analysis and/or visualization.

However, the analysis of the students' semester projects from both years revealed recurring shortcomings. While students did apply external data appropriately to their work, frequently these data were not cited properly. Although students correctly documented traditional published literature, they might not consider data to be a valid, citable scholarly source or have a clear understanding of how to cite a data set.

Students also struggled to fully comprehend the importance and complexity of data sharing, though the course was geared toward pushing this point explicitly. The following issues appeared multiple times over the two separate semesters:

1. *Preservation/archiving.* The students' final task in 2008 was to submit their data to the GEON Portal (www.geongrid .org) for safekeeping and redistribution. In 2010, GEON was merely a suggestion and students were encouraged to identify a repository in their domain to which they could submit their project data. Although many students attempted these submissions in good faith (despite some technical difficulties with GEON both years), several students shared the sentiments of one in particular, who argued that a department-run website that "everybody in the [domain] community knows about" was a better ultimate destination for their data than any more formal data repository.
2. *Metadata.* Although the time allocated for metadata was limited, the instructors managed to include the concepts of schema, authoritative terminology, XML, indexing, and searchability. Each course offering had a metadata unit during which instructors introduced students to several proper examples of metadata. The students then completed a lab in which they wrote their own simple metadata documents. While some students did write good accompanying metadata for their final project materials, most did not. One deficit seemed to arise from students creating metadata from the perspective of "how I did it," rather than striving to make the data more discoverable by the next scientist down the line.
3. *The technologies and workflows of data sharing.* Students (despite instructor warnings) expected to accomplish far more than they were able during a single semester. This was an outcome of students' expectations that, once analyzed, their data could be visualized fairly easily and shared online. The complexity of building data-driven, interactive Web applications was not apparent until it was too late.

DISCUSSION

The authors sought to triangulate the needs related to DIL through interviews with research faculty and analysis of the results of our own geoinformatics-themed DIL course. We found a substantial amount of overlap between the needs identified: databases, metadata, data sharing, preservation and curation of data, and formatting and documentation of data.

The assessments also uncovered differences that were more clearly a focus for one group than the other. For example, the interviews with faculty members primarily focused on data they created themselves, while a significant portion of the Geoinformatics course involved locating data from external sources. An analysis of course work showed that students needed to learn "the basics" of much of information technology, even before broaching data issues. Additionally, to manipulate the data, students had to learn how to use analysis and visualization tools, use workflow management tools, and develop a minimum computing background to take advantage of the available cyberinfrastructure. On the other hand, the production- and publication-focused faculty researchers described the need for data curation and management, such as good versioning, documentation, and quality assurance and the merging of data. In addition, the faculty surfaced the concept of data ethics: when to share data, who owns data, and how to appropriately acknowledge data. To that extent, these two investigations provide complementary information about perceived DIL needs.

We have argued that an understanding of either faculty or student practices and needs alone is insufficient to develop the foundational objectives necessary for a DIL program. Instead, both faculty and student perspectives must be understood and analyzed in tandem to inform a more complete understanding of what is needed in DIL. We now reintroduce another foundational component toward developing objectives for a DIL program: the perspective of the librarian. The organization, description, dissemination, curation, and preservation of information resources, which increasingly includes research data, are the hallmark of librarians. Although DIL must be grounded in real-world needs as expressed by students and faculty, the librarian brings the broader perspective and a connection to the larger "information ecology" that exists beyond the single research project or classroom. This connection can ensure that holistic best practices strengthen current practices.

Comparison of Data Information Literacy With ACRL IL Standards

To help articulate and ground our core DIL objectives, we found it useful to examine these topics through the prism of the ACRL (Association of College and Research Libraries) information literacy competency standards (2000), which have been widely adopted by many institutions and accreditation agencies and guide many library instruction initiatives. To that end, the next section first lists the ACRL standards, then briefly examines each standard for its relevance to these DIL objectives.

One readily identifiable gap in applying the ACRL information literacy standards to a DIL program is the difference in focus. The ACRL standards focus on educating information consumers—people seeking information to satisfy an information need. Although faculty and students do consume research data, our analysis of faculty and students indicates a strong need to address their roles as data producers as well. Therefore, the underlying objectives for any DIL program need to accommodate both the data producer's viewpoint as well as that of the data consumer.

The ACRL standards state that information literate individuals are able to:

1. Determine the extent of information need.
2. Access needed information efficiently and effectively.
3. Evaluate information and its sources critically and incorporate selected information into one's knowledge base and value system.

4. Use information effectively to accomplish a specific purpose.
5. Understand the economic, legal, and social issues surrounding the use of information, and access and use information ethically and legally. (ACRL, 2000, pp. 2–3)

ACRL Standard One: Determining Nature and Extent of Information Need

When gathering information, one often skips the research question formulation stage that is the foundation of the information search process (Kuhlthau, 2004). However, without articulating and understanding the question deeply, one cannot arrive at a relevant answer. The instructors addressed this concept in the semester project for the Geoinformatics course—for example, the overall assignment asked students to identify their research question and determine what data they needed to address that question. In the case of geospatial data, students needed to determine whether to use raster or vector data, because each type has its own strengths and weaknesses for analysis and presentation. Thus, the authors' curricular topic of *databases and data formats* fit best into this competency standard, as it is fundamental to understanding the nature of the information needed. In fact, Standard One already explicitly addresses data, stating that a student "realizes that information may need to be constructed with raw data from primary sources."

From the data producer's standpoint, identifying the nature and extent of the potential needs and uses of the data being generated provides the foundation for effectively sharing, reusing, curating, and preserving data. The cultural practices and norms of the producer's discipline, including being aware of any existing community resources, standards, or tools, inform these data functions.

ACRL Standard Two: Access Needed Information Efficiently and Effectively

Students need to consult common disciplinary and general data repositories as well as understand the formats and services through which data can be accessed in order to access information efficiently and effectively. In the Geoinformatics course, students investigated several data sources and were required to use external data extensively to supplement their own data. In addition to finding data relevant to their research question, the variety and complexity of data formats made the process of locating supplementary data challenging for the students. Several students needed assistance converting data from one format to another and understanding how to merge data sets with different resolutions or timescales.

Standard Two addresses these issues, as an information literate student "extracts, records, and manages the information and its sources," including using "various technologies to manage information selected and organized" (ACRL, 2000, pp. 10–11). Not only will DIL students need to know where data exist, but they also must harvest, convert, possibly merge, and ultimately feed it into analysis or visualization tools that may or may not require still other formats. Although a direct graft of classic information literacy competency standards to DIL would focus on the process of bringing data *into* one's research, as the faculty interviews revealed, these concepts are similar for publishing data to the world. Thus, DIL concepts related to this competency standard include data repositories, data conversion, data organization, sharing data, and interoperability.

ACRL Standard Three: Evaluate Information Critically

When evaluating data, students understand and critically evaluate the source. Students must determine whether the research group that provided the data is known to be reliable and/or if the data repository or its members provide a level of quality control for its content. Users also need to evaluate the data for relevancy and compatibility with their own research. As part of the quality assurance component of data evaluation, students need to evaluate associated metadata. Among other attributes, metadata specifies the details of the experiment or data product, including the following: the conditions under which the data were collected or created; the apparatus or procedures used to generate the data; distribution information and access rights; and spatial and temporal resolution, units, and parent sources. It is a vital tool in the evaluation of the quality and authority of the resource. While the ACRL standards would approach this from a data user perspective, the faculty interviewed made it clear that data producers need to provide quality assurance for data and metadata as well.

ACRL Standard Four: Use Information to Accomplish a Specific Purpose

In this standard, students carry out a project and need to "communicate the product or performance effectively to others." As such, students should use a format and employ information technologies that best support the purpose of the work. Here, in the expansive verb "communicate" and phrase "appropriate information technologies," one can assume the concepts of data sharing, reuse, and curation, as well as connections to analysis and visualization tools.

In addition, this standard includes the application of information toward the planning and creation of a product, revising the development process as appropriate along the way. These components parallel the statements made by faculty on the importance of documenting the processes used to develop research data (the "product" in this case). Researchers also identified the careful management and organization of data as essential in enabling its eventual transfer "from their original locations and formats to a new context" (as stated in Standard Four) for internal use by others in the project, or for reuse by others.

ACRL Standard Five: Understand Economic, Legal, and Social Issues and Use Information Ethically

Data ethics are certainly an important component of a well-rounded DIL program, especially since intellectual property issues concerning data are much less defined than, for example, those concerning traditional textual works. Students need to not only determine when and how to share data, which varies among disciplines, but also document their own sources of data. We found students struggled with the latter in the Geoinformatics course, as exhibited primarily by a failure to acknowledge those parties responsible for the data they consumed and reused. The ethical issues surrounding students as data producers and publishers, a concern raised by research faculty, appears to be entirely absent from the ACRL standards and would be a largely novel component of a DIL curriculum.

CORE COMPETENCIES FOR DATA INFORMATION LITERACY

With information gleaned from the faculty interviews, the Geoinformatics course, and the ACRL Information Literacy Competency Standards, the authors propose the following educational objectives for a DIL program. Disciplinary implementation of these outcomes would naturally incorporate technologies or techniques specific to that discipline. The following are the proposed core competencies, organized by major theme.

Introduction to databases and data formats. Understands the concept of relational databases and how to query those databases, and becomes familiar with standard data formats and types for the discipline. Understands which formats and data types are appropriate for different research questions.

Discovery and acquisition of data. Locates and utilizes disciplinary data repositories. Identifies appropriate data sources and can import data and convert it when necessary, so that it can be used by downstream processing tools.

Data management and organization. Understands the life cycle of data, develops DMPs, and records the relationship of subsets or processed data to the original data sets. Creates standard operating procedures for data management and documentation.

Data conversion and interoperability. Proficient in migrating data from one format to another. Understands the risks and potential loss or corruption of information caused by changing data formats. Understands the benefits of making data available in standard formats to facilitate downstream use.

Quality assurance. Recognizes and resolves any apparent artifacts, incompletion, or corruption of data sets. Utilizes metadata to anticipate potential problems with data sets.

Metadata. Understands the rationale for metadata and proficiently annotates and describes data so it can be understood and used by members of the work group and external users. Develops the ability to read and interpret metadata from external disciplinary sources. Understands the structure and purpose of ontologies in facilitating better sharing of data.

Data curation and reuse. Recognizes that data may have value beyond the original purpose, (i.e., to validate research or for use by others). Understands that curating data is a complex, often costly endeavor that is nonetheless vital to community-driven e-research. Recognizes that data must be prepared for its eventual curation at its creation and throughout its life cycle. Articulates the planning and actions needed to enable data curation.

Cultures of practice. Recognizes the practices, values, and norms of the chosen field, discipline, or subdiscipline as they relate to managing, sharing, curating, and preserving data. Recognizes relevant data standards of a field (metadata, quality, formatting, and so forth) and understands how these standards are applied.

Data preservation. Recognizes the benefits and costs of data preservation. Understands the technology, resource, and organizational components of preserving data. Utilizes best practices in preservation appropriate to the value and reproducibility of data.

Data analysis. Becomes familiar with the basic analysis tools of the discipline. Uses appropriate workflow management tools to automate repetitive analysis of data.

Data visualization. Proficiently uses basic visualization tools of the discipline and avoids misleading or ambiguous representations. Understands the advantages of different types of visualization—for example, maps, graphs, animations, or videos—for different purposes.

Ethics, including citation of data. Understands intellectual property, privacy, and confidentiality issues and the ethos of the discipline related to sharing data. Appropriately acknowledges data from external sources.

The authors compared the DIL core objectives with the course syllabus from the Science Data Literacy curriculum of Qin and D'Ignazio (2010) and found similarities between the two formulations. The chief difference appeared to be the depth of treatment of different topics. While the SDL course concentrated on metadata, for example, our approach focuses as much on the consumption of data (tools) as it does on documenting and annotating data. The Geoinformatics course perhaps had too little coverage of metadata, but we found that students and faculty both needed as much help with data manipulation as they did with enhancing the documentation of their data. Naturally, instructors must balance using tools and creating interoperable infrastructure in teaching this type of course.

We have alluded to the notion that a comprehensive DIL program may not be entirely the responsibility of librarians. However, librarians who have the skills to teach database management and data analysis, for example, could teach those concepts. Indeed, learning those skills supports the educational mission of the university. However, the authors recommend collaboration between disciplinary faculty and librarians as the best practice for teaching DIL skills. DIL needs to be grounded in the culture of the discipline in which it is embedded, and also imbued with the greater, communal perspective possessed by a librarian.

CONCLUSION

Thirty years ago, it was good laboratory practice [that] you had a bound paper manual, you took good notes, you took fifteen or twenty data points, maybe a hundred, and you had a nice little lab book. But we've scaled now to getting this mega amount of information and we haven't scaled our laboratory management practices. . . . It makes perfect sense to me that . . . you get this [data management skills] in people's consciousness, make them aware it's a problem early on in their careers as graduate students, before they go on and do all the other things and get too set in their ways. . . . And . . . that takes a fair amount of education . . . and training. (Civil Engineer)

The authors uncovered a growing need among research faculty and students for DIL skills. As a result, the authors brought together data from different audiences to propose a suite of core DIL skills that future e-researchers need to fully actualize the promise of the evolving cyberinfrastructure.

DIL represents an opportunity to expand information literacy from the library into the laboratory. In much the same way that libraries' information literacy programs have gone beyond the "one-size-fits-all" approach, librarians will need to go beyond a "one-size-fits-all" approach to data management and curation literacy. The Data Curation Profiles project (Cragin, Palmer, Carlson, & Witt, 2010; Witt, Carlson, Brandt, & Cragin, 2009) indicated that different disciplines and subdisciplines have different norms and practices for conducting their research and working with data. These differences are manifest in the myriad ways they manage (or don't manage), share (or don't share), curate, and preserve their research data. While we have provided a general summary of common themes from these interviews, we understand that any DIL program focused on a specific discipline needs to identify, incorporate, and address these specific differences in the curriculum. Models will help ascertain the educational needs of subdisciplines with regard to their data and then design DIL programs that will address these needs. These results serve to start a conversation and propose general concepts, rather than to provide a final, detailed curriculum.

Upon examination of the ACRL standards for information literacy, it is clear that DIL falls within the scope of standard library practice. The conceptual overlap between the ACRL standards and the DIL objectives indicates that these skills are very much aligned with librarianship. With some exceptions, the ACRL standards are written generally enough to accommodate DIL skills, and indeed the standards do have several specific outcomes related to data. Still, given the ballooning interest in data management for e-research, the new iteration of the standards should incorporate more data-related outcomes, especially from the perspective of the user as publisher of information.

Additional research should be done to identify the skill sets librarians need to support the DIL objectives, either as stated here or as they develop in practice. This will not only speed the development of DIL curricula, but also push the library community to work to adapt the collective DIL practice to trends in e-research.

ACKNOWLEDGMENTS

The authors wish to acknowledge support from the Institute of Museum and Library Services, Grant #IMLS LG-06-07-0032-07, for the faculty assessment portion of this chapter, and the work of Anupma Prakash, University of Alaska Fairbanks, whose Geoinformatics course provided insight into the development of our own.

NOTE

This chapter was originally published in 2011 (Carlson, J., Fosmire, M., Miller, C., & Sapp Nelson, M. [2011]. Determining data information literacy needs: A study of students and research faculty. *portal: Libraries and the Academy, 11*[2], 629–657. http://dx.doi.org/10.1353/pla.2011.0022) as an article describing the needs assessment research done by the Purdue University Libraries. The authors' articulation of DIL competencies and how they relate to information literacy served as the springboard for the Data Information Literacy project. The editors feel that this work serves as an important milestone in DIL history, and as such it is reprinted here with minimal revision.

REFERENCES

Association of College and Research Libraries (ACRL). (2000). *Information literacy competency standards for higher education.* Retrieved from http://www.ala.org/acrl/files/standards/standards.pdf

Atkins, D. E., Droegemeier, K. K., Feldman, S. I., Garcia-Molina, H., Klein, M. L., Messerschmitt, D. G., . . . Wright, M. H. (2003). *Revolutionizing science and engineering through cyberinfrastructure: Report of the National Science Foundation Blue-Ribbon Advisory Panel on Cyberinfrastructure.* Retrieved from National Science Foundation website: http://www.nsf.gov/cise/sci/reports/atkins.pdf

Cragin, M. H., Palmer, C., Carlson, J., & Witt, M. (2010). Data sharing, small science and institutional repositories. *Philosophical Transactions of the Royal Society A, 368*(1926), 4023–4038. http://dx.doi.org/10.1098/rsta.2010.0165

Friedlander, A., & Adler, P. (2006). *To stand the test of time: Long-term stewardship of digital data sets in science and engineering.* Retrieved from Association of Research Libraries website: http://www.arl.org/storage/documents/publications/digital-data-report-2006.pdf

Gabridge, T. (2009). The last mile: Liaison roles in curating science and engineering research data. *Research Library Issues: A Bimonthly Report from ARL, CNI, and SPARC, 265,* 15–21. Retrieved from http://old.arl.org/bm~doc/rli-265-gabridge.pdf

Gold, A. K. (2007). Cyberinfrastructure, data, and libraries, part 2: Libraries and the data challenge: Roles and actions for libraries. *D-Lib Magazine, 13*(9/10). http://dx.doi.org/10.1045/september2007-gold-pt2

Graham, A., McNeill, K., & Stout, A. (2011). *Managing research data 101.* Retrieved from MIT Libraries website: http://libraries.mit.edu/guides/subjects/data-management/Managing_Research_Data_101_IAP_2011.pdf

Gray, J., Szalay, A. S., Thakar, A. R., Stoughton, C., & vandenBerg, J. (2002). *Online scientific data curation, publication, and archiving* [Arxiv preprint cs/0208012]. Retrieved from http://arxiv.org/abs/cs/0208012

Grimes, D. J., & Boening, C. H. (2001). Worries with the Web: A look at student use of Web resources. *College & Research Libraries, 62*(1), 11–22.

HathiTrust Research Center. (n.d.). Our Research Center. Retrieved from http://www.hathitrust.org/htrc/

Hey, T., & Hey, J. (2006). E-science and its implications for the library community. *Library Hi Tech, 24*(4), 515–528. http://dx.doi.org/10.1108/07378830610715383

Hunter, C., Lake, S., Lee, C., & Sallans, A. (2010). A case study in the evolution of digital services for science and engineering libraries. *Journal of Library Administration, 50*(4), 335–347. http://dx.doi.org/10.1080/01930821003667005

Hunt, K. (2004). The challenges of integrating data literacy into the curriculum in an undergraduate institution. *IASSIST Quarterly* (Summer/Fall), 12–15. Retrieved from http://www.iassistdata.org/downloads/iqvol282_3hunt.pdf

Jones, E., Lougee, W., Rambo, N., & Celeste, E. (2008). *E-science talking points for ARL deans and directors.* Retrieved from Association of Research Libraries website: http://www.arl.org/storage/documents/publications/e-science-talking-points.pdf

Kuhlthau, C. C. (2004). *Seeking meaning: A process approach to library and information services* (2nd ed.). Westport, CT: Libraries Unlimited.

Lougee, W., Choudhury, S., Gold, A., Humphrey, C., Humphreys, B., Luce, R., . . ., & Young, P. (2007). *Agenda for developing e-science in research libraries.* Retrieved from Association of Research Libraries website: http://old.arl.org/bm~doc/ARL_EScience_final.pdf

Miller, C. C. (2010). Geoinformatics course site. Retrieved from Purdue University Libraries website: http://oldsite.lib.purdue.edu/gis/geoinformatics

Miller, C., & Fosmire, M. (2008). *Creating a culture of data integration and interoperability: Librarians collaborate on a geoinformatics course.* Paper presented at the International Association of University Libraries 29th Annual IATUL Conference, Auckland, New Zealand. Retrieved from http://www.iatul.org/conferences/pastconferences/2008proceedings.asp

National Research Council. (2009). *Ensuring the integrity, accessibility, and stewardship of research data in the digital age* [The National Academies Press Openbook version]. Retrieved from http://www.nap.edu/catalog.php?record_id=12615

National Science Board. (2005). *Long-lived digital data collections enabling research and education in the 21st century.* Retrieved from http://www.nsf.gov/pubs/2005/nsb0540/

National Science Foundation Cyberinfrastructure

Council. (2007). *Cyberinfrastructure vision for 21st century discovery.* Retrieved from http://www.nsf.gov/pubs/2007/nsf0728/nsf0728.pdf

National Science Foundation. (2011). Chapter II— Proposal preparation instructions. In *Grant proposal guide.* Retrieved from http://www.nsf.gov/pubs/policydocs/pappguide/nsf11001/gpg_2.jsp

National Virtual Observatory. (2010). What is the NVO? Retrieved from http://www.us-vo.org/what.cfm

Ogburn, J. L. (2010). The imperative for data curation. *portal: Libraries and the Academy, 10*(2), 241–246. http://dx.doi.org/10.1353/pla.0.0100

Qin, J., & D'Ignazio, J. (2010, June). *Lessons learned from a two-year experience in science data literacy education.* Paper presented at the International Association of Scientific and Technological University Libraries, 31st Annual Conference, West Lafayette, IN. Retrieved from http://docs.lib.purdue.edu/iatul2010/conf/day2/5

Schield, M. (2004). Information literacy, statistical literacy and data literacy. *IASSIST Quarterly, 28*(2/3), 6–11.

Schield, M. (2010). Assessing statistical literacy: Take CARE. In P. Bidgood, N. Hunt, & F. Jolliffe (Eds.), *Assessment methods in statistical education: An international perspective* (pp. 133–152). Chichester, England: John Wiley & Sons.

Science Data Literacy Project (2010). Syllabus. Retrieved from http://sdl.syr.edu/?page_id=23

Stephenson, E., & Caravello, P. S. (2007). Incorporating data literacy into undergraduate information literacy programs in the social sciences: A pilot project. *RSR: Reference Services Review, 35*(4), 525–540. http://dx.doi.org/10.1108/00907320710838354

Walters, T. O. (2009). Data curation program development in U.S. universities: The Georgia Institute of Technology example. *International Journal of Digital Curation, 4*(3), 83–92. http://dx.doi.org/10.2218/ijdc.v4i3.116

Welshons, M. (Ed.). (2006). *Our cultural commonwealth: The report of the American Council of Learned Societies Commission on cyberinfrastructure for the humanities and social sciences.* Washington, DC: American Council of Learned Societies.

Witt, M., Carlson, J., Brandt, D. S., & Cragin, M. H. (2009). Constructing data curation profiles. *International Journal of Digital Curation, 4*(3), 93–103. http://dx.doi.org/10.2218/ijdc.v4i3.117

CHAPTER **2**

DEVELOPING THE DATA INFORMATION LITERACY PROJECT

Approach and Methodology

Jake Carlson, University of Michigan

Lisa R. Johnston, University of Minnesota

Brian Westra, University of Oregon

INTRODUCTION

In Chapter 1 we described the foundational research that generated an early articulation of data information literacy (DIL) and the resulting 12 DIL competencies. The next step was to explore how our conceptions of DIL could be applied in practice. To do this we developed a 3-year Institute of Museum and Library Services (IMLS)–funded study to further the DIL concept and to create and implement educational programs for graduate students in science, technology, engineering, and mathematics (STEM). The purpose of the project was to answer two overarching questions. First, what data management and curation skills are needed by future scientists to fulfill their professional responsibilities and take advantage of collaborative research opportunities in data-driven research environments? Second, how can academic librarians apply their expertise in information retrieval, organization, dissemination, and preservation to teaching these skills? This chapter explains the methods and approaches that we used in the Data Information Literacy project.

KEY ASSUMPTIONS OF THE DATA INFORMATION LITERACY PROJECT

Before describing the methodology of the DIL project in detail, we must begin by listing our key assumptions for this project. These assumptions served as our guiding principles in developing and carrying out our work. They are that (a) information literacy is a foundation for DIL; (b) graduate students are a receptive audience for DIL programs; (c) librarians are in a prime position to teach DIL skills; (d) the need for DIL programs has not been fully documented; and finally, (e) to meet this need successfully, librarians must align with disciplinary cultures and local practices.

Information Literacy as a Foundation for Data Information Literacy

One of the key assumptions that we made in developing the DIL project was that we should take advantage of librarians' experiences and long, well-documented history with information literacy (Rader, 2002). We deliberately named our project "Data Information Literacy" rather than simply "Data Literacy" for two reasons. First, we wanted to recognize that the library and education communities have invested a great deal of time and energy in understanding how students learn to acquire, evaluate, and use information; this investment was certainly relevant in exploring how students develop, manage, and curate research data. Information literacy has a long history of exploring, assessing, and transforming instructional models and strategies to ensure their relevancy to particular situations and environments. Explorations in information literacy have been conducted at a broad scale to make sure the frameworks are in sync with the aims of higher education (Pausch & Popp, 2000) or to align with advances in technologies, societal norms, and learning theories (Martin, 2013). Others are more tightly focused on particular models such as embedded librarianship (Kvenild & Calkins, 2011) or offering instruction in an online environment (Hahn, 2012). Data as a type of information have distinctions and idiosyncrasies that merit special consideration, but we believed the information literacy field could provide a solid foundation for our work.

Second, DIL is an area in which librarians can make important contributions. However, teaching students information literacy competencies in relation to working with research data may seem daunting to many librarians. By directly connecting work with data to a familiar and accepted area (e.g., information literacy), we hope to encourage more librarians to take action to develop DIL programs of their own. We believe that DIL is a logical outgrowth of information literacy and therefore expanding the scope of information literacy to include data management and curation is a logical extension of information literacy concepts.

There are a number of other initiatives that affirm our approach to linking data and information literacy. The Society of College, National and University Libraries (SCONUL) Seven Pillars of Information Literacy model (SCONUL Working Group on Information Literacy, 2011), and the Researcher Development Framework by Vitae (2014), a UK-based nonprofit organization, each incorporate data management skills into their definitions of information literacy and support holistic approaches to helping doctoral candidates acquire skills and knowledge in data management. A report from the Research Information Network (Goldstein, 2011) argued that a broader interpretation of information literacy is needed—one that recognizes research data as information—to ensure that students gain the skills they will need to be successful in their careers. The 2012 LIBER working group on e-science selected research data as a critical area for involvement by libraries in e-science support and recommended that libraries assist faculty with the integration of data management into the curriculum (Christensen-Dalsgaard et al., 2012).

Graduate Students as a Receptive Audience

Another key assumption was the immediate benefit that graduate-level students may gain

from building their skill sets in DIL concepts. For example, in the STEM disciplines, graduate students carry out the data management tasks for their own research, and frequently participate in data activities to support lab/team projects as well (Akmon, Zimmerman, Daniels, & Hedstrom, 2011; Westra, 2010). But Gabridge (2009, p. 17) observed that graduate students composed "a constantly revolving community of students who arrive with . . . uneven skills in data management."

Graduate students participate in varying levels of mentoring or apprenticeship. However, research data skill and competency development focuses on more traditional skills such as research design, equipment use, data analysis, and problem solving in the laboratory or field setting rather than those addressed by the DIL competencies (Feldman, Divoll, & Rogan-Klyve, 2013; Leon-Beck & Dodick, 2012). Furthermore, the process through which novice researchers acquire these skills may be influenced by social and cultural factors in their research teams or communities of practice (Feldman et al., 2013). Therefore, acquisition of DIL competencies by graduate students appears to be uneven at best.

When thinking about target audiences for DIL training, it is essential to evaluate the local landscape. Researchers appreciate training that has an immediate impact on their particular disciplinary setting; training which lacks this will be ignored by graduate students (Molloy & Snow, 2012). Interviews, surveys, and post-training feedback can help libraries confirm the types of research services which may be of interest and beneficial to graduate students and research faculty (Bresnahan & Johnson, 2013; Johnson, Butler, & Johnston, 2012). Finding the best approach to target graduate students with training was a major component of the DIL project.

Knowing that graduate students were a prime audience, the next question was: How and when could we engage this audience? There are a number of pathways by which training can be provided to future scientists. For example, graduate students may be introduced to basic data management concepts via a data management module in "responsible conduct of research" training (Frugoli, Etgen, & Kuhar, 2010). This may lead to other consultations and training opportunities. Institutions are also embedding training in other required courses and programs. While it is important to provide early training (Molloy & Snow, 2012), significant gains may be achieved by engaging students when they are grappling with issues in their own practices (Scott, Boardman, Reed, & Cox, 2013). Most students are interested in training with a strong component of immediacy and practical application (Byatt, Scott, Beale, Cox, & White, 2013; Parsons, 2013).

Librarians Are in an Excellent Position to Teach Data Information Literacy Skills

Librarians are in a unique position to teach DIL in academic environments. Graduate-level courses with a librarian embedded within them have been linked to improved student learning (Kumar & Edwards, 2013; Kumar, Wu, & Reynolds, 2014), and informationists have been successful in deploying services to graduate students and research teams (Hoffmann & Wallace, 2013; Polger, 2010). However, surveys conducted on data management show that very few students consult with a librarian on research data management (RDM) issues (Doucette & Fyfe, 2013). A Research Information Network (RIN) initiative applied the SCONUL Seven Pillars model of information literacy and Vitae's Research Development Framework to the development of data

management skills in postgraduate courses in the United Kingdom. The results demonstrated that a wide range of disciplines need data management skills and that core skills as well as discipline-specific training should be embedded into the postgraduate curricula (Goldstein, 2010). These findings indicate an opportunity for librarians to engage graduate students about the issues they face in working with research data.

Demand for Data Information Literacy Programs Needs Further Exploration

The approaches to teaching data management and curation for graduate students in the sciences are either stand-alone courses or programs or one-shot workshops. The stand-alone course approach has been used by several schools of information science, including Syracuse University (Qin & D'Ignazio, 2010), the University of Michigan (n.d.), and the Rensselaer Polytechnic Institute. Syracuse designed a course to teach science data literacy, defined as "the ability to understand, use, and manage science data" (Qin & D'Ignazio, 2010, p. 3), with a focus on preparing students for employment in science or as data management professionals. The University of Michigan developed a research fellowship program, Open Data, centered on building a community of practice around managing, sharing, and reusing scientific data. The curriculum includes a core course on data curation and elective courses from multiple disciplines. The Tetherless World Constellation (n.d.) research center at Rensselaer Polytechnic Institute offers a course in "data science" for graduate students that includes metadata, discovery, workflow management, data analysis, and data mining. One advantage of the stand-alone approach to teaching data skills is the depth of coverage. However, it may be difficult for students to commit to a course, especially if the course is outside of their discipline.

Becoming prevalent at academic institutions, "one-shot" workshops represent a second approach to data management and curation education. Many of these workshops, such as those offered by MIT (Graham, McNeill, & Stout, 2011) and the University of Minnesota (Johnston, Lafferty, & Petsan, 2012), help faculty and graduate students address requirements for data management plans by funding agencies. Other workshops cover data management as one component of a broader training in research ethics or responsible conduct of research, as required by the National Science Foundation and the National Institutes of Health (Coulehan & Wells, 2006; Frugoli et al., 2010). Workshops require less of a time commitment and are likely to reach more people, but they cannot provide as much breadth or depth.

As the need for students who are capable of managing and curating data sets continues to expand, we are seeing the development of alternative methods. In some cases, online and print materials provide guidance on core data management practices. For instance, the Australian National University created a Data Management Manual that is now in its eighth edition. The university's Information Literacy Program uses this manual as a resource for teaching graduate students (Australian National University, 2013). Other programs have taken a multi-tier approach, providing seminars, lectures, and workshops; integrating data management into research professional development courses; and incorporating discipline-specific content for particular audiences (Byatt et al., 2013).

The DIL project was a means for exploring the strengths and weaknesses of different approaches in educating students about the data concepts they would need to be successful in their careers. We explored a number of possibilities for developing and delivering effective educational programs. Similarly, we recognized that DIL programs would be shaped by educational objectives and constraints due to time, circumstances, and resources. Comparing multiple approaches to developing and implementing DIL programs helps with identifying common themes and differences across approaches.

Alignment With Disciplinary Cultures and Local Practices

Perhaps our most important assumption in developing and implementing the DIL project was that its success depended on our ability to understand and align with existing cultures of practice. We recognized that a DIL education program would cause the students to change the processes and workflows that they had learned previously. This deviation could potentially affect others who depended on the students' work. We wanted to ensure that the DIL project would have a positive effect, not just for the students, but for the faculty and others in the lab. We needed to understand not only the current practices of the students but also faculty perceptions and reactions to the 12 DIL competencies that we had developed. If the faculty or the students saw little value in a particular competency then there was no point in including it in a DIL program (at least initially).

In addition to local practices, we needed to incorporate the perspectives and resources of the disciplines. Each of the disciplines with which we worked had articulated its own set of values, beliefs, and practices with regard to working with research data. Our DIL programs had to be informed by these disciplinary concepts to have the desired impact.

The need to take context into consideration in developing educational programming has received attention in information literacy research. Librarians have largely embraced information literacy as one of their core missions; however, Lloyd and Williamson (2008) argued that conceptions of information literacy that have come out of the library and information science fields are too narrow. Recognizing information skills as a part of sociocultural practices within broader contexts enables practitioners to better understand how people engage with information in ways that are meaningful to them (Lloyd, 2010). Hoyer (2011) also argued for moving away from a generic skills-based conception of information literacy and toward a framework that goes beyond the academic sector into the workplace and other arenas. As the social interactions and relationships within the workplace are factors in how information is accessed, evaluated, and used in workplace environments, social context ought to be accounted for in how information literacy is taught to students.

The idea that curation specialists need to understand the nuances and disciplinary practices of the research communities they serve is also taking root (Martinez-Uribe & Macdonald, 2009; Molloy & Snow, 2012). This is extending into education in data management and curation as well. Several initiatives in data management and curation education are taking this approach. The Research Data MANTRA project at the University of Edinburgh developed online programs based on needs assessments from postgraduate programs in social science, clinical psychology, and geoscience (EDINA, n.d.). The University of Massachusetts Medical School and Worcester Polytechnic Institute developed *Frameworks for a Data Management Curriculum* for teaching research data management to undergraduate- and graduate-level students in the sciences, health sciences, and engineering disciplines (Piorun et al., 2012).

In some cases, training can leverage materials created within certain research domains to promulgate RDM best practices, tools, and resources. For instance, ecologists and evolutionary biologists can find a number of articles about basic practices they can take to improve data sharing and reproducibility (Borer, Seabloom, Jones, & Schildhauer, 2009; Dryad, 2014; White et al., 2013). Disciplinary frameworks may be useful for synthesizing a guidance document, such as the *Principles for Engineering Research Data Management* created by the University of Bath (Darlington, Ball, Howard, Culley, & McMahon, 2010).

DEVELOPING THE DIL PROJECT

To address our goals of better understanding what data management and curation skills are needed by graduate students in science and engineering disciplines, and more specifically, what roles libraries and information science professionals could play in addressing these skills, we developed the DIL project. If we were successful in answering these two questions, then the DIL project could take the next steps of testing an approach for library-run education for DIL skills. We ultimately strove to build a case for models that academic libraries could implement for their own curricula and programming by designing and implementing case studies of DIL programs. Through our experiences and assessment of these programs, we would then move beyond the unique, individual needs of our home institutions and attempt to create a dialog of these experiences at the community level in order to address data management and curation issues more broadly. Our findings presented in Chapter 3 and the case studies in Chapters 4 through 8 describe our work toward meeting these ambitious goals.

The DIL project got its start by recruiting an initial cohort of librarians to partner with and create a series of educational programs. These librarians, the five DIL project teams illustrated in Table 2.1, developed expertise in this area through following a shared methodological framework. Reviewing the process and outcomes of the our five case study findings, we then created a guide for developing DIL programs (Chapter 9) comprising the materials and resources we created or applied, along with a detailed description of the construction and implementation of each of the educational programs that were created. In addition, we analyzed our work and experiences collectively to identify commons themes or challenges, as well important differences, to generate a guide for others seeking to develop their own DIL programs. Our intent in producing a guide for developing DIL programs and in sharing the materials we developed was to have them serve as resources for librarians and as a catalyst for creating a community of practice.

Structure of the Project

To carry out the DIL project we recruited librarians to form five project teams based at four different locations: two at Purdue University and one each at Cornell University, the University of Minnesota, and the University of Oregon. We recognized that a diverse set of perspectives and skill sets would be required to ensure the success of each project team and so each team was composed of three people: a data librarian, a subject librarian or information literacy librarian, and a faculty researcher from a science or engineering discipline. The data librarians applied their knowledge of data management and handling and data curation standards and best practices to inform a DIL program for the project team. The subject specialist librarians brought their knowledge of the information ecologies of the particular disciplines they served to ensure that their DIL program would be relevant to the specific disciplinary needs. On two of the project teams the data librarian and subject specialist roles were represented in one person, given the nature of their job responsibilities. On these teams, we recruited a librarian with knowledge and expertise in information literacy to serve as a resource in developing the team's DIL program. The information literacy experts on the project also served as resources to the DIL project as a whole and were invaluable in shaping the overall direction of the project. The third team member, a faculty researcher, contributed to the team's understanding of their research community standards and practices in working with data. They allowed their research group to be interviewed and observed, and were interviewed themselves to enable us to obtain this understanding. In addition, they collaborated with their project team on the construction and deployment of the educational programs for their students. We believed that having a direct connection with a faculty researcher was essential to ensure that the resulting DIL program was directly relevant to their students. The five DIL teams in this project are outlined in Table 2.1.

IMPLEMENTING THE DATA INFORMATION LITERACY PROJECT

Our proposal to carry out the DIL project was awarded by the IMLS in October of 2011. The project was implemented in five stages:

TABLE 2.1 *The Five DIL Project Teams and Their Composition*

Institution	Discipline	Data Librarian	Subject Librarian/ Information Literacy Specialist
Purdue University	Electrical and computer engineering	Jake Carlson	Megan Sapp Nelson
Purdue University	Agricultural and biological engineering	Marianne Bracke	Michael Fosmire
Cornell University	Natural resources	Sarah Wright	Camille Andrews
University of Minnesota	Civil engineering	Lisa R. Johnston	Jon Jeffryes
University of Oregon	Ecology/landscape architecture	Brian Westra	Dean Walton

1. Conducting an environmental scan and literature review
2. Interviewing faculty and students
3. Creating the DIL program
4. Teaching the DIL program
5. Assessing its impact

The details of the work performed by each of the project teams in developing and implementing their individual DIL programs are in the case studies presented in Chapters 4 through 8.

Conducting an Environmental Scan and Literature Review

Each of the five teams identified disciplinary resources and perspectives by conducting an environmental scan of the scholarly literature, reports, and other material produced by researchers in the discipline and subdiscipline of their faculty partner for information pertaining to the DIL competencies. Each team performed an environmental scan of existing data repositories, digital libraries, metadata schema, and other resources, standards, and best practices for their discipline or subdiscipline. They shared and discussed results of the literature review and environmental scan to identify common themes.

Interviews of Faculty and Students

The next stage was to conduct interviews with our faculty partners and graduate students. These interviews were question-based using a script and workbook; however, interactive elements were incorporated when possible, allowing the interviewers and interviewees to share stories and ask questions (Ellis, 2008). We had two objectives in conducting the interviews. First, we wanted to gain an understanding of current practices with regard to handling, managing, and curating data in the labs of our faculty partners. In addition to getting a sense of the kinds of data being generated in the lab, we sought to better understand local policies and practices with data. In particular we wanted to understand where and how graduate students acquired their knowledge and skills in working with data and how effective they were in doing so. Second, we wanted to gain an understanding of the educational needs of graduate students with regard to data from the perspective of the faculty and the graduate students. We sought to obtain this understanding through applying the 12 DIL competencies that we had generated from previous research (see Chapter 1) and asking our interviewees to review and react to them. In developing the interview protocol, we revisited our initial conceptions of the 12 DIL competencies and revised them both to streamline them and to ensure adequate coverage to potential areas of coverage for our educational programs.

Our belief, which was later confirmed in the literature reviews and environmental scans, was that individual disciplines would have unique interpretations, perspectives, and motivations surrounding the management, dissemination, and curation of data. In the interviews, we asked faculty and students to use a 5-point Likert scale to indicate how important they felt it was for graduate students to acquire each of these competencies before they graduated. We then followed up with several questions to learn why they assigned each competency the rating they did.

We also believed that faculty and students would have their own terminologies and definitions for the concepts and activities that encompassed research data from their disciplinary practices, which may vary from the terms and definitions used by library science and information professionals. These two factors made it difficult, if not impossible, for us to craft definitions for each of the 12 competencies. For example, there is yet to be a universally recognized definition for *data quality* that would be understood by everyone we intended to interview. In fact, having such firm definitions would have been counterproductive for our purposes. We wanted the faculty and students to provide us with *their* perspectives on the

Our interview instruments are available for download at http://dx.doi.org/10.5703 /1288284315510.

knowledge and skills that were important to them and to their discipline. Asking them to react to a definition as articulated by librarians could have resulted in responses with limited value in informing educational programming for that discipline. Ultimately, we viewed the 12 DIL competencies as starting points for a broader conversation between the librarians on the DIL project and the faculty and students.

Instead of attempting to craft authoritative and universal definitions of the competencies, we listed particular skills or abilities that could be included as a component of the competency. We invited the interviewees to suggest other skills that they would consider to fall under each of the competencies. Although this led to some overlapping discussions, this approach enabled us to gain a more thorough and nuanced understanding of faculty and student perspectives. The 12 data competencies and the skills that we associated with each of them for the purposes of the interview are listed in Table 2.2.

The interview protocol was based on the structure of the Data Curation Profiles Toolkit developed at Purdue University (http:// datacurationprofiles.org). It consisted of an interview worksheet, with questions for the interviewee to complete in writing during the interview, and an interviewer's manual, which contained follow-up questions for the interviewer to ask based on the written responses of the interviewee. Our interview instruments are are available for download at http://dx.doi.org /10.5703/1288284315510.

The interviews were conducted in the spring and summer of 2012. Eight of the interviews were with faculty. The other 17

TABLE 2.2 *The 12 DIL Competencies and the Skills Used to Associate With Each Competency for the DIL Project Interviews*	
Cultures of practice	Recognizes the practices, values, and norms of field, discipline, or subdiscipline as they relate to managing, sharing, curating, and preserving data Recognizes relevant data standards of field (e.g., metadata, quality, formatting) and understands how these standards are applied
Data conversion and interoperability	Is proficient in migrating data from one format to another Understands the risks and potential loss or corruption of information caused by changing data formats Understands the benefits of making data available in standard formats to facilitate downstream use
Data curation and reuse	Recognizes that data may have value beyond the original purpose, to validate research, or for use by others Is able to distinguish which elements of a data set are likely to have future value for self and for others Understands that curating data is a complex, often costly endeavor that is nonetheless vital to community-driven e-research Recognizes that data must be prepared for its eventual curation at its creation and throughout its life cycle Articulates the planning and activities needed to enable data curation, both generally and within his or her local practice Understands how to cite data as well as how to make data citable
Data management and organization	Understands the life cycle of data, develops data management plans, and keeps track of the relation of subsets or processed data to the original data sets Creates standard operating procedures for data management and documentation
Data preservation	Recognizes the benefits and costs of data preservation Understands the technology, resources, and organizational components of preserving data Utilizes best practices in preparing data for its eventual preservation during its active life cycle Articulates the potential long-term value of own data for self or others and is able to determine an appropriate preservation time frame Understands the need to develop preservation policies and is able to identify the core elements of such policies
Data processing and analysis	Is familiar with the basic data processing and analysis tools and techniques of the discipline or research area Understands the effect that these tools may have on the data Uses appropriate workflow management tools to automate repetitive analysis of data
Data quality and documentation	Recognizes, documents, and resolves any apparent artifacts, incompletion, or corruption of data Utilizes metadata to facilitate an understanding of potential problems with data sets Documents data sufficiently to enable reproduction of research results and data by others Tracks data provenance and clearly delineates and denotes versions of a data set

Continued

TABLE 2.2   *The 12 DIL Competencies and the Skills Used to Associate With Each Competency for the DIL Project Interviews—cont'd*

Data visualization and representation	Proficiently uses basic visualization tools of discipline Avoids misleading or ambiguous representations when presenting data in tables, charts, and diagrams Chooses the appropriate type of visualization, such as maps, graphs, animations, or videos, based on an understanding of the reason/purpose for visualizing or displaying data
Databases and data formats	Understands the concept of relational databases and how to query those databases Becomes familiar with standard data formats and types for the discipline Understands which formats and data types are appropriate for different research questions
Discovery and acquisition of data	Locates and utilizes disciplinary data repositories Evaluates the quality of the data available from external sources Not only identifies appropriate external data sources, but also imports data and converts it when necessary, so it can be used locally
Metadata and data description	Understands the rationale for metadata and proficiently annotates and describes data so it can be understood and used by self and others Develops the ability to read and interpret metadata from external disciplinary sources Understands the structure and purpose of ontologies in facilitating better sharing of data
Ethics and attribution	Develops an understanding of intellectual property, privacy and confidentiality issues, and the ethos of the discipline when it comes to sharing and administering data Acknowledges data from external sources appropriately Avoids misleading or ambiguous representations when presenting data

interviews were with current or former graduate students or postdocs of the interviewed faculty, or in one case with a lab technician. Each DIL project team compiled and analyzed its own ratings and responses to inform the development of its program. Each team wrote a summary of results and shared it with other members of the DIL project at an in-person project meeting. The overall findings for each of the 12 competencies are reported in Chapter 3.

With what was learned from the environmental scan and the interviews, each team developed a DIL program that included defined learning goals, educational interventions, and metrics for assessment. In addition to crafting the content of their DIL program, each team negotiated an approach for delivering the content with their faculty partners, as shown in Table 2.3. The approach selected by each team depended on a number of factors, including existing norms and structures of the lab, the amount of time the faculty and students had available to accommodate a DIL program, and available resources to support the program.

TABLE 2.3   *Approaches for Delivering a DIL Program Taken by the Five DIL Teams*

Institution	Discipline	Approach
Purdue University	Electrical and computer engineering	Embedded librarianship
Purdue University	Agricultural and biological engineering	Series of workshops
Cornell University	Natural resources	6-Week mini-course
University of Minnesota	Civil engineering	Hybrid in-person/online course
University of Oregon	Ecology/landscape architecture	One-shot seminar

Each of the project teams delivered their educational program in the fall of 2012, with the exception of the project team at Cornell, which delivered their program in the spring of 2013. The team members recorded their experiences with what worked well and what might be improved, as well as their general impressions and feelings about the delivery of their program. As a part of their program, each team developed assessment mechanisms to determine their success in implementing their learning goals and objectives. In addition to student achievement, student and faculty attitudes were assessed to determine the relevancy and effectiveness of the instruction. The five teams then conducted a collective analysis of the educational interventions to identify patterns and commonalities across experiences in developing DIL programs, as well as account for any significant differences. Finally, the teams wrote detailed reports on their programs and educational approaches. Each account was analyzed and recommendations were made for future iterations of their program. The lessons learned were built into a guide for other practicing librarians presented in this book in Chapter 9.

The DIL project wrapped up in the fall of 2013 with a 2-day Data Information Literacy Symposium held at Purdue University. The intent of the symposium was to exchange information and consider ways and means of building a community of practice on DIL. At the symposium, each of the DIL teams presented their work and shared their experiences through presentations, discussions, and hands-on exercises. The 80-plus librarian and information professional participants were invited to share their own experiences in teaching data competencies at their institutions through multiple directed discussions and activities. Chapter 11 reports on the many areas of consideration for the continued development of DIL that were identified at the symposium and suggests possible avenues for moving forward.

CONCLUSION

Our overarching goals with implementing the DIL project were to gain a better understanding of how librarians could develop educational programs on data management and curation topics and then to articulate directions for the academic library community to act on the opportunities presented in this area. We developed the overarching methodology and approach outlined in this chapter for this purpose. However, we found that the five DIL project teams diverged from each other in content and approach to develop a high-quality DIL program for their project partner. The second section of this book describes the work of each of the DIL project teams. The third section articulates what we learned collectively from our experiences and charts a course to further developing the 12 DIL competencies and toward forming a community of practice on DIL.

NOTE

Portions of this chapter are reprinted from Carlson, J., Johnston, L., Westra, B., & Nichols, M. (2013). Developing an approach for data management education: A report from the Data Information Literacy project. *International Journal of Digital Curation, 8*(1), 204–217. http://dx.doi.org/10.2218/ijdc.v8i1.254

REFERENCES

Akmon, D., Zimmerman, A., Daniels, M., & Hedstrom, M. (2011). The application of archival concepts to a data-intensive environment: Working with scientists to understand data management and preservation needs. *Archival Science, 11*(3–4), 329–348. http://dx.doi.org/10.1007/s10502-011-9151-4

Australian National University (2013). *ANU data management manual: Managing digital research data at the Australian National University*. Retrieved from http://anulib.anu.edu.au/_resources/training-and-resources/guides/DataManagement.pdf

Borer, E. T., Seabloom, E. W., Jones, M. B., & Schildhauer, M. (2009). Some simple guidelines for effective data management. *Bulletin of the Ecological Society of America, 90*(2), 205–214. http://dx.doi.org/10.1890/0012-9623-90.2.205

Bresnahan, M. M., & Johnson, A. M. (2013). Assessing scholarly communication and research data training needs. *Reference Services Review, 41*(3), 413–433. http://dx.doi.org/10.1108/RSR-01-2013-0003

Byatt, D., Scott, M., Beale, G., Cox, S. J., & White, W. (2013). *Developing researcher skills in research data management: Training for the future—A DataPool project report*. Retrieved from University of Southampton research repository: http://eprints.soton.ac.uk/351026/1/REPORT-Supporting_Researchers-RDM-Training-Final.docx

Christensen-Dalsgaard, B., van den Berg, M., Grim, R., Horstmann, W., Jansen, D., Pollard, T., & Roos, A. (2012). *Ten recommendations for libraries to get started with research data management* [Final report of the LIBER working group on e-science/research data management]. Retrieved from http://www.libereurope.eu/sites/default/files/The research data group 2012 v7 final.pdf

Coulehan, M. B., & Wells, J. F. (2006). *Guidelines for responsible data management in scientific research*. Retrieved from Office of Research Integrity, U.S. Department of Health and Human Services website: http://ori.hhs.gov/images/ddblock/data.pdf

Darlington, M., Ball, A., Howard, T., Culley, S., & McMahon, C. (2010). *Principles for engineering research data management*. Retrieved from University of Bath Online Publication Store: http://opus.bath.ac.uk/22201/1/erim6rep101028mjd10.pdf

Doucette, L., & Fyfe, B. (2013). *Drowning in research data: Addressing data management literacy of graduate students*. Paper presented at ACRL 2013, "Imagine, Innovate, Inspire,"

Indianapolis, IN. Retrieved from http://www
.ala.org/acrl/sites/ala.org.acrl/files/content
/conferences/confsandpreconfs/2013/papers
/DoucetteFyfe_Drowning.pdf

Dryad. (2014). Joint data archiving policy (JDAP).
Retrieved from http://datadryad.org/pages/jdap

EDINA (n.d.) About MANTRA. Retrieved from
University of Edinburgh website: http://datalib
.edina.ac.uk/mantra/about.html

Ellis, C. S. Interactive interview. (2008). In L. M.
Given (Ed.), *The SAGE encyclopedia of qualitative
research methods* (pp. 444–446). http://dx.doi
.org/10.4135/9781412963909.n222

Feldman, A., Divoll, K. A., & Rogan-Klyve, A.
(2013). Becoming researchers: The participation
of undergraduate and graduate students in scientific research groups. *Science Education, 97*(2),
218–243. http://dx.doi.org/10.1002/sce.21051

Frugoli, J., Etgen, A. M., & Kuhar, M. (2010). Developing and communicating responsible data
management policies to trainees and colleagues.
Science and Engineering Ethics, 16(4), 753–762.
http://dx.doi.org/10.1007/s11948-010-9219-1

Gabridge, T. (2009). The last mile: Liaison roles
in curating science and engineering research
data. *Research Library Issues: A Bimonthly Report
from ARL, CNI, and SPARC, 265,* 15–21. Retrieved from http://old.arl.org/bm~doc/rli-265
-gabridge.pdf

Goldstein, S. (2010). Data management, information literacy and DaMSSI. Retrieved from Research Information Network website. http://www
.rin.ac.uk/our-work/researcher-development
-and-skills/data-management-and-information
-literacy

Goldstein, S. (2011). The role of research supervisors
in information literacy. Retrieved from Research
Information Network website: http://www.rin
.ac.uk/our-work/researcher-development
-and-skills/information-handling-training
-researchers/research-superv

Graham, A., McNeill, K., & Stout, A. (2011).

Managing research data 101. Retrieved from
MIT Libraries website: http://libraries.mit.edu
/guides/subjects/data-management/Managing
_Research_Data_101_IAP_2011.pdf

Hahn, E. (2012). Video lectures help enhance online information literacy course. *Reference Services Review, 40*(1), 49–60.

Hoffmann, D., & Wallace, A. (2013). Intentional
informationists: Re-envisioning information
literacy and re-designing instructional programs around faculty librarians' strengths as
campus connectors, information professionals, and course designers. *Journal of Academic
Librarianship, 39*(6), 546–551. http://dx.doi
.org/10.1016/j.acalib.2013.06.004

Hoyer, J. (2011). Information is social: information literacy in context. *Reference Services Review, 39*(1), 10–23. http://dx.doi
.org/10.1108/00907321111108088

Johnson, L. M., Butler, J. T., & Johnston, L. R.
(2012). Developing e-science and research services and support at the University of Minnesota
Health Sciences Libraries. *Journal of Library Administration, 52*(8), 754–769. http://dx.doi.org
/10.1080/01930826.2012.751291

Johnston, L., Lafferty, M., & Petsan, B. (2012).
Training researchers on research data management: A scalable cross-disciplinary approach.
Journal of eScience Librarianship, 1(2), Article 2.
http://dx.doi.org/10.7191/jeslib.2012.1012

Kumar, S., & Edwards, M. E. (2013). Information literacy skills and embedded librarianship
in an online graduate programme. *Journal of
Information Literacy, 7*(1), 3–18. http://dx.doi
.org/10.11645/7.1.1722

Kumar, S., Wu, L., & Reynolds, R. (2014). Embedded librarian within an online health informatics
graduate research course: A case study. *Medical
Reference Services Quarterly, 33*(1), 51–59. http://
dx.doi.org/10.1080/02763869.2014.866485

Kvenild, C., & Calkins, K. (Eds.). (2011). *Embedded librarians: Moving beyond one-shot instruc-*

tion. Chicago, IL: Association of College and Research Libraries.

Leon-Beck, M., & Dodick, J. (2012). Exposing the challenges and coping strategies of field-ecology graduate students. *International Journal of Science Education, 34*(16), 2455–2481. http://dx.doi.org /10.1080/09500693.2012.713145

Lloyd, A. (2010). *Information literacy landscapes: Information literacy in education, workplace and everyday contexts.* Oxford, UK: Chandos Publishing.

Lloyd, A., & Williamson, K. (2008). Towards an understanding of information literacy in context: Implications for research. *Journal of Librarianship and Information Science, 40*(1), 3–12. http://dx.doi.org/10.1177/0961000607086616

Martin, J. (2013). Refreshing information literacy: Learning from recent British information literacy models. *Communications in Information Literacy, 7*(2), 114–127.

Martinez-Uribe, L., & Macdonald, S. (2009). User engagement in research data curation. In M. Agosti, J. Borbinha, S. Kapidakis, C. Papatheodorou, & G. Tsakonas (Eds.), *Research and advanced technology for digital libraries* (Lecture Notes in Computer Science, Vol. 5714, pp. 309–314) [SpringerLink version]. http://dx.doi .org/10.1007/978-3-642-04346-8_30

Molloy, L., & Snow, K. (2012). The Data Management Skills Support Initiative: Synthesising postgraduate training in research data management. *International Journal of Digital Curation, 7*(2), 101–109. http://dx.doi.org/10.2218/ijdc .v7i2.233

Parsons, T. (2013). Creating a research data management service. *International Journal of Digital Curation, 8*(2), 146–156. http://dx.doi.org /10.2218/ijdc.v8i2.279

Pausch, L., Popp, M. P. (2000). *Assessment of information literacy: Lessons from the higher education assessment movement* [White paper]. Retrieved from Association of College and Research Libraries website: http://www.ala.org/acrl/publi cations/whitepapers/nashville/pauschpopp

Piorun, M., Kafel, D., Leger-Hornby, T., Najafi, S., Martin, E., Colombo, P. & LaPelle, N. (2012). Teaching research data management: An undergraduate/graduate curriculum. *Journal of eScience Librarianship, 1*(1), 46–50. http:// dx.doi.org/10.7191/jeslib.2012.1003

Polger, M. (2010). The informationist: Ten years later. *Journal of Hospital Librarianship, 10*(4), 363–379. http://dx.doi.org/10.1080/15323269 .2010.514556

Qin, J., & D'Ignazio, J. (2010, June). *Lessons learned from a two-year experience in science data literacy education.* Paper presented at the International Association of Scientific and Technological University Libraries, 31st Annual Conference, West Lafayette, IN. Retrieved from http://docs.lib .purdue.edu/iatul2010/conf/day2/5

Rader, H. B. (2002). Information literacy 1973–2002: A selected literature review. *Library Trends, 51*(2), 242–259.

SCONUL Working Group on Information Literacy. (2011). *The SCONUL seven pillars of information literacy: Core model for higher education.* Retrieved from http://www.sconul.ac.uk/sites /default/files/documents/coremodel.pdf

Scott, M., Boardman, R., Reed, P., & Cox, S. (2013). Research data management education for future curators. *International Journal of Digital Curation, 8*(1), 288–294. http://dx.doi .org/10.2218/ijdc.v8i1.261

Tetherless World Constellation (TWC). (n.d.). Data science course. Retrieved from Rensselaer Polytechnic Institute website: http://tw.rpi.edu /web/Courses/DataScience

University of Michigan (n.d.). Open data: Scientific data management, sharing and reuse [Website]. Retrieved from http://opendata.si.umich.edu/

Vitae. (2014). About the Vitae Researcher Development Framework. Retrieved from https://www .vitae.ac.uk/rdf

Westra, B. (2010). Data services for the sciences: A needs assessment. *Ariadne, 64*. Retrieved from http://www.ariadne.ac.uk/issue64/westra/

White, E. P., Baldridge, E., Brym, Z. T., Locey, K. J., Mcglinn, D. J., & Supp, S. R. (2013). Nine simple ways to make it easier to (re)use your data. *PeerJ PrePrints, 1,* e7v2. http://dx.doi.org /10.7287/peerj.preprints.7v2

CHAPTER **3**

AN EXPLORATION OF THE DATA INFORMATION LITERACY COMPETENCIES

*Findings From the
Project Interviews*

Jake Carlson, University of Michigan
Jon Jeffryes, University of Minnesota
Lisa R. Johnston, University of Minnesota
Mason Nichols, Purdue University
Brian Westra, University of Oregon
Sarah J. Wright, Cornell University

INTRODUCTION

This chapter delves into the results of the user needs assessments we conducted for the Data Information Literacy (DIL) project and introduces the instructional interventions we developed to address those needs. Between March 2012 and June 2012, the five DIL project teams collectively interviewed 25 researchers (8 faculty and 17 graduate students or postdocs) on their DIL (instrument available at http://dx.doi.org/10.5703/1288284315510). We begin this chapter by presenting the broad themes that were uncovered across the interviews from our analysis. We then turn our attention to the responses given to each of the 12 DIL competencies by the faculty and students that we interviewed.

RESULTS OF THE DATA INFORMATION LITERACY INTERVIEWS

The results of the five case studies (presented in Chapters 4 through 8) revealed similarities and differences between faculty and students in how they perceived the importance of the DIL competencies for graduate students. Due to the small sample size and the use of convenience sampling, these results cannot be generalized outside of these case studies as indicators of each disciplines' importance ranking. Nevertheless the findings offer a useful starting point for larger investigations into the current environment of the educational needs of graduate students.

The DIL competency ratings based on a 5-point Likert scale are displayed in Figure 3.1. They show that, on average, participants valued each competency as either "important," "very

important," or "essential." However, there was considerable variance in the responses received as indicated by the high standard deviations (ranging from .75 to 1.02). The competencies that pertained more directly to keeping a research lab operational and to publishing outputs, such as *data processing and analysis, data visualization and representation,* and *data management and organization,* tended to be rated more important than competencies that are less central to these activities, such as *discovery and acquisition* and *data preservation.* Although deemed important, some of the lower rated competencies, such as data preservation, are difficult to address. In the interviews, many faculty stated that they lacked the experience or knowledge to educate students effectively about these competencies. Several of the faculty and students questioned whether their field had a culture of practice in managing, handling, or curating data.

Figure 3.1 also shows the differences in how the participants viewed some of the competencies. Faculty generally placed a higher value on student development of competencies in actively working with data (e.g., *data processing and analysis, data visualization and representation*) and in competencies that would sustain the value of the data over time (e.g., *metadata and data description, data quality and documentation*) than the students did. Students gave the *discovery and acquisition of data* competency a higher rating than did the faculty. Students indicated in the interviews that this was an important component of learning their field and contextualizing their research. Two of the faculty who worked with code as their data gave *data management and organization* a lower rating than did the other participating faculty. One faculty member believed that, individually, students should know how to manage their own data but did not necessarily need to know

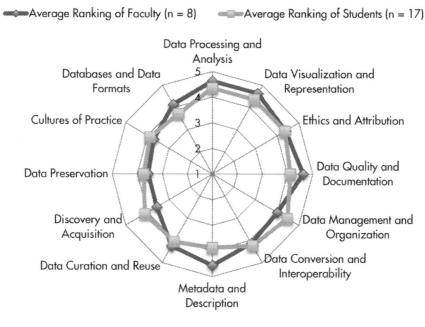

Figure 3.1 Graphical comparison of faculty and student ratings of importance of DIL competencies. Scale: 5 = essential; 4 = very important; 3 = important; 2 = somewhat important; 1 = not important.

how to develop systems or management plans for larger units. The other found it difficult to respond, not knowing what constituted good management practice and therefore unable to say if it would be worth the investment of his and the students' time.

THEMES FROM THE DATA INFORMATION LITERACY INTERVIEWS

Analyzing the interview transcripts revealed several commonalities across the five case studies: the lack of formal training in data management, the absence of formal policies governing lab data, self-directed learning through trial and error, and a focus on mechanics over concepts.

None of the five research groups provided their students formal training in data management. Instead, faculty reported that they expected that their students had acquired most of these and other competencies prior to joining their lab. As a University of Oregon faculty member noted, "[students may have] picked up [their skills] at on-the-job training, because a lot of them had a former life in a professional field . . . or [it's] something they got as an undergraduate." In contrast, student interviews revealed wide variations in their prior experiences with data. Most of the students had attended a seminar on responsible conduct of research (research ethics) but reported that data practices were not covered in the seminar. Moreover, these students could not recall the specifics of what was stated about data practices. It should be noted here that none of the five case studies involved data that would require training on dealing with human subjects or sensitive data.

In lieu of formal training, most graduate students learned data management through trial and error, reading manuals, asking their peers for help, or searching the Internet. Of the five labs participating in this project, only one had written policies for the treatment and handling of data. Respondents predominantly expressed disciplinary norms and processes for data management as underlying expectations that tended to be delivered informally and verbally. Some of the students interviewed had inherited data from previous students or others in the lab; this transference process also tended to be informal with minimal introduction to the data.

Faculty expected their graduate students to be independent learners. For example, one faculty member summed up the skills acquisition process as the "pain and suffering method," which she described as "[graduate students] try it, they fail, they see what failed, they come back to their advisor and you say, 'Ah, well maybe you should try X.' It is not something that we have attempted to teach, certainly."

When asked how well their students had mastered the DIL competencies, faculty stated that students tended to focus more on the mechanics of working with or analyzing data rather than the theories and assumptions underlying the software or tools they used. For this reason, some of the faculty expressed concern that students' understanding of these competencies may be somewhat superficial. For instance, one faculty member stated that students may be able to collect data from a sensor, but they did not necessarily understand the equipment variables that might impact data quality or accuracy. They may be more focused on getting the data than on understanding the steps and settings that created it. Similarly, some faculty felt that though students may be able to use tools to work with data, they did not always use them very effectively or efficiently. For example, one faculty member commented,

"I certainly think that they learn basic visualization tools, but there's a difference between learning how to draw a histogram and how to draw a histogram that's informative and easy to read."

This differentiation between basic project-driven skills and deeper, transferable understanding is found in questions about managing and curating data. Most students described idiosyncratic methods of data management, and generally overestimated the capacity of their methods to support local collaboration. Only 3 of the 7 faculty interviewed felt that their students provided enough information about their data for the faculty member to understand it. Only one faculty member thought that students provided enough information for a researcher outside of the lab to understand and use the data. In contrast, 15 of the 17 students believed that they provided sufficient information for someone outside of the lab to understand and use the data.

Faculty wanted their students to acquire a richer understanding and appreciation for good data management practices, but there were several barriers that restricted faculty from taking action. First, spending time on data management was not a priority if it distracted from or delayed the research process. Faced with this pressure, faculty accepted that a minimal skill set was sufficient for their students to succeed in school. One faculty member stated, "[Students] can do their work without understanding this. It's not essential that they have this. It's best if they do, but they don't. I guess I could be doing more, but we don't talk about all of these functions. . . . I'm not sure they all understand why data has to be curated."

Second, faculty did not see themselves as having the knowledge or resources to impart these skills to their students themselves. One faculty member mentioned requirements by funding agencies for data management plans and journals accepting supplemental data files as positive steps, but researchers in her field were ill-prepared to respond. Most of the faculty stated that there were no best practices in data management in their particular field. Faculty in this study did not believe that funding agencies, publishers, or scholarly societies in their discipline provide the guidance or resources to support effective practices in managing, sharing, or curating data. In the absence of such support, the data practices in their labs remain centered on local needs.

It is interesting to note similarities between our findings and the findings of others who have studied faculty perceptions of student competencies in information literacy. Shelley Gullikson (2006) surveyed faculty at institutions in eastern Canada to understand their perceptions of the ACRL Information Literacy Competency Standards. Her results indicated a consensus that information literacy competencies were important overall, but little agreement on when they should be taught. Claire McGuiness (2006) conducted semi-structured interviews with sociology and civil engineering faculty in the Republic of Ireland and found that faculty believed that students were acquiring information literacy competencies without formal or direct instruction but through other existing learning situations and course work. More recently, Sharon Weiner (2014) surveyed faculty at Purdue University to develop an understanding of to what extent information literacy concepts were taught by faculty across the disciplines. In addition to revealing significant differences between what aspects of information literacy were taught between the schools, faculty responses indicated that they expected their students to know how to avoid plagiarism, search for information, and define a research topic before enrolling in their courses.

FINDINGS ON EACH OF THE 12 DATA INFORMATION LITERACY COMPETENCIES

The rest of this chapter will discuss findings on the 12 DIL competencies across the interviews conducted by the five DIL project teams. Subsequent chapters describe the more specific findings by each project team and how the teams translated these findings into educational programs. Each of the competencies presented here includes the loosely worded skills description that was provided to the interviewees to ground the discussion, as well as any additional skills that they themselves articulated. Next, we summarize a curated list of responses from both faculty and students.

Cultures of Practice

Table 3.1 summarizes the results of our interviewee responses regarding the *cultures of practice* competency.

Faculty Responses

A major concern of faculty was the amount of prior training graduate students received with respect to cultures of practice for data. One faculty member described students' knowledge in this area as "underwhelming." Faculty felt that though students adequately saved their files and made backup copies, they were not as competent with sharing, curating, and preserving data. On the other hand, several faculty members commented that they themselves were unaware of any established practices, values, or norms for a data "culture of practice" in their discipline. For example, a computer science faculty member pointed out that knowing how to document research properly, and being able to go back to it in the future, is a discipline-wide issue.

TABLE 3.1 *Faculty and Student DIL Competency Ratings of Importance: Cultures of Practice*	
Competency-related skills:	Recognizes the practices, values, and norms of chosen field, discipline, or subdiscipline as they relate to managing, sharing, curating, and preserving data Recognizes relevant data standards of field (e.g., metadata, quality, formatting) and understands how these standards are applied
Additional skills:	Identifies standard protocols in the lab that may or may not match discipline-wide standards
Faculty and student ratings:*	Faculty average = 3.71 Student average = 3.88

*Ratings based on a 5-point Likert scale: 5 = essential; 4 = very important; 3 = important; 2 = somewhat important; 1 = not important.

Overall, faculty believed that guidance in this area would be beneficial. While it's true that faculty recognized the importance of obtaining skills through experience or peer teaching, they would like to have formal training available so that established practices and norms might be followed in the lab and the discipline. One participant described an ideal course for learning cultures of practice in the discipline that would include attitudes, shared skills (e.g., scripting language), visualization techniques, and technical writing training for describing results according to cultural norms.

Student Responses

The students we interviewed were unaware of any standards or discipline-wide norms for organizing, documenting, and sharing data. Yet, they recognized that this would be useful and important. One student stated that if researchers did not adhere to the standards of their field, "the results will not mean as much." And several students mentioned that they would follow standards if such standards exist. One computer science student mentioned that metadata standards in academia and industry appear to be at odds, with a greater amount of metadata being required in industry. As many graduate students take positions outside of academia after graduation, developing an understanding of industry norms and expectations in working with data is a critical element of effective educational programs.

Data Conversion and Interoperability

Table 3.2 summarizes the results of our interviewee responses regarding the *data conversion and interoperability* competency.

Faculty Responses

Most faculty reported that competencies with *data conversion and interoperability* were generally underdeveloped in students. Faculty reported that their students acquired their knowledge and skills in this competency through classes, peers, and experience. One faculty member stated that his students needed more experience with how conversion can affect their data. Another mentioned that students need to be aware of issues surrounding data loss during data migration and have an understanding of appropriate open standards for file formats.

Potential data loss in the conversion process was mentioned repeatedly. Faculty reported

TABLE 3.2 *Faculty and Student DIL Competency Ratings of Importance: Data Conversion and Interoperability*

Competency-related skills:	Is proficient in migrating data from one format to another Understands the risks and potential loss or corruption of information caused by changing data formats Understands the benefits of making data available in standard formats to facilitate downstream use
Additional skills:	Understands the advantages of different file formats Ability to code
Faculty and student ratings:*	Faculty average = 4.13 Student average = 4.24

*Ratings based on a 5-point Likert scale: 5 = essential; 4 = very important; 3 = important; 2 = somewhat important; 1 = not important.

that students were not considering the potential for loss or corruption when converting their data files. One faculty member made a connection between understanding how data can be manipulated and ensuring the quality of the data. Another saw this as an important skill for students to develop not just for working in his lab but also for gaining employment after graduation.

Student Responses

Nearly all of the students (14 out of 17) reported converting data as a part of their work in the lab, though most did not mention conversion as a distinct stage of the data life cycle. Students responded to questions of data conversion and interoperability by discussing conversion techniques for raw data (i.e., Microsoft Access files to plain text files; proprietary sensor data to Microsoft Excel) as well as processed data (i.e., converting images created in gnuplot to GIF or JPEG; converting a figure to a table). Conversions ranged from a simple cut-and-paste transportation of data to identifying the meaningful elements of the data and extracting them into a usable format. Students were less concerned with data loss during the conversion process than faculty. A few students reported

checking the data after converting them to ensure that data loss had not occurred.

Data Curation and Reuse

Table 3.3 summarizes the results of our interviewee responses regarding the *data curation and reuse* competency.

Faculty Responses

Faculty viewed *data curation and reuse* as an important subject, but commented that both students and the researchers themselves lacked these skills. In fact, several commented that the idea of data reuse is just beginning to take hold. One faculty member commented that the entire research lab needed a better understanding of who would benefit from data curation. Another felt that students generally don't have to concern themselves with these skills as the researcher decides when and how to make the data available for reuse.

Faculty also had a more personal reason for believing data curation and reuse to be important. In their experience, their data could not be recreated over the course of extended experiments and consequently must be curated. Therefore they were the number one

TABLE 3.3 *Faculty and Student DIL Competency Ratings of Importance:*
Data Curation and Reuse

Competency-related skills:	Recognizes that data may have value beyond the original purpose, to validate research, or for use by othersIs able to distinguish which elements of a data set are likely to have future value for self and for others Understands that curating data is a complex, often costly endeavor that is nonetheless vital to community-driven e-research Recognizes that data must be prepared for its eventual curation at its creation and throughout its life cycle Articulates the planning and activities needed to enable data curation, both generally and within local practice Understands how to cite data as well as how to make data citable
Additional skills:	None
Faculty and student ratings:*	Faculty average = 4.25 Student average = 4.06

*Ratings based on a 5-point Likert scale: 5 = essential; 4 = very important; 3 = important; 2 = somewhat important; 1 = not important.

reuse consumers of their own data. Similarly, faculty commented that the academic culture places less emphasis on functionality of data for public use and rather focuses more on the researchers' needs. Not all data are viable for curation, however, as one faculty member noted; nonstandard code was not reusable and didn't promote future research.

Faculty were also asked whether they or their graduate students had ever deposited data into a data repository. Of the eight faculty interviewed, three had deposited data in a repository, three had not, and two did not answer the question. Those that had, deposited their code into SourceForge or Google Code. However, faculty reported that getting the software in a format in which it could be shared was difficult.

Student Responses

Students identified at which stages their data (raw vs. processed vs. published) would be most valuable to save, but the potential value for reuse in the data they created was not an immediate concern. Rather, students did not

appear to understand the practices and skills that would be needed to support the reuse of their digital information. For example, one student believed that individuals in the lab were taking the necessary steps to prepare the generated data for eventual reuse, but was unsure of "exactly what they're doing."

Of the 18 students interviewed, 7 indicated that they had deposited data into a repository for reuse, though some of them indicated that these repositories were for a particular agency and not publicly accessible. Students were almost evenly split about their intent to deposit data into a repository in the future, with 7 indicating that they were planning to do so and 6 stating that they were not. Four students responded "I don't know" to the question. Almost all of the students we interviewed were willing to share their data with someone outside of their lab, with only one student responding "no" and one other stating "I don't know." Several students said they would need their advisor's approval before sharing their data. However, 12 of the 15 students who indicated they

TABLE 3.4 *Faculty and Student DIL Competency Ratings of Importance: Data Management and Organization*

Competency-related skills:	Understands the life cycle of data, develops data management plans, and keeps track of the relation of subsets or processed data to the original data sets Creates standard operating procedures for data management and documentation
Additional skills:	Familiarity with tools for data management Ability to annotate data sets at a higher level to keep track of changes and analyses performed
Faculty and student ratings:*	Faculty average = 4.00 Student average = 4.47

*Ratings based on a 5-point Likert scale: 5 = essential; 4 = very important; 3 = important; 2 = somewhat important; 1 = not important.

would share their data also stated that they would place conditions on sharing the data. The other 3 students responded "I don't know." The most common condition was that the student or the lab receives proper credit through a citation if the data were used in a publication. Other conditions mentioned were no redistribution of the data before publication of the findings of the lab of origin, and assurance that the data would not be misinterpreted by the recipient.

Data Management and Organization

Table 3.4 summarizes the results of our interviewee responses regarding the *data management and organization* competency.

Faculty Responses

Faculty described data management skills as standard operating procedures passed on from one student to the next. They believed that students gain rudimentary skills in data management in statistics courses prior to their graduate school career. "Learning by doing" was cited by many faculty as how students obtained these skills. If students were not proficient in this area, several problems

arose, including code overwrites, haphazard organization, and the inability to locate specific data. Faculty also cited participation in internships as a way that students obtained proficiency.

Data management plans ranked as very important; however, faculty clarified that students should able to follow them rather than develop and create them. When it came to the life cycle of data, faculty had different perspectives. One believed that students did not necessarily have to understand the life cycle to manage the data. Another cited the data life cycle as the reason students lacked skills: they did not see the full picture of why data management and organization becomes important further in the data life cycle. Another faculty member maintained that it was important for students to understand the entire process so that they can backtrack if a mistake is made.

Student Responses

Students rated *data management and organization* skills as the highest competency in terms of importance. In general, the students described the processes of data management and not necessarily the reasons behind it. For example, most students kept copies of their data in

TABLE 3.5 *Faculty and Student DIL Competency Ratings of Importance: Data Preservation*

Competency-related skills:	Recognizes the benefits and costs of data preservation Understands the technology, resources, and organizational components of preserving data Utilizes best practices in preparing data for its eventual preservation during its active life cycle Articulates the potential long-term value of own data for self or others and is able to determine an appropriate preservation time frame Understands the need to develop preservation policies and is able to identify the core elements of such policies
Additional skills:	None
Faculty and student ratings:*	Faculty average = 3.57 Student average = 3.75

*Ratings based on a 5-point Likert scale: 5 = essential; 4 = very important; 3 = important; 2 = somewhat important; 1 = not important.

multiple locations, but the ad hoc methods of saving created confusion rather than security. Almost all students stated that they learned data management skills through trial and error. They learned through word-of-mouth about standards for managing and organizing their data, if they existed at all. Of the 15 students, 9 mentioned that there were no formal policies or that they did not know of any in place for managing the data in their lab (2 students did not respond to the question). Even those students working in labs with policies were unaware of formal standards in the discipline. The students recognized organization of data as an issue recognized for day-to-day tasks. For example, it was difficult for one student to locate particular files. That student reported occasionally needing to go back and rerun coding to find the authoritative version.

Data Preservation

Table 3.5 summarizes the results of our interviewee responses regarding the *data preservation* competency.

Faculty Responses

Depending on context, data preservation was considered either "essential" or not a major concern for faculty. Faculty whose work included sustainability of results over time tended to view preservation of their data as a priority. Other faculty saw the importance of preservation in theory, but did not necessarily see the need to take action to preserve their data. Faculty noted a lack of student knowledge or interest in this area. One faculty member mentioned a need for more resources to tell students about current best practices. Some faculty reported that they themselves did not have strong knowledge in this area. One rated this competency as both "important" and "I don't know," as he felt he did not fully understand data preservation. Another faculty member reported that since technology changed so quickly, some of the data would become obsolete quickly.

Student Responses

Many of the students were unsure of a long-term use for their data. Students gave a range of responses when asked how long their data set should be preserved (see Table 3.6).

The length of preservation of data differed among the labs. For example, the students in the natural resources lab recognized the unique quality of their research and their role in supporting long-term research, and answered "indefinitely" to the question. Students in the agricultural and biological engineering lab were generally less certain of the long-term value of the data. Four of the five students responded either "less than 3 years" or "I don't know" to the question. There was some uncertainty about what was being done to preserve the data in the civil engineering lab. Two students indicated that no steps were being taken to preserve the data, one indicated that steps were being taken, and one did not know. Overall, students believed that the principal investigator, others in the lab, or a data repository handled data preservation.

Data Processing and Analysis

Table 3.7 summarizes the results of our interviewee responses regarding the *data processing and analysis* competency.

Faculty Responses

Data processing and analysis is considered a direct component of conducting science in most disciplines; therefore it received the highest rating of importance by faculty. Overall, respondents viewed this competency as critical for students to avoid mistakes in evaluating data and to gain efficiency in their work. Several faculty mentioned that students were unfamiliar with processing and analysis tools in the lab as well as within their discipline.

Faculty estimated that their students' skill levels in this competency ranged from "not systematic" and "inefficient" to "highly experienced"

TABLE 3.6   *How Long Should Your Data Set Be Preserved? (n = 17)*

Student Response	Number of Respondents
I don't know	4
Less than 3 years	2
10–20 years	2
20–50 years	3
50–100 years	1
For the life of the bridge being studied	1
Indefinitely	4

upon entering the program. One faculty member described students as good in this area, but not necessarily efficient, meaning that it took students longer than it should to perform tasks. Potential resources for graduate students included workshops and classes, but peer-to-peer learning was noted as most influential. Another faculty member responded that he did not typically teach these skills because students absorbed the material better by engaging with it themselves—even though they may fail repeatedly.

As with many of the competencies, the nature of training depends on local and disciplinary practices and culture. There was an emphasis on developing processing and analysis skills and critical thinking through personal engagement with the data and tools. Some of the pathways to skill acquisition mentioned were peer-to-peer and advisor contacts; formal courses, such as statistics; and self-teaching/trial and error.

Student Responses

As with faculty, students recognized that these skills were generally at the core of scientific practice in their domains. One student from

TABLE 3.7   *Faculty and Student DIL Competency Ratings of Importance: Data Processing and Analysis*

Competency-related skills:	Familiar with the basic data processing and analysis tools and techniques of the discipline or research area Understands the effect that these tools may have on the data Uses appropriate workflow management tools to automate repetitive analysis of data
Additional skills:	None
Faculty and student ratings:*	Faculty average = 4.63 Student average = 4.35

*Ratings based on a 5-point Likert scale: 5 = essential; 4 = very important; 3 = important; 2 = somewhat important; 1 = not important.

the ecology lab commented: "One of the—I think—biggest mistakes that people make in our field is improperly analyzing data." Students indicated that they were asked to perform a wide variety of tasks in processing and analyzing data. Several students reported teaching themselves to use tools to perform these tasks. Statistical programs dominated the list of tools that students described (R, SPSS, SAS), as did Microsoft Excel. In addition, they described a variety of other programs and tools for collecting and transforming data specific to the particular research domain and project, including ArcGIS, data loggers, ENVI for analyzing Landsat images, MATLAB, and various coding languages such as Python and C++.

Data Quality and Documentation

Table 3.8 summarizes the results of our interviewee responses regarding the *data quality and documentation* competency.

Faculty Responses

Many faculty felt that their students knew to check for any discrepancies in their data to resolve issues before analysis; however, faculty did not express much confidence in their students'

abilities to do the job well, nor to document the steps taken. One interviewee commented that it was "very hard to motivate students to write documentation," mostly because the students' focus was not on reproducibility, but on getting the work done and graduating. Faculty described self-documentation of code (a log of commands used and the parameters) as being important so that students could reproduce results. Another faculty member cited that a lack of tools for automating the process was a real challenge. This interviewee also noted that students consistently found themselves more concerned with the outputs of an experiment rather than the steps taken to get to the outputs. Still another faculty interviewee was confident that students were learning the skills needed to write the methods section of a paper, but that there was not enough documentation concerning the research process itself. This interviewee felt that students were overconfident when it came to artifacts and corruptions, and that they generally thought that their data was in good shape. One of the labs used error-checking procedures to ensure that measurements fell within known boundaries. The students in this lab participated in basic data quality checks, which included steps to ensure

TABLE 3.8   *Faculty and Student DIL Competency Ratings of Importance: Data Quality and Documentation*

Competency-related skills:	Recognizes, documents, and resolves any apparent artifacts, incompletion, or corruption of data Utilizes metadata to facilitate an understanding of potential problems with data sets Documents data sufficiently to enable reproduction of research results and data by others Tracks data provenance and clearly delineates and denotes versions of a data set
Additional skills:	None
Faculty and student ratings:*	Faculty average = 4.63 Student average = 4.12

*Ratings based on a 5-point Likert scale: 5 = essential; 4 = very important; 3 = important; 2 = somewhat important; 1 = not important.

that measurements were not out-of-bounds. Five out of the seven faculty we interviewed reported using some kind of version control practices in the lab, whether a specific system such as Subversion (SVN) or SharePoint, or file naming practices that included the version.

Student Responses

Overall, the students were aware of and/or participated in quality control steps. Out of 16 students, 14 felt that they created a sufficient amount of documentation for someone with similar expertise to understand and use their data (1 student did not provide a response). However, this may reflect one faculty member's assertion that students were overconfident in this area. Students in the computer engineering program were aware that this is an area that could benefit from "drastic improvement" (in the words of 1 student), but they also reported that their faculty advisor stressed documentation of the steps taken during research. For them, logging of calculations, thoughts, and the *entire* research process began early. These students were also more likely to use versioning software; students in ecology and natural resources were more likely to use file naming

strategies for versioning. They learned these skills through trial and error, from peers, and from the principal investigator. All 16 of the students who provided a response planned to leave a copy of their data with their advisor after they graduate.

Data Visualization and Representation

Table 3.9 summarizes the results of our interviewee responses regarding the *data visualization and representation* competency.

Faculty Responses

Faculty saw data visualization and representation as a critical competency for students to master. They identified a need for more advanced instruction for students to learn how to create effective, and ethical, graphical representations of data. Several of the faculty reported that students learned the mechanical aspects of using visualization tools, but were not as skilled in knowing what makes a good visualization. As one faculty member stated, "visualization is communication." Students also struggled in making use of representations to evaluate the quality of their data or to "impact a specific decision."

TABLE 3.9 *Faculty and Student DIL Competency Ratings of Importance: Data Visualization and Representation*

Competency-related skills:	Proficiently uses basic visualization tools of discipline
	Avoids misleading or ambiguous representations when presenting data in tables, charts, and diagrams
	Chooses the appropriate type of visualization, such as maps, graphs, animations, or videos, on the basis of an understanding of the reason/purpose for visualizing or displaying data
Additional skills:	Understands the mechanics of specific data visualization software programs
Faculty and student ratings:*	Faculty average = 4.63
	Student average = 4.35

*Ratings based on a 5-point Likert scale: 5 = essential; 4 = very important; 3 = important; 2 = somewhat important; 1 = not important.

Faculty reported that students received little to no formal training in this area as graduate students. Instead, students used the skills they acquired from undergraduate course work with their intuition to create visualizations and representations of their data. There were some exceptions. One faculty member recommended a book on the topic to incoming students. Another faculty member taught advanced techniques in the lab.

Student Responses

Student responses indicated a general recognition of the importance of data visualization to convey their findings in publications and other venues. All 17 of the students we interviewed indicated that they generated visual representations of their data. Several students mentioned the need to connect their work to their intended audiences. One student mentioned that "it's pretty much impossible to interpret the data without turning it into something." Students reported informal training on data visualization—advisors, lab mates/peers, and online help were resources for learning. Students mentioned a desire for software-specific instruction for creating their data visualizations

in R, MATLAB, Python, GMT, ArcGIS, Excel, SPSS, GIMP, and SigmaPlot.

Databases and Data Formats

Table 3.10 summarizes the results of our interviewee responses regarding the *databases and data formats* competency.

Faculty Responses

Faculty stated that students needed competency with databases and data formats but that their abilities were generally underdeveloped. Faculty gravitated to the "databases" elements of this competency rather than the more general "data formats" aspects. This may be due to the order in which we presented our information; however, it can also be inferred that not every faculty member interviewed employed databases in his or her work. Not surprisingly, those who did tended to give a higher overall rating of importance to this competency than those who did not.

Of the faculty who discussed databases, most mentioned understanding how to query databases as an important skill for students. Any faculty thoughts and concerns about

TABLE 3.10   *Faculty and Student DIL Competency Ratings of Importance: Databases and Data Formats*

Competency-related skills:	Understands the concept of relational databases and how to query those databases Becomes familiar with standard data formats and types for discipline Understands which formats and data types are appropriate for different research questions
Additional skills:	Understands how to maximize performance of databases based on own design
Faculty and student ratings:*	Faculty average = 3.71 Student average = 3.88

*Ratings based on a 5-point Likert scale: 5 = essential; 4 = very important; 3 = important; 2 = somewhat important; 1 = not important.

databases were generally shaped by the way that they themselves made use of them in their labs. For example, the natural resources faculty member commented that without the use of databases, it's as if his data does not exist. In contrast, the agricultural and biological engineering faculty member was striving to incorporate all of the lab's data sets into a database and noted that both he and his students needed to spend more time learning about the capabilities of databases. Some fields offer courses in databases, and faculty expect that students take these courses and to know how to work with databases prior to joining the lab. The faculty we interviewed from fields in which such courses are not offered speculated that students acquired skills by working with others, rather than through formal classroom experience.

Student Responses

Students handled a variety of data formats in their respective labs. The vast majority of students used Microsoft Excel or .csv files, as well as ASCII text file formats. Other data formats mentioned were Microsoft Access databases, MATLAB files, images (TIFF and JPEG), raster data, SPSS files, SigmaPlot, and NetCDF,

as well as the programming languages C and C++. Students tended not to focus on the data formats in the interviews. Therefore, they did not discuss larger issues in formatting data and databases in depth.

Discovery and Acquisition of Data

Table 3.11 summarizes the results of our interviewee responses regarding the *discovery and acquisition of data* competency.

Faculty Responses

Overall, faculty rated discovery and acquisition of data lowest of the 12 competencies. The assignment of importance to these skills seemed to align to the degree to which the individual and team used external data for research. Two of the faculty we interviewed indicated that the data they used were generated entirely in their labs, and they assigned a lower rating to this competency. Others indicated that external data might be brought into the lab to compare with or augment the data they generated. Or they might support an analysis done in the lab. Faculty used external data from sources such as the Census

TABLE 3.11 *Faculty and Student DIL Competency Ratings of Importance: Discovery and Acquisition of Data*	
Competency-related skills:	Locates and utilizes disciplinary data repositories Evaluates the quality of the data available from external sources Not only identifies appropriate external data sources, but also imports data and converts it when necessary so it can be used locally
Additional skills:	Understands and navigates data use agreements for reuse of data sets from external sources
Faculty and student ratings:*	Faculty average = 3.57 Student average = 4.12

*Ratings based on a 5-point Likert scale: 5 = essential; 4 = very important; 3 = important; 2 = somewhat important; 1 = not important.

Bureau, SourceForge, and repositories of geo-spatial data.

Faculty thought that student skills were highly variable in this competency. They believed that students acquired skills through trial and error and consultations with advisors and peers. No dominant theme emerged across faculty responses, but some valued the ability to evaluate data quality and have an "appropriate level of skepticism of outside data sources." Some faculty thought that locating and using data sources, if necessary, was an easily acquired skill.

Student Responses

This competency was highly rated overall by students despite a lack of experience for some with locating and using data from external sources. Students reported that their skills were developed primarily from consultations with peers and advisors. Students' experiences in acquiring data varied. Some found data that had been well documented, thus making it easy to understand and use. Others noted that it was difficult to understand the external data they had acquired or the data used different measurement scales that had to be converted. Overall, 14 out of 17 students

made use of data acquired outside of their lab. The major data repositories used by students were more varied than those listed by faculty. In addition to geospatial data repositories and SourceForge, students used the Environmental Protection Agency, the National Oceanic and Atmospheric Administration, Oregon State University's PRISM Climate Group, and the U.S. Department of Agriculture's Soil Survey Geographic (SSURGO) databases.

Seven out of the 17 students inherited data generated from others, reporting both positive and negative experiences in the transition. A student in computer engineering mentioned doing literature reviews as a means of searching for code.

Ethics and Attribution

Table 3.12 summarizes the results of our interviewee responses regarding the *ethics and attribution* competency.

Faculty Responses

Few faculty commented on the "misrepresentations of data" component of this competency, focusing instead on the citation, intellectual

TABLE 3.12 *Faculty and Student DIL Competency Ratings of Importance: Ethics and Attribution*

Competency-related skills:	Develops an understanding of intellectual property, privacy and confidentiality issues, and the ethos of the discipline when it comes to sharing and administering data Acknowledges data from external sources appropriately Avoids misleading or ambiguous representations when presenting data
Additional skills:	Identifies what data not to show for privacy purposes
Faculty and student ratings:*	Faculty average = 4.38 Student average = 4.35

*Ratings based on a 5-point Likert scale: 5 = essential; 4 = very important; 3 = important; 2 = somewhat important; 1 = not important.

property (IP), privacy, and confidentiality elements. Citing data was rated as "essential" to "very important" but faculty stated that their disciplines lacked standards for citing data. Most felt that students were good enough at citing data. One of the faculty members felt that ethics and attribution were discussed consistently in the lab and at the university and believed that students recognized that ethics extended beyond literature and included data sets. Two of the faculty felt that students cited outside sources sufficiently. One of them noted that students may not know how to cite a data set versus a piece of literature, and he himself didn't know of a disciplinary standard for citing data.

Several faculty noted that graduate students received ethics training either at the university or departmental level. The majority of the faculty noted that the question of who owned the data is "somewhat shaky" or "up in the air." One of the faculty members we interviewed felt that ethics training adequately covers privacy and IP issues, but more detailed, practical instruction for handling sensitive data is necessary. Another stated that students needed to understand the differences between copyrights, trademarks, and patents.

Student Responses

Several students reported citing the research paper associated with a data set rather than a data set itself, although many of the graduate students interviewed (11 out of 17 students) expressed a general feeling of being competent at citing data. It is encouraging that 11 students reported receiving training or instruction for ethics and IP issues, although they had mixed opinions about the usefulness of the training about data. Of the 17 students interviewed, only 3 indicated that they had a good understanding of their university's policies on research data, which echoed the faculty's statements on the need for more substantive graduate education in this area. One of the computer science students mentioned that the lab sought software code with open GNU or PSD licenses to ensure that they could properly use code generated by others. This aligned well with the faculty assertion that it was very important that these students understood issues with IP and copyright, trademarks, and patents. Of potential concern was that one student asserted that she didn't need to cite external code that she consulted but never used outright. About half of the students interviewed were not aware of any journals that

TABLE 3.13 *Faculty and Student DIL Competency Ratings of Importance: Metadata and Data Description*

Competency-related skills:	Understands the rationale for metadata and proficiently annotates and describes data so it can be understood and used by self and others
	Develops the ability to read and interpret metadata from external disciplinary sources
	Understands the structure and purpose of ontologies in facilitating better sharing of data
Additional skills:	Individuals who publish research must be ready at any point to answer questions from others regarding the data set
Faculty and student ratings:*	Faculty average = 4.57
	Student average = 3.88

*Ratings based on a 5-point Likert scale: 5 = essential; 4 = very important; 3 = important; 2 = somewhat important; 1 = not important.

might accept data sets for publication or as supplements to a journal article.

Metadata and Data Description

Table 3.13 summarizes the results of our interviewee responses regarding the *metadata and data description* competency.

Faculty Responses

Faculty described students as barely proficient or worse in the area of metadata and data description, and most felt that this was an area that needed improvement. Nearly every faculty member interviewed (seven out of eight) reported that the amount of documentation and description that their graduate students currently provided was not sufficient for someone outside of the lab to understand and make use of the data. Three of the faculty reported that they themselves had some trouble understanding and making use of the data because of the lack of description. One of the faculty felt

As an artifact of the research process, data sets are reflections of the decisions and actions made consciously or unconsciously by humans.

that this competency was of primary importance and that much could be gained by addressing the need; he expressed personal interest in learning more because he was unsure of the meaning of the term *metadata* and felt that a lack of knowledge in this area could be damaging. Another stated that "currently, researchers spend more time doing the work than explaining the work [they] are doing." For ongoing projects in one of the labs in which students pass code to other students each semester, the faculty member stated that current documentation was "definitely" not enough for someone outside of the lab to understand and make use of the data. Faculty considered this to be a major issue during project transition between semesters.

Student Responses

Out of the 17 students interviewed, 12 were familiar with the concept of metadata, though most stated that they had not received any formalized training. Some actually provided an inaccurate definition when pressed to explain it. (Two confused it with meta-analysis.) Student knowledge of metadata evolved from past projects, trial and error, and even past work in industry at least for one graduate student. For example, a natural resources graduate student explained that her method for describing data had been learned through a "personal coping strategy," meaning, through trial and error. One graduate student familiar with metadata noted that the metadata he creates often is not detailed because he "doesn't have enough time." Several students reported no trouble understanding the metadata that accompanied the external data they have used. None of the students reported using a metadata standard, although one student applied a standardized taxonomy.

CONCLUSION

Overall the DIL competencies were an effective means of exploring the environments and needs of our faculty partners and their students. The DIL competencies were not intended to serve as a universally applied set of skills or as prescriptive standards. The DIL competencies will continue to evolve as we learn more about disciplinary and local practices. Chapter 10 addresses future directions for developing the DIL competencies.

We observed many commonalities between faculty and students from different fields of study and from different academic institutions. Conducting interviews informed not only our respective DIL programs but also our collective understanding of the environments in which research data are generated, administered, and utilized. As an artifact of the research process, data sets are reflections of the decisions and actions made consciously or unconsciously by humans. Understanding the environments,

challenges, and needs of the people who work with data is an integral part of developing educational programs about data. The next section of this book presents the work of the five DIL project teams, describes the specific findings from their interviews, and their responses to the findings. These case studies illustrate how important the interviews were to the success of the DIL project.

NOTE

Portions of this chapter are reprinted from Carlson, J., Johnston, L., Westra, B., & Nichols, M. (2013). Developing an approach for data management education: A report from the Data Information Literacy project. *International Journal of Digital Curation, 8*(1), 204–217. http://dx.doi.org/10.2218/ijdc.v8i1.254

REFERENCES

Gullikson, S. (2006). Faculty perceptions of ACRL's Information Literacy Competency Standards for Higher Education. *Journal of Academic Librarianship, 32* (6), 583–592. http://dx.doi.org/10.1016/j.acalib.2006.06.001

McGuinness, C. (2006). What faculty think: Exploring the barriers to information literacy development in undergraduate education. *Journal of Academic Librarianship, 32*(6), 573–582. http://dx.doi.org/10.1016/j.acalib.2006.06.002

Weiner, S. A. (2014). Who teaches information literacy competencies? Report of a study of faculty. *College Teaching, 62*(1), 5–12. http://dx.doi.org/10.1080/87567555.2013.803949

PART II

Data Information Literacy Case Studies

CHAPTER 4

DEVELOPING A FOR-CREDIT COURSE TO TEACH DATA INFORMATION LITERACY SKILLS

A Case Study in Natural Resources

Sarah J. Wright, Cornell University
Camille Andrews, Cornell University

INTRODUCTION

The Cornell University Data Information Literacy (DIL) project team worked with a faculty member and graduate students in natural resources. The faculty member's lab collects data on longitudinal changes in fish species and zooplankton—namely their occurrence, population abundance, growth, and diet—in Lake Ontario. After interviewing the faculty member, a former student, and a lab technician, we determined that the DIL needs for this area were primarily *data management and organization* and *data quality and documentation,* including *metadata and data description.* We also placed a secondary focus on *databases and data formats, data visualization and representation,* and *cultures of practice,* including data sharing.

To address these needs, the Cornell team focused on two separate educational tracks. The first was a series of DIL workshops, open to the whole Cornell community, which was an introduction to data management and data management plans (DMPs), data organization, and data documentation. The second was a 6-week credit course on data management for graduate students in natural resources taught by the faculty member and the data librarian, Sarah J. Wright, in the spring of 2013. The course built on the previous workshop topics and also included sections on data quality, data sharing, data analysis, and visualization.

Assessment for the workshops involved using post-instruction surveys. The for-credit course assessment included formative "1-minute papers," very short, anonymous exercises performed at the end of each class; instructor feedback on active learning exercises (including an optional DMP exercise graded by a rubric—see Appendix A to this chapter); and a final survey that asked students to self-report on perceived skills before and after taking the class. The feedback was generally very positive, with the majority of students in the credit course indicating that they would recommend it to other graduate students in natural resources. They also reported an increase in their skill levels for all outcomes.

This chapter will discuss the Cornell case study and our instructional approaches. The strengths of our program were that we

- introduced graduate students to major concepts in data management;
- built and gathered modules, exercises, and tools that can be used in a range of educational situations;
- exposed current gaps in data management training;
- allowed students to network and exchange information;
- built awareness and relationships with faculty.

Ways in which we can improve are to

- provide more hands-on exercises so that students can apply the skills they learn to their research data;
- tailor the outcomes of the workshops and the course to specific skill levels and other disciplines;
- build and gather more curriculum resources and activities at both low- and high-skill levels;
- increase outcomes-based assessment and experiment with ways to make sessions more student-centered and peer-led.

LITERATURE REVIEW AND ENVIRONMENTAL SCAN OF DATA MANAGEMENT IN NATURAL RESOURCES AND ECOLOGY

The faculty member who worked with our Cornell team has a lab that collects data on longitudinal changes in fish species and zooplankton. This faculty member has long been an advocate of improving the data management skills of graduate students, and therefore was a natural partner for this project. Our faculty member's concern with data management reflected general trends in the larger field of ecology, which has increasingly emphasized data management and curation at both a macro and a micro level. For example, Wolkovich, Regetz, and O'Connor (2012) note:

> Because an ecological dataset [is] collected at a certain place and time [it] represents an irreproducible set of observations. Ecologists doing local, independent research possess . . . a wealth of information about the natural world and how it is changing. Although large-scale initiatives will increasingly enable and reward open science, . . . change demands action and personal commitment by individuals—from students and PIs [principal investigators]. (p. 2102)

A great deal of the literature focused on higher level issues, such as big data, cyberinfrastructure, and the development of metadata standards, or on an individual project as a microcosm of these issues. Given the heterogeneous and interdisciplinary nature of ecological data and the need for integrative studies in areas such as climate change, several authors (Carr et al., 2011; Jones, Schildhauer, Reichman, & Bowers, 2006; Michener & Jones, 2012; Wolkovich et al., 2012) addressed bioinformatics, ecoinformatics, and data sharing writ large, including the current state of the art and the need for better data management and coordination between various areas of ecological research. Others (Gil, Hutchison, Frame, & Palanisamy, 2010; Michener, Brunt, Helly, Kirchner, & Stafford, 1997) explored the variety of metadata standards for ecological data, the need for structured metadata and crosswalks to facilitate integration and interoperability of heterogeneous data sets, and the existing and needed partnership efforts necessary to advance this. In other cases, the literature outlines cyberinfrastructure needs for long-term ecological research, including particular technical solutions and issues with data collection, modeling, and management, such as the difficulties of collecting and harvesting heterogeneous data from a network of sites, building cross-searchable digital repositories, and accurately modeling with existing data (Barros, Laender, Gonçalves, Cota, & Barbosa, 2007; Magnusson & Hilborn, 2007; McKiernan, 2004). Institutions such as The Long Term Ecological Research Network (2012; Michener, Porter, Servilla, & Vanderbilt, 2011), DataONE (n.d.a), the Knowledge Network for Biocomplexity (2005), and for limnology the Global Lake Ecological Observatory Network (n.d.) championed high-level efforts toward providing researchers with centralized repositories, resources, tools, and training to address data management needs. For example, the Ecological Metadata Language (EML) and data management tools such as Morpho from the Knowledge Network for Biocomplexity are standards and tools that are widely available (Fegraus, Andelman, Jones, & Schildhauer,

2005; Knowledge Network for Biocomplexity, n.d.).

Among the natural resources graduate students we interviewed, there was a lack of awareness of existing practices, tools, or standard best practices in other areas, as well as a demand for point-of-need information and instruction at a very basic level. Although compilations of basic guidelines exist, such as those published in the *Bulletin of the Ecological Society of America* (Borer, Seabloom, Jones, & Schildhauer, 2009) and the DataONE (n.d.a) Best Practices database, the information on data management and curation practices is scattered across various publications, websites, and training curricula.

Similarly, an environmental scan of data management and curation at Cornell University revealed that the available resources, training, and services on data management at Cornell are scattered (Block et al., 2010). Hence, Cornell formed the Research Data Management Service Group in 2010 to be "a collaborative, campus-wide organization that links Cornell University faculty, staff and students with data management services to meet their research needs" (Research Data Management Service Group, n.d., "Mission"). In the area of formal graduate student training, our scan found that several workshops and classes are available that cover various components of data management, and it is conceivable that pieces of the process may be addressed in research methods classes and research labs. For example, in the Department of Natural Resources at Cornell, there are courses that cover basic biological statistics, wildlife population analysis, hydrologic data and tools, data collection and analysis for forest and stream ecology, and spatial statistics. Other departments across the College of Agriculture and Life Sciences have courses that address geographic information

systems (GIS), remote sensing, spatial modeling and analysis, temporal statistics, genomics and bioinformatics. In terms of non-curricular opportunities, units such as the Cornell University Library, Cornell Statistical Consulting Unit, and Cornell Institute for Social and Economic Research offer open workshops and consultation on GIS, basic data analysis, Bayesian statistical modeling, multilevel modeling, logistic regression analysis, linear regression parameters, path analysis, mediation analysis, experimental design, longitudinal data analysis, and other statistical techniques, as well as training on GIS software packages such as ArcGIS and Manifold, and statistical software such as SAS, SPSS, Stata, and R. However, despite these opportunities, there is still a lack of comprehensive training that addresses the major elements of data management for natural resources students in a holistic fashion.

CASE STUDY OF GRADUATE STUDENT DATA INFORMATION LITERACY NEEDS IN NATURAL RESOURCES

To discover more about data management needs at Cornell University, we used the DIL interview protocol (available for download at http://dx.doi.org/10.5703/1288284315510) to interview the faculty member in natural resources, one of his former graduate students, and a current lab technician during the period of March through May, 2012. Each participant rated how important DIL skills were to their data. The following section provides an overview of the responses we received.

The lab performed longitudinal studies of fish and zooplankton species. Some of the data sets contained information collected over decades,

TABLE 4.1   *DIL Competency Ratings of Participants in Natural Resources Case Study (n = 3)*

DIL Competency	Faculty Member	Former Graduate Student	Lab Technician
Discovery and acquisition of data	Somewhat important	Essential	Very important
Databases and data formats	Essential	Essential	Important
Data conversion and interoperability	Essential	Essential	Very important
Data processing and analysis	Essential	Essential	Very important
Data visualization and representation	Essential	Essential	Important
Data management and organization	Essential	Essential	Essential
Data quality and documentation	Essential	Essential	Essential
Metadata and data description	N/A	Essential	Important
Cultures of practice	Important	Essential	Essential
Ethics and attribution	Essential	Very important	Essential
Data curation and reuse	Very important	Essential	Very important
Data preservation	Important	Essential	Important

emphasizing the crucial need for data curation and maintenance over the extended life span of the data. Because these longitudinal data cannot be reproduced, a more formalized approach to data curation and management would be of great utility to students in the lab. The faculty member and lab staff also used databases extensively to organize and manage their longitudinal data sets. For this reason, they described acquiring the *data management and organization* skills necessary to work with databases and data formats, document data, and handle accurate data entry as essential (see Table 4.1). Otherwise, as the faculty member memorably stated, "it's [as if] the data set doesn't exist."

Interviewees noted *data conversion and interoperability* as a particularly important skill for importing data into statistical packages. Two out of three of our respondents mentioned that they lacked an understanding of the differences between raw and processed data and how they were used. The faculty member felt that students lacked a good understanding of data visualization theory, an interesting emerging area. Less important to the faculty member was that students had an understanding of how to access external data (other than geospatial data), how to find and evaluate data repositories, and version control. The reasons varied: in some cases the faculty member felt that there was little need for the skill on that particular project; the students learned the skill informally (e.g., finding external data or data repositories through trial and error); or one or two people in the lab handled the task for everyone (e.g., entering data into Excel and the Access database).

Metadata was of high importance to all of our interviewees. When asked about metadata, the faculty member responded that he wasn't even sure what it meant; however, he hoped to learn about it over the course of the collaboration. The former graduate student and the current lab technician placed even more emphasis on data documentation and description skills than the faculty member. The lab technician attributed much of the documentation and description he performed to a "personal coping strategy," so that when he came back to the data later he could understand what he did and where he was in the process.

The former graduate student indicated that accessing and using external data sets, depositing data into repositories, data preservation, and intellectual property were important areas of knowledge. He learned most of what he knew through trial and error, from colleagues, and in peer-to-peer learning. Perhaps this was one of the reasons that he was adamant about best practices and training students early in graduate school. In answering our question about what he wished he'd known or been taught before graduate school, he said:

> By graduate school, that's the point in which you are putting data in [spreadsheets], [so] your best management practices should be in place. But I recognize they're probably not. . . . So [data management skills] should be the very first thing you learn when you come to grad school.

When asked about the importance of the DIL skills, the former graduate student listed all as essential (see Table 4.1) but noted that some were covered better than others. For example,

skill development in the *discovery and acquisition of data* happened pretty well, but he found education about *databases and data formats* and *data conversion and interoperability* in its infancy. Within certain skill sets, like *data processing and analysis,* the degree program included tools, techniques, and their effects on interpretation, but did not include more advanced concepts like workflow management tools. He also noted that there was a lack of norms, or weak norms, in the field regarding its *cultures of practice.* There was a need for those in the field, especially faculty and principal instigators (PIs) of research projects, to push for higher standards in data management issues. He felt that most of the outcomes he mentioned as essential were taught poorly or not at all.

In fact, across most of the competencies discussed, lack of formal training for acquiring important skills arose as a common theme. The student and technician noted that they acquired most of their skills informally, especially in areas such as generating visualizations and ascribing metadata to files, as there was no formal on-campus training and few readily identifiable people with expertise. Although there were classes and workshops available, students were not aware of them and were more receptive to just-in-time training or troubleshooting. When we discussed the availability of Cornell courses to learn about R, one respondent said, "I don't know if there are actual courses on it. I imagine there are somewhere, but I haven't pursued that and I don't know that I really have time to take a course." The student described the optimal situation as one where he would have access to an expert who was using R in a similar way, much like the library has a GIS librarian available for GIS users.

There were some disconnects between what we learned from the faculty member and what we heard from the lab technician and the former graduate student. *Discovery and acquisition of external data* was only somewhat important to the faculty member. He felt that "if they didn't know these [databases] existed, it wouldn't matter," explaining that they seldom used external data in their research. However, the student and the lab technician reported using external data *and* exhibited limited knowledge of disciplinary repositories. Our discussion of *cultures of practice* skills followed the same path: it had less importance to the faculty member, but was essential to the student and the lab technician. The former graduate student's level of awareness of the skills and their necessity was very high, especially since he had had a great deal of experience as an administrator of a large data set. For example, the faculty member and the lab technician placed less emphasis on understanding formal metadata standards and data preservation (counting them as important, but not essential), in contrast to the former graduate student and what we found in the environmental scan and literature review. They also did not mention workflows or tools like Morpho a great deal. This disconnect between faculty and student views is unsurprising, since faculty tend to assume everyone understands the culture that they've been embedded in for years. Additionally, those who are not database administrators or who have not had occasion to need certain skills will naturally tend to downplay their importance.

While respondents considered nearly all of the skills we covered in our interview important, those that were not as highly prioritized included *discovery and acquisition of data* and *data preservation*. Interestingly, there were a few differences in opinion between our faculty collaborator and the others we interviewed. The most dramatic difference was around

discovery and acquisition of data, which the student and the lab technician felt was very important or essential. In contrast, our faculty collaborator felt that students should already have a good grasp of where to obtain data sets and therefore considered it only somewhat important (with the lowest rating of any of the competencies). *Cultures of practice* was another example of a competency that the faculty member felt the students should understand (and he rated it as "important"). This is one that the student and the lab technician felt was essential and needed to be addressed in educational interventions.

A TWOFOLD INSTRUCTIONAL APPROACH TO DATA INFORMATION LITERACY NEEDS

In fall 2012 and spring 2013 we implemented instructional interventions based on our findings to address the gaps that we found in the curriculum covering data management skills. Given the wide range of competencies of interest to the faculty and students interviewed, the Cornell DIL team narrowed the skills down according to the following principles:

1. Does the competency address a gap we found in the curriculum?
2. Did we have the expertise to address the need? If not, could we include someone else who did have the expertise?
3. Where could we add the most value?

After asking these questions in concert with our faculty collaborator, the four DIL-related areas on which we focused were *data management and organization, data analysis and visualization, data sharing,* and *data quality and documentation.* Our instructional approach was twofold: in the fall we offered workshops in the library addressing several data management topics; in the spring we offered a six-session, one-credit course for graduate students in natural resources.

Instruction Approaches: 1-Hour Workshops and 6-Week Course

In the fall, we offered a series of 1-hour library-sponsored workshops aimed at graduate students in the sciences, each introducing a different data management topic. The first workshop focused on data management planning and was an unqualified success: 30 students attended and we had an additional 13 on a wait list. The subsequent workshops had lower attendance: 8 attended the data organization workshop, 10 attended the data documentation workshop, and only 4 signed up for the data sharing workshop, so it was canceled. Despite the decreased attendance at the later workshops, we felt we were successful because the later session subjects were more specific, addressing topics that appealed to a more limited audience than had the broader workshop on data management (see Table 4.2). The students who attended were active and enthusiastic participants and expressed appreciation after the workshops.

In the spring, the Cornell DIL team offered the six-session, one-credit course for graduate students in natural resources, Managing Data to Facilitate Your Research. The data librarian and the faculty collaborator co-taught the course. The content was similar to the fall semester library workshops, but we were able to build on prior classes as we progressed through the material. For example, in the workshop format, we introduced the basics of data management as part of each workshop; in the course format we introduced data management in the first session and were focused on additional content in each subsequent class. At the beginning of each session, we recapped what we covered in the last session and offered time to respond to questions. Because we listed the course through the Department of Natural Resources, we had a more subject-specific focus and drew on examples from ecology and fisheries research. For example, during the session on data analysis and visualization, the faculty collaborator demonstrated linking stable isotope data from the Cornell University Stable Isotope Laboratory to the master database file from the Adirondack Fisheries Research Program. This involved discussing data import, linking the new table to master tables in the database, developing a query, and exporting the data into Microsoft Excel. All of these topics could have been discussed without the context of real research data, but using real-life examples drawn from the discipline helped the students understand what was happening in the data management process and, more importantly, why it should happen. We created a library guide for the course, available at http://guides.library .cornell.edu/ntres6940.

We drew on several resources to build the course and workshop content. For example, DataONE (n.d.b) created education modules covering data management topics that are openly available at http://www.dataone .org/education-modules. We relied heavily on those that matched our identified needs. We did make changes to the slides, adjusting for the discipline and for the time allotted. We also made use of an Ecological Society of America (ESA) publication about best practices in data management (Borer et al., 2009).

Twenty-five students enrolled in the course. Most of the students were from the natural resources department, though there were students from biological and environmental

TABLE 4.2 *Weekly Course Topics and Readings in the Spring 2013 One-Credit Cornell Course NTRES 6940: Managing Data to Facilitate Your Research*

Topic	Description and Readings
1. Introduction to data management	We will use the first class session for introductions and logistics. The instructors will give a brief explanation of DMPs and reasons for using them. We'll then have a group discussion of research, data problems encountered, and data management needs. Readings: Wolkovich, E. M., Regetz, J., & O'Connor, M. I. (2012). Advances in global change research require open science by individual researchers. *Global Change Biology, 18*(7), 2102–2110. http://dx.doi.org/10.1111/j.1365-2486.2012.02693.x National Science Foundation (n.d.). Dissemination and sharing of research results. http://www.nsf.gov/bfa/dias/policy/dmp.jsp Research Data Management Service Group (n.d.). Data management planning: Guide to writing a data management plan (DMP). http://data.research.cornell.edu/content/data-management-planning
2. Data organization	Organizing your data at the front end of a research project will save time and increase your ability to analyze data. This session will introduce you to the principles involved in creating a relational database and will provide examples to help you organize your own data in this manner. Topics will include best practices for data entry, data types, how to handle missing data, organization by data type, and data file formats. Readings: Borer, E. T., Seabloom, E. W., Jones, M. B., & Schildhauer, M. (2009). Some simple guidelines for effective data management. *Bulletin of the Ecological Society of America, 90*(2), 205–214. http://dx.doi.org/10.1890/0012-9623-90.2.205 Research Data Management Service Group (n.d.). Preparing tabular data for description and archiving. http://data.research.cornell.edu/content/tabular-data
3. Data analysis and visualization	Analyze existing data and create graphs using R in order to effectively communicate findings. Readings: DataONE (n.d.). Education modules: Lesson 10—Analysis and workflows. http://www.dataone.org/education-modules Noble, W. S. (2009). A quick guide to organizing computational biology projects. *PLoS Computational Biology, 5*(7), e1000424. http://dx.doi.org/10.1371/journal.pcbi.1000424

Continued

engineering, ecology and evolutionary biology, crop and soil sciences, and civil and environmental engineering. The students ranged from first-year to fourth-year graduate students. Two faculty and staff members attended. Fifteen students attended four or more of the six sessions in the course (see Figure 4.1).

Given that it was only a one-credit, 6-week-long course, we could only briefly touch upon the major issues. A mix of higher level,

TABLE 4.2 *Weekly Course Topics and Readings in the Spring 2013 One-Credit Cornell Course NTRES 6940: Managing Data to Facilitate Your Research*—cont'd

Topic	Description and Readings
4. Data sharing	The NSF and other funding agencies have already adopted data sharing policies. Publishers also have data sharing requirements, whether they host data themselves, or expect researchers to deposit data in a data center or to make it available upon request. So where to share? During this class session, we'll discuss disciplinary databases, Cornell's eCommons digital repository, and some other sharing strategies, and will talk about evaluation criteria upon which to base your decision about where to share your data. Readings: Center for Research Libraries. (2005). General factors to consider in evaluating digital repositories. *Focus on Global Resources, 25*(2). http://www.crl.edu/focus/article/486 Databib | searchable catalog of research data repositories (http://databib.org/index.php) eCommons@Cornell (http://ecommons.library.cornell.edu/)
5. Data quality and documentation	While written documentation—for example, in a lab notebook—is still important, the platforms on which modern researchers are working and collecting data are increasingly complex. How do you document your digital data and the steps you take to analyze it? Are your files sufficiently organized and well described so that others can interpret what you've done? What about yourself, 3 months from now? During this class session on data documentation, we'll discuss the challenge of remembering details relevant to interpreting your data, and offer some best practices and strategies to adopt in order to organize and describe your data for yourself and others. Readings: Disciplinary Metadata | Digital Curation Centre (http://www.dcc.ac.uk/resources/metadata-standards) Kozlowski, W. (2014). *Guidelines for basic "readme" style scientific metadata.* http://data.research.cornell.edu/sites/default/files/SciMD_ReadMe_Guidelines_v4_1_0.pdf Rudstam L. G., Luckey, F., & Koops, M. (2012). *Water quality in offshore Lake Ontario during intensive sampling years 2003 and 2008: Results from the LOLA (Lake Ontario Lower Foodweb Assessment) Program.* http://hdl.handle.net/1813/29691
6. Final wrap-up: data management plans	For the final class session, participants will have the opportunity to present a DMP for peer discussion and review. Depending on interest, presentations may range from 6 to 15 minutes. Readings: Sample DMP from Inter-University Consortium for Political and Social Research (ICSPR) (http://www.icpsr.umich.edu/icpsrweb/content/datamanagement/dmp/plan.html) Sample DMPs from University of California San Diego (http://idi.ucsd.edu/data-curation/examples.html) Sample DMPs from the University of New Mexico (http://libguides.unm.edu/content.php?pid=137795&sid=1422879)

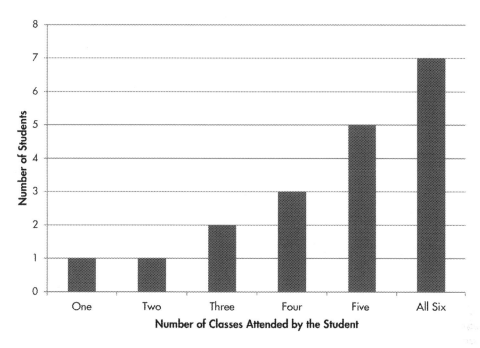

Figure 4.1 Self-reported attendance by students enrolled in the spring 2013 one-credit Cornell course NTRES 6940: Managing Data to Facilitate Your Research (n = 19).

conceptual articles gave context to our discussions, along with more practical resources for students to explore on their own and pointers to Cornell University resources for training and just-in-time help.

Learning Objectives for the Cornell Course

The aim of our instruction for the course was to introduce students to data management best practices in natural resources and to help students create plans to manage their data effectively and efficiently while meeting funder and publisher requirements. The learning objectives were as follows:

By the end of this course, students will be able to

- describe data management and why it is important;

- describe their research and data collection process in order to identify their data life cycle and complete the initial part of the DMP;
- evaluate a DMP to recognize the necessary components of a successful plan;
- describe and follow best practices in structuring relational databases to make analysis and retrieval easier/more efficient for long-term studies;
- analyze existing field data and create graphs using R to effectively communicate findings;
- evaluate disciplinary data repositories to determine requirements and fitness for data deposit;
- evaluate the annotation/documentation accompanying a data set to recognize the appropriate level necessary for long-term understanding by self and others;
- create a DMP to manage and curate

TABLE 4.3   *Needs and Learning Outcomes Addressed in the Cornell For-Credit Class per Session*

Session	Needs Identified	Outcomes Addressed
1. Introduction to data management	Basic introduction to data management: importance in the research context of the audience	Understands the life cycle of data, develops DMPs, and keeps track of the relation of subsets or processed data to the original data sets Creates standard operating procedures for data management and documentation
2. Data organization	Acquiring the data management and organization skills necessary to work with databases and data formats, document data, and handle accurate data entry is described as essential, otherwise, "it's as if the data set doesn't exist"	Understands the concept of relational databases, how to query those databases, and becomes familiar with standard data formats and types for discipline Understands which formats and data types are appropriate for different research questions
3. Data analysis and visualization	A good understanding of higher end data visualization, though not positioned as currently essential but as an interesting emerging area by the instructor, was in short supply. The lab primarily uses R for data analysis and visualization, but training is limited, and not aimed specifically at students in natural resources	Becomes familiar with the basic analysis tools of the discipline Uses appropriate workflow management tools to automate repetitive analysis of data Proficiently uses basic visualization tools of discipline
4. Data sharing	Areas such as accessing external data (except for background geospatial data) and finding and evaluating data repositories were of less importance to the faculty member than to the students, but the faculty member expressed interest in learning more about Cornell's institutional repository	Recognizes that data may have value beyond the original purpose, to validate research or for use by others Locates and utilizes disciplinary data repositories

Continued

their own data for effective long-term use and reuse as well as to meet funding requirements.

Each session attempted to meet the learning outcomes outlined by the DIL project (see Table 4.3). We addressed them through a variety of activities; however, we were not able to address all of them in great depth. Some sections of the course were more traditional. For example, students read an article on effective data management practices (Borer et al., 2009)

TABLE 4.3 *Needs and Learning Outcomes Addressed in the Cornell For-Credit Class per Session—cont'd*

Session	Needs Identified	Outcomes Addressed
5. Data quality and documentation	Skills such as ascribing metadata to files are acquired informally; furthermore, the faculty member noted he wasn't even sure what was meant by metadata, and he hoped to learn about it over the course of the collaboration	Recognizes that data may have value beyond the original purpose, to validate research or for use by others Understands the rationale for metadata and proficiently annotates and describes data so it can be understood and used by self and others Develops the ability to read and interpret metadata from external disciplinary sources Understands the structure and purpose of ontologies in facilitating better sharing of data
6. Data management plans	Funders and other organizations are increasingly requiring DMPs, and few graduate students are aware of the components of a good DMP	Understands the life cycle of data, develops DMPs, and keeps track of the relation of subsets or processed data to the original data sets Creates standard operating procedures for data management and documentation Articulates the planning and actions needed to enable data curation

before class and commented to a discussion forum on points they found interesting or that needed more clarification. Then we reviewed the comments and discussed them in class.

We considered graduate students to be expert learners; therefore we employed collaborative learning techniques, including think-pair-share and group problem solving (Center for Teaching Excellence, 2013b). For example, as a class activity students discussed their research data life cycle in detail and then drew a diagram of the stages of research. For "evaluate disciplinary data repositories" students worked in groups to identify possible repositories for data deposit for their subject. (See Appendix B to this chapter for a full description of the exercise.) For the session on data documentation, students worked in groups with examples of metadata and evaluated what was done well and what could be improved. Finally, we asked those who chose to complete the optional DMP exercise to complete a different section of the DMP each week, and participants received feedback from the librarian instructors.

Assessment

We used a combination of formative and summative assessment tools, including 1-minute reflections after each session, feedback on outputs from active learning exercises, and a

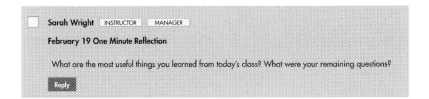

Figure 4.2 One Minute Reflection assignment via a course Blackboard site.

final survey (Center for Teaching Excellence, 2013a; Downey, Ramin, & Byerly, 2008). A 1-minute reflection was administered either as a survey after each library workshop, or as a discussion question via the course Blackboard site. Figure 4.2 shows a typical 1-minute reflection assignment.

In addition to the 1-minute reflection posts, we used the discussion board for students to ask questions after each class session. There were 68 posts, with 21 participants—representing the majority of the students enrolled. We gained many substantial and useful comments using this method. In fact, the comments were so useful that it became our practice to review the most pertinent comments at the beginning of each class as a way to emphasize content from the last class or to lead into content for that day's class. After the class on data organization and the use of relational databases, we received positive feedback from students enthusiastically discussing the changes they would make due to what they had just learned.

> The "rules of thumb" were a great summary of various best practices for data management. It was interesting to read that computer code was actually a form of metadata in itself. I suppose I had never looked at it in that light before but from now on I will take my commenting more seriously! I was also grateful for the explanation of best practices for relational databases. I've heard of the term but this paper did a great job walking through the formation of one, step by step. Finally, I'm finding that by taking this class and doing these readings

I'm becoming more aware of different data management services in my own field.

> Three points from Borer et al. (2009) that were particularly useful: [1] the merits of using scripted analyses. Having used JMP for 4 years, I know too well the agony of trying to replicate drop-down menu instructions months after doing an analysis. I plan to switch to R. [2] standardized file naming system using the international date format. While I use descriptive folder names, I do not always use descriptive file names and I am not consistent with date format . . . [which] makes searching for files on my computer inefficient . . . [and] also means that when I send others my data it loses some descriptive information . . . [3] full taxonomic names in data files. A few years ago I did an experiment in which I identified 100+ plant species in the field. I used abbreviations in my data. Flash forward 3 years, and it took me days to reconstruct what all my abbreviations were. Some taxonomic names had changed. Never again!

We received comments that required followup and more conversation:

> The relational database method seems great but will take some getting used to. Is there a way to connect excel and access files that would allow you to input data and automatically update in the relational database?

> Learning about relational databases was very useful. Efficient organization of spreadsheets

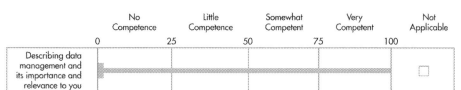

Figure 4.3 Example self-assessment survey question using a slider scale.

was also helpful. I would like to learn more about how to organize metadata, but I think this is an upcoming class discussion. Also, I am still lacking clear reasons why Access is preferable to Excel. What does Access offer that Excel does not? What are the features that make Access particularly useful?

After reading the last comment, we felt that we had not clearly explained the advantages of a relational database, so we addressed that point at the beginning of the next class. As these examples illustrate, the 1-minute reflections proved to be a powerful form of formative assessment that allowed us to respond to the learning needs of the students.

We also provided active learning exercises so that students could receive outcomes-based assessments of their work and understanding. Some of these were in-class exercises that we collected and delivered feedback on for the students. Others were optional out-of-class assignments, which included rubrics for assessment. Though few students completed the optional assignment (n = 5), all who tried it found it useful; those who didn't complete it indicated that it probably should be required in the class. In most cases, we simply discussed what students found during the exercises and gave feedback during discussion.

Finally, we administered a self-assessment survey at the end of the class to gauge the success of our experimental course (see the full instrument in Appendix C to this chapter).

We invited and received constructive criticism via the survey instrument, much of which will guide our next attempt at offering similar instruction.

Here, we also asked the students to self-evaluate their skill levels concerning the course outcomes both before and after taking the class (see an example in Figure 4.3). Rather than performing pre- and post-evaluations, we asked students to rate their skill levels before and after, after instruction occurred. This method avoided the problem of overestimation of skill that is common before learning a new topic (Kruger & Dunning, 1999). Having learned more about the course outcomes, students could then better compare what they actually knew at the beginning to what they had learned during the course.

On average, responses (n = 17) showed marked increases in the skills, knowledge, and abilities that the students felt they possessed after taking the class, as shown in Figure 4.4. However, there was room for improvement since on average students rated none of the outcomes in the "somewhat competent" to "very competent" range after the course. In fact, several outcomes received an average rating of "little competence" and "somewhat competent" following the course. And, the most frequently voiced criticism of the class was that we touched on a lot of important topics, but we didn't have time to go in-depth and failed to provide enough opportunities to practice what we'd discussed. Still, feedback was

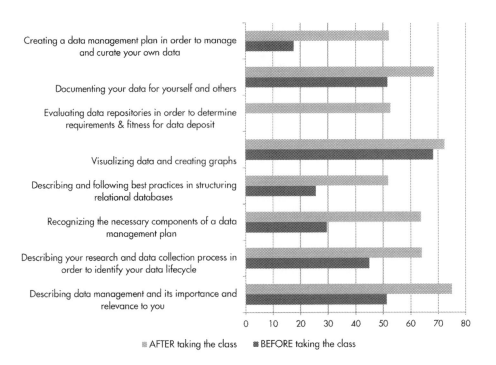

Figure 4.4 Average responses (before and after) to the survey question, "How would you rate your knowledge/skills/ability in the following areas?" (n = 17). (NOTE: Due to a technical error in the survey, the student response to "Evaluating data repositories in order to determine requirement & fitness for data deposit" before taking the class could not be included in this figure.)

overwhelmingly positive, and the majority of students (13 out of 16) would recommend this course to others in natural resources.

RESULTS

Overall, the response to the workshops and the course was very positive. Students reported a better awareness of data management skills and the resources and tools available to them. One student noted, "I think the topic of this class is SO ESSENTIAL [to] the way scientific research is being carried out and shared now. . . . [This course] fills a hole in Cornell grad education." Filling a need in the curriculum is exactly what the Cornell DIL team was trying to do, and it was gratifying that students recognized

the importance of the topic and appreciated our educational efforts!

The self-reported increase in skill for all of the learning outcomes was another positive outcome of the course. The marked increase in students' abilities to articulate the importance of data management, to create their own DMP, and to describe and document their own data collection practices was an important step forward. Their comments in the end-of-class survey bore this out and indicated their increased awareness of many areas of data management. As one student said:

I think just the exposure to the different aspects of data management and the discussion about the usefulness of relational databases and analysis software like R can be of great benefit to students, especially those that are relatively new to research and may not be aware of the types and benefits of resources available to them.

Benefits for the DIL project included uncovering areas in which there was a need for more exploration, such as curation of training resources and opportunities, direct instruction on tools (e.g., conversion from Excel to database programs, database tools for Mac users, data visualization tools, qualitative analysis tools like Atlas.ti), and allowing students to exchange information and network with each other. Interestingly, in the final class students exchanged information about ad hoc training in data visualization in departments beyond natural resources. This shows the library's potential role in facilitating peer-to-peer training in addition to the formal, instructor-led educational initiatives. The library is experimenting with the role of facilitator to crowd source tips and workflows from students who have expertise and to schedule project clinics with interested and skilled students and staff. This facilitator role could be fruitfully applied to DIL and would address the need to balance a great need for specialized instruction with a small library staff that has limited time and skills.

Before the course ended, the project team at Cornell discussed how to continue providing data management instruction and what could be done to improve it. This project has been an exciting experiment, but there is much interest beyond the library. Our faculty collaborator discussed how to offer this course next time—indicating even before we had finished the course that he was invested in doing it again. Building a stronger relationship with this faculty member and investigating the students' need for hands-on training (in areas that faculty assumed the students knew or would learn informally along the way) was one of the most rewarding parts of this experience.

The course also gained wider recognition among faculty and students; it was the focus of a short article in the *Cornell Chronicle* titled "Course Teaches Grad Students How to Manage Their Data," which sparked inquiries from faculty and graduate students in other departments (Glazer, 2013). This prompted the library to hold more one-time sessions and to add modules to online guides that hopefully will lead to more course- and curriculum-integrated instruction.

Although the student feedback was very positive, there is room for improvement. For example, the scope of the course should be more focused, and it would work better with a smaller group that has a similar level of experience. We would like to expand the course beyond six sessions, or eliminate content if we are unable to increase the number of sessions. In the current course, we included more material than we could reasonably cover. These changes would also allow us to introduce more exercises and to provide more opportunities for hands-on learning. This was a major criticism received of the course. Including more practical exercises in the course and holding project clinics and peer-led workshops would provide students the opportunity to experiment with and learn using their own research data. These formats would also allow students more time for discussion and peer exchange around personal workflows and existing practices. They would make the sessions less prescriptive and instructor-led and more student-led and free-flowing. Discussions would also allow for more just-in-time exchange of information for students who are interested in particular areas, and for more advanced students who might not want to take a full course.

With these goals in mind, we plan to provide general, beginner-level data management library workshops in the fall, open to anyone, focused on topics like creating a DMP or writing a readme file to describe your data. We'll then provide a disciplinary course (possibly in other departments that have expressed interest) where we can provide more focused, in-depth instruction and require active learning components, such as the creation of a DMP. The peer-to-peer workshop model and project clinics are also a possibility for the future.

It is clear that DIL skills are important skills that graduate students feel are not being taught sufficiently in their programs. A former graduate student brought up the need for data management instruction even earlier, stating, "I think it starts as an undergraduate. It's an easily understood discipline at even a high school or junior high level, and I would start it that early, if possible." We would like to incorporate data management instruction into undergraduate laboratory classes, similar to the way we've incorporated information literacy into the curriculum at multiple points in programs. This is a long-term goal that has grown out of the current project, and it will require collaboration and the investment of groups both inside and outside the library.

DISCUSSION

The Cornell DIL team entered this project with a general idea of the DIL competencies; however, interacting with students and teaching the competencies resulted in some changes to our original impressions. Much as the ACRL's (2000) information literacy competency standards outline high-level outcomes for information literacy across an entire curriculum, the DIL competencies are a starting point for articulating what data management concepts students should understand and apply throughout their research careers. How this

plays out at varying stages of a researcher's education and for each discipline is a much more detailed and idiosyncratic issue. We found that many of the students in the course, especially those at the beginning skill levels in a particular competency, wanted much more specific (and often very tool-based) skills (e.g., how to better use spreadsheet and database packages like Excel and Access), rather than the higher level conceptual DIL skills, especially in the absence of an immediate real-world application (e.g., funder data sharing requirements).

Since the competencies outlined in the DIL project covered such a wide range in a quickly changing field, they placed an emphasis on the recognition and understanding of general best practices and much less emphasis on the skills needed at the disciplinary and lab/project level. Working with the general DIL competencies and tailoring them to course and class session outcomes forced us to refine and articulate what we wanted students to be able to do and how we wanted them to demonstrate and apply their understanding to their disciplinary-specific situation. For example, we recognized that skills build in a progression, so we derived the following outcomes from the general DIL competency "understands the life cycle of data, develops DMPs, and keeps track of the relation of subsets or processed data to the original data sets":

- Describe research and data collection process to identify data life cycle and complete initial part of DMP
- Evaluate a DMP to recognize the necessary components of a successful one
- Create a DMP to manage and curate own data for effective long-term use and reuse as well as to meet funding requirements

In the course, we briefly addressed tracking subsets of data, but addressing this topic alone was much more involved than it first appeared. This pattern emerged in working with the competencies.

The range of skill levels in the class and the wide variety of types of data with which they worked (e.g., quantitative and qualitative; small and large data sets in multiple formats) showed the need for competencies that progressed over time from basic understanding and tool-based skills to higher level competencies in analysis and synthesis, as well as for outcomes that addressed particular disciplines or kinds of data. This work is the beginning of that effort.

Questions we asked ourselves in the process of creating the workshop series and the for-credit course map well to areas that we need to address to integrate DIL competencies into the curriculum:

- *What skills do students currently have and where are their most pressing needs?* The interviews we conducted with the faculty member and students in natural resources gave us an in-depth view of the skills and attitudes of a very small sample. A larger survey of graduate students and faculty in natural resources (and other disciplines) would give a better idea of the needs of the campus community.
- *What are the gaps in the curriculum? What outcomes are already addressed, where, and at what levels?* As part of the environmental scan, we identified the training available, but a closer look at the syllabi of courses that incorporated DIL outcomes and a census of available workshops and other training could help us target our efforts.
- *Do we have the expertise to address student and researcher needs? If not, could we include someone else in or provide staff professional development to gain the missing*

expertise? It does no good to plan instruction if we do not have the expertise to deliver it, so we asked ourselves: Who is the best person to answer this need?

- *Where can we add the most value? Where can we find partners to supplement areas that are outside our purview?* Strategic partnerships with other departments on campus can help reach students at the time of need.
- *What curriculum resources already exist to meet particular DIL outcomes and at what level?* Instead of reinventing the wheel, we should try to find, centralize, and adapt available curriculum resources for DIL educational content. A repository or directory of curriculum resources for DIL would be useful.

CONCLUSION

We are only beginning to specify the competencies in DIL that will develop the data management skills that future researchers and scientists will need, and many barriers to identifying them still exist. The rapidly changing nature of the field, the heterogeneity of skills within the disciplines, and the intensive and long-term nature of the task of integrating DIL skills within (and alongside) the curriculum present challenges to academic librarians seeking to take on this task. The questions posed in our discussion are a start. Similarly, the workshop series and for-credit course that we piloted at Cornell University are just a beginning. And the harsh reality is that it is impossible to scale or sustain workshops or credit courses to reach graduate students in all disciplines. These interventions may work best as gateways to introduce students to the range of skills they need to acquire through other more targeted workshops and classes, throughout their academic career. However, by taking the lessons learned in these preliminary initiatives, and by using the modules we created or adapted, we can build on this foundation to create an integrated, progressive DIL program that will prepare students for the challenges and changes ahead.

NOTE

This case study is available online at http://dx.doi.org.10.5703/1288284315476.

REFERENCES

Association of College and Research Libraries (ACRL). (2000). *Information literacy competency standards for higher education.* Retrieved from http://www.ala.org/acrl/sites/ala.org.acrl/files/content/standards/standards.pdf

Barros, E., Laender, A., Gonçalves, M., Cota, R., & Barbosa, F. (2007). Transitioning from the ecological fieldwork to an online repository: A digital library solution and evaluation. *International Journal on Digital Libraries, 7*(1–2), 109–112. http://dx.doi.org/10.1007/s00799-007-0024-7

Block, W. C., Chen, E., Cordes, J., Dietrich, D., Krafft, D. B., Kramer, S., . . . Steinhart, G. (2010). *Meeting funders' data policies: Blueprint for a research data management service group (RDMSG).* Retrieved from Cornell University Library eCommons website: http://hdl.handle.net/1813/28570

Borer, E. T., Seabloom, E. W., Jones, M. B., & Schildhauer, M. (2009). Some simple guidelines for effective data management. *Bulletin of the Ecological Society of America, 90*(2), 205–214. http://dx.doi.org/10.1890/0012-9623-90.2.205

Carr, M. H., Woodson, C. B., Cheriton, O. M.,

Malone, D., McManus, M. A., & Raimondi, P. T. (2011). Knowledge through partnerships: Integrating marine protected area monitoring and ocean observing systems. *Frontiers in Ecology and the Environment, 9*(6), 342–350. http://dx.doi.org/10.1890/090096

Center for Teaching Excellence. (2013a). Active learning. Retrieved from http://www.cte.cornell.edu/teaching-ideas/engaging-students/active-learning.html

Center for Teaching Excellence. (2013b). Collaborative learning. Retrieved from http://www.cte.cornell.edu/teaching-ideas/engaging-students/collaborative-learning.html

DataONE. (n.d.a). Best practices. Retrieved from https://www.dataone.org/best-practices

DataONE. (n.d.b). Education modules. Retrieved from http://www.dataone.org/education

Downey, A., Ramin, L., & Byerly, G. (2008). Simple ways to add active learning to your library instruction. *Texas Library Journal, 84*(2), 52–54.

Fegraus, E. H., Andelman, S., Jones, M. B., & Schildhauer, M. (2005). Maximizing the value of ecological data with structured metadata: An introduction to ecological metadata language (EML) and principles for metadata creation. *Bulletin of the Ecological Society of America, 86*(3), 158–168. http://dx.doi.org/10.1890/0012-9623(2005)86[158:MTVOED]2.0.CO;2

Gil, I. S., Hutchison, V., Frame, M., & Palanisamy, G. (2010). Metadata activities in biology. *Journal of Library Metadata, 10*(2–3), 99–118. http://dx.doi.org/10.1080/19386389.2010.506389

Glazer, G. (2013, Feb. 21). Course teaches grad students how to manage their data. *Cornell Chronicle.* Retrieved from http://www.news.cornell.edu/stories/2013/02/course-teaches-grad-students-how-manage-their-data

Global Lake Ecological Observatory Network (n.d). Understand, predict and communicate the role and response of lakes in a changing global environment. Retrieved from http://www.gleon.org/

Jones, M. B., Schildhauer, M. P., Reichman, O. J., & Bowers, S. (2006). The new bioinformatics: Integrating ecological data from the gene to the biosphere. *Annual Review of Ecology Evolution and Systematics, 37*(1), 519–544. http://dx.doi.org/10.1146/annurev.ecolsys.37.091305.110031

Knowledge Network for Biocomplexity. (n.d.). Knowledge network for biocomplexity. *National Science Foundation.* Retrieved from https://knb.ecoinformatics.org/

Knowledge Network for Biocomplexity. (2005). The knowledge network for biocomplexity (KNB) and our graduate student research training seminar series. Retrieved February, 15, 2013, from https://knb.ecoinformatics.org

Kruger, J., & Dunning, D. (1999). Unskilled and unaware of it: How difficulties in recognizing one's own incompetence lead to inflated self-assessments. *Journal of Personality and Social Psychology, 77*(6), 1121–1134. http://dx.doi.org/10.1037/0022-3514.77.6.1121

Long Term Ecological Research Network, The. (2013). The LTER network. Retrieved from http://www.lternet.edu/

Magnusson, A., & Hilborn, R. (2007). What makes fisheries data informative? *Fish and Fisheries, 8*(4), 337–358. http://dx.doi.org/10.1111/j.1467-2979.2007.00258.x

McKiernan, G. (2004). Ecological and environmental data. *Science & Technology Libraries, 23*(4), 95–104. http://dx.doi.org/10.1300/J122v23n04_08

Michener, W. K., Brunt, J. W., Helly, J. J., Kirchner, T. B., & Stafford, S. G. (1997). Nongeospatial metadata for the ecological sciences. *Ecological Applications, 7*(1), 330–342. http://dx.doi.org/10.1890/1051-0761(1997)007[0330:NMFTES]2.0.CO;2

Michener, W. K., & Jones, M. B. (2012). Ecoinformatics: Supporting ecology as a data-intensive science. *Trends in Ecology & Evolution, 27*(2), 85–93. http://dx.doi.org/10.1016/j.tree.2011.11.016

Michener, W. K., Porter, J., Servilla, M., & Vanderbilt, K. (2011). Long term ecological research and information management. *Ecological Informatics, 6*(1), 13–24. http://dx.doi.org/10.1016/j.ecoinf.2010.11.005

Research Data Management Service Group. (n.d.). About the Research Data Management Service Group. Retrieved from http://data.research.cornell.edu/content/about

Wolkovich, E. M., Regetz, J., & O'Connor, M. I. (2012). Advances in global change research require open science by individual researchers. *Global Change Biology, 18*(7), 2102–2110. http://dx.doi.org/10.1111/j.1365-2486.2012.02693.x

APPENDIX A: Rubric for the Spring 2013 One-Credit Course

Rubric for Evaluating Data Management Plans*

This rubric includes the National Science Foundation's requested components of a data management plan (DMP). Note that a DMP should be no longer than two pages and should be clear and concise. Therefore, it will be very difficult to achieve an "excellent" rating for every section of the DMP—satisfactory is satisfactory for the majority of the components. A thorough, high-quality DMP will contain several "excellent" components and many "satisfactory" components.

Excellent	Satisfactory	Unsatisfactory
DESCRIPTION		
Provides brief, nontechnical description of data produced during *all stages* of project (i.e., data collection, processing, analysis, sharing, and archiving) Indicates *in detail* which data will be shared and when for each stage of the project; if no data to be shared, states this and indicates why not Describes *in detail* impact of data sharing on larger community (including examples of possible interdisciplinary use of the research data) and how strategy helps to disseminate research to that larger community; if no impact or community exists, statement to that effect and explanation about why	Provides brief, nontechnical description of data produced during *most key stages* of project Indicates which data will be shared and schedule at *basic level;* may be lacking detail for some data stages; if no data to be shared, states this Describes general impact of data sharing on research community and how strategy helps to disseminate research to that larger community; if no impact or community exists, statement to that effect	Missing or incomplete description of data produced during key stages of project that would hinder understanding of data life cycle Missing any indication of data to be shared and timeline Missing description of data importance; no mention of broader community that might benefit from data sharing (or if no impact or community exists, no statement to that effect and or explanation about why)
CONTENT AND FORMAT		
Describes data collection and processing plans *in full,* step-by-step detail (e.g., raw/processed/reduced/analyzed data, software code, samples, curricula)	Describes data collection and processing plans *in general* detail (e.g., raw/processed/reduced/analyzed data, software/code)	Missing or incomplete description of data collection and processing plans

Continued

* Rubric adapted from the Cornell Research Data Management Service Group's Data Management Planning Overview, available at http://data.research.cornell.edu/content/data-management-planning.

Excellent	Satisfactory	Unsatisfactory
CONTENT AND FORMAT—cont'd		
Identifies *all* file formats used throughout the course of the project (including those for collection, use, conversion, and formatting for sharing and archiving); selects file formats for sharing and archiving that maximize potential for reuse and longevity; describes plans for conversion, if necessary Identifies *in detail* metadata (documentation) standards (if applicable) or supplementary documentation necessary to make data understandable; indicates who will document data and when; explains reason for choosing documentation strategy	Identifies *most* file formats used over the course of the project (including those for collection, use, conversion, and formatting for sharing and archiving) Identifies *basic* metadata standards and/or basic documentation needed to make data understandable; lacks details of who is responsible for documentation and when it will occur	Missing or incomplete description of file formats Missing or incomplete identification of basic metadata and documentation
PROTECTION AND INTELLECTUAL PROPERTY (IP)		
Describes *full* data management and storage procedures (e.g., identification of storage facilities, backup policies (including frequency, automated or manual), need for secure or restricted access, confidentiality and privacy issues (including anonymizing and protecting personally identifiable data, and any legal or ethical requirements); includes explanation of advantages of strategy chosen Indicates and documents licensing and IP for data (including use of licenses such as Creative Commons or Open Data Commons or formal policies on data usage and creation of derivative works) Plans to include *full* rights statements in metadata and/or other documentation	Describes *basic* data management and storage procedures (e.g., identification of storage facilities, backup policies [frequency, automated or manual], need for secure or restricted access) Indicates and documents basic policies on data usage, reuse, and creation of derivative works (e.g., data can be shared and reused noncommercially with credit) Mentions *basic* reuse requirements; may not explain how terms will be communicated	Missing description of data management and storage procedures Missing any statement on licensing and IP policies Missing any mention of terms of reuse

Continued

Excellent	Satisfactory	Unsatisfactory
ACCESS		
Describes *detailed* plan and infrastructure (i.e., hardware, campus services, commercial services, or disciplinary data centers) for storing and providing access to data; Provides *detailed* description of access mechanisms and policies, including any potential restrictions to access; describes the rationale behind them; provides a timeline for providing access Indicates *in detail* how access strategy will maximize the value and the discoverability of the data to interested audiences; provides examples of potential audiences	Describes *basic* plan and infrastructure (i.e., hardware, campus services, commercial services, or disciplinary data centers) for storing and providing access to data Provides a *general* description of access mechanisms and policies; missing potential restrictions, the rationale behind them, and applicable timeline Indicates in *general* how access strategy will maximize the value of the data to interested audiences; lacks examples of potential audiences	Missing or incomplete description of plan for access and infrastructure Missing any information on access mechanisms and policies Missing any indication of how access strategy will maximize value of data
PRESERVATION AND TRANSFER OF RESPONSIBILITY		
Identifies data to be preserved after end of project (including *thorough* explanation of selection rationale) Describes preservation resources (e.g., hardware or campus or commercial services, institutional commitment or funding), *selection rationale, policies,* expertise, and plans for transfer of responsibility to keep data accessible long term	Identifies data to be preserved after end of project (including *cursory* description of selection rationale) Describes preservation resources (e.g., hardware or campus or commercial services, institutional commitment or funding) and plans for transfer of responsibility to keep data accessible long term	Missing or incomplete description of data to be preserved and no description of selection rationale Missing or incomplete description of preservation resources (e.g., hardware or campus or commercial services, institutional commitment or funding) and no plans for transfer of responsibility

APPENDIX B: Data Sharing Exercise Outline for "Evaluating Repositories"

This outline provides an example of the in-class exercise on evaluating repositories in the Data Sharing session of the Cornell for-credit course in the spring of 2013. Students were instructed as follows:

1. Use DataBib (http://databib.org) to identify a repository of interest to explore.
2. Next, take 10 minutes to look at the repository individually, noting why you think it would be a good or bad fit for your data. Check the repository for:
   a. Supporting organization.
   b. Usage rights, licenses, or other policies related to reuse and redistribution of data.
   c. Technical systems/data security (policies and methods for backup, redundancy, authentication, formats accepted).
   d. Preservation commitment.
3. In groups of 3–4, take the next 10 minutes to discuss your findings in your group.
4. Use 5–10 minutes per group to report out to the class your group's answers to the following:
   a. Repositories chosen.
   b. The top reasons for choosing a repository.
   c. The top reason for not choosing a repository.
   d. Whether or not DataBib was helpful. Other information you would like to have to make your choices easier.

APPENDIX C: Assessment Tool

NTRES 6940 End-of-Class Evaluation

Thank you for taking NTRES 6940! This survey will help us measure to what degree we accomplished our goals, discover what we can do to improve the class for future students, and inform our grant project. It is completely anonymous and doesn't reflect on your grade. Thank you for taking the time to complete the survey.

Q1 Primary departmental affiliation (e.g., NTRES) _____

Q2 Year in program
- ☐ First (1)
- ☐ Second (2)
- ☐ Third (3)
- ☐ Fourth (4)
- ☐ Fifth (5)
- ☐ Sixth (6)
- ☐ N/A or Other (7) _____

Q3 How many class sessions did you attend?
- ☐ One (1)
- ☐ Two (2)
- ☐ Three (3)
- ☐ Four (4)
- ☐ Five (5)
- ☐ Six (6)

Q4 How would you rate your knowledge/skills/ability in the following areas *before* taking this class?
No competence (1), Little competence (2), Somewhat competent (3), Very competent (4), Not applicable (0)
_____ Describing data management and its importance and relevance to you
_____ Describing your research and data collection process to identify your data life cycle
_____ Recognizing the necessary components of a data management plan
_____ Describing and following best practices in structuring relational databases
_____ Visualizing data and creating graphs
_____ Evaluating data repositories to determine requirements and fitness for data deposit
_____ Documenting your data for yourself and others
_____ Creating a data management plan to manage and curate your own data

Q5 How would you rate your knowledge/skills/ability in the following areas *after* taking this class?

No competence (1), Little competence (2), Somewhat competent (3), Very competent (4), Not applicable (0)

_____ Describing data management and its importance and relevance to you

_____ Describing your research and data collection process to identify your data life cycle

_____ Recognizing the necessary components of a data management plan

_____ Describing and following best practices in structuring relational databases

_____ Visualizing data and creating graphs

_____ Evaluating data repositories to determine requirements and fitness for data deposit

_____ Documenting your data for yourself and others

_____ Creating a data management plan to manage and curate your own data

CHAPTER 5

ADDRESSING SOFTWARE CODE AS DATA

An Embedded Librarian Approach

Jake Carlson, University of Michigan

Megan Sapp Nelson, Purdue University

INTRODUCTION

This Data Information Literacy (DIL) team, one of two Purdue University teams in the Institute of Museum and Library Services (IMLS)–funded project, partnered with software design teams involved with Engineering Projects in Community Service (EPICS), a course for undergraduate students from a variety of disciplines. We primarily worked with the graduate teaching assistants (TAs) who graded undergraduate design submissions produced during the design cycle. The software teams created code-based data sets and supporting documentation in a variety of languages and platforms. The creation of code documentation was the primary DIL need of the software teams.

To respond to these needs, the Purdue DIL team developed a rubric that provided guidance for students to create and TAs to evaluate the documentation. Our team created a series of suggested exercises for students that tied specific data management activities to phases of the engineering design cycle used by EPICS (Lima & Oakes, 2006). We then implemented an embedded librarian service within the software teams. We handed out the rubrics and suggested exercises, offered a skill-training session to further enrich the students' knowledge, met with the TAs to help them understand the document, and then served as design reviewers (outside assessors) for the teams.

To assess the intervention, we used the design notebooks created by individual team members to identify instances where the students demonstrated DIL objectives. We created a coding schema that standardized notebook analysis across teams. The assessment concluded that on the individual level, students did not adequately record their coding decisions or articulate the rationale behind these decisions.

While students showed a range in skill level in personal mastery of DIL, widespread weakness was evident in the competencies of *data management and organization, data curation and reuse,* and *data quality and documentation.* The core of our program was the integration of librarians within a preexisting, highly structured course. In the future, we plan to focus on implementing a role within the team that is responsible for ensuring that the documentation is of sufficient quality that it can be easily understood and is complete enough to ensure continued development of the project.

ENVIRONMENTAL SCAN OF DATA MANAGEMENT PRACTICES FOR SOFTWARE CODE

Data curators and digital preservation experts are paying more attention to software code as it is not uncommon for code to be an important component of a data set or other electronic object (Matthews, Shaon, Bicarregui, & Jones, 2010). If the data set is to be curated effectively, it logically follows that the accompanying code must be accounted for in all curation planning and activities. Managing and curating software code as a component of a data set presents several challenges in addition to the ones that would otherwise be encountered in curating data. These challenges include the myriad of components and dependencies of code (such as externally focused documentation, internal documentation, multiple versions of iterative code created, and so forth), the practice of building on or incorporating code developed over time or from multiple authors, and the rapid pace of new technologies that are introduced and adopted by software code writers. Therefore, data sets that include software code may require additional planning and consideration.

Although the literature on the curation of software code as a component of a data set specifically is relatively limited, there is a great deal of literature that touches on the 12 DIL competencies and software code more generally. *Data management and organization,* and what we referred to in the DIL project as *data quality and documentation* in particular, have received a significant amount of attention. We focused our environmental scan on a subset of material that appeared most relevant to address the issues faced by EPICS. We also selected a range of materials that touched on each of the 12 competencies in some way. The selected materials in our review included scholarly articles, trade publications, reports, books, and websites to incorporate the perspectives of both academics and professionals in the field.

This environmental scan was helpful in informing our work in several ways. Code developers have a reputation for sharing their work with others as a matter of practice. For example, the ideas of "open source" and "open access" are assumed to be a strong component of the culture of practice of developers, which was largely supported in our literature review (Crowston, Annabi, & Howison, 2003; Halloran & Scherlis, 2003). However, despite an ethos and willingness to share code, many developers do not provide the documentation necessary for others to understand or make use of their code easily (Sojer & Henkel, 2010; von Krogh, Spaeth, & Haefliger, 2005). Furthermore, code comments or other descriptions are often absent, or do not reflect the intent of the coder sufficiently, making it difficult if not impossible to understand the decisions made in developing the code (Marcus & Menzies, 2010; Menzies & Di Stefano, 2003). This is despite the availability of resources to assist in the documenting process in software repositories and the availability of tools such as Doxygen (n.d.). Software coding is frequently a collaborative activity, particularly in the workplace, as coders will often be assigned to work on existing code as a part of a team whose membership will change as collaborators transition in and out of a project. Documentation, description, and organization of code are all recognized as important activities for a software group, but they are often activities that are neglected (Lethbridge, Singer, & Forward, 2003). Many researchers in the computer science field present these issues as research questions to solve and suggest technology based solutions to address them (Bettenburg, Adams, Hassan, & Smidt, 2010; Grechanik et al., 2010; Hasan, Stroulia, Barbosa, & Alalfi, 2010). However, these proposed technology-based solutions are often more theoretical than applied in nature by design and therefore of limited practical value.

The environmental scan led to several other observations and findings that informed our work with EPICS. We noted some related interests within the curation and software communities but found that they used different terminologies in expressing these interests. For example, the idea of "software traceability"—or the practice of recording design decisions including the who, what, where, when, and why and explicitly connecting these decisions to the software for the purposes of quality assurance (Ali, Gueheneuc, & Antoniol, 2011; Bashir & Qadir, 2006)—has commonalities with the data curation idea of "provenance," or tracking and accounting for actions and decisions made in curating a digital object (Bashir & Qadir, 2006). Traceability is a quality assurance process ensuring that design decisions are readily identified and accounted for over the course of developing the code. Provenance is tracked to ensure the integrity of the existing object and to demonstrate compliance with the policies and practices of the repository. It is the difference between developing something and maintaining it. We also came across a school of thought that advocated for "literate programming" and "human readable code." The essence of the argument was that rather than creating code to solely be machine readable, developers should create code with the deliberate intent of making it suitable for human reading as well (Knuth, 1984). An offshoot of this idea, "clean code," was particularly useful in planning our educational programming (Martin, 2008). Finally, the need to preserve software code seems to be catching on in the data curation field, though we did not observe this as much in the software literature, where there seems to be a "technology moves too fast" mentality (Chen, 2001). One particularly useful resource in this area of preservation is the Software Sustainability Institute (http://www.software.ac.uk/), which provides services and resources to ensure that software used in research is available and supported beyond its original life span.

METHODOLOGY

Our project partner was Engineering Projects in Community Service (EPICS), a service-learning center at Purdue University (https://engineering .purdue.edu/EPICS). EPICS is focused on teaching undergraduates engineering design concepts and skills by working with community service agencies to develop customized engineering solutions that address real-life needs. EPICS brings students from a variety of disciplines across the university and academic years to work together on a common project. Therefore EPICS capitalizes on the diversity of strengths that the participating students bring

each semester, but also must manage the gaps in their knowledge and abilities. This is a highly transitory group of students, with project personnel turning over each semester as projects continue till completion. One of the librarians on this project, Megan Sapp Nelson, worked with EPICS on previous projects and had developed a strong understanding of their information needs generally, as well as their working culture. As an advisor to EPICS software teams for 4 years, she was familiar with the highly structured nature of the design course and had previously developed information literacy education interventions to improve the quality of the conceptual design performed in the projects (Sapp Nelson, 2009, 2013). From past experiences, she was aware that students had difficulty managing their software code and documenting their work, which presented problems for all involved, including future students coming into the project, faculty advisors and administrators in EPICS, and the community partners who will make use of the students' projects.

The DIL team interviewed four faculty and two graduate students in the spring of 2012 (the instrument is available for download at http://dx.doi.org/10.5703/1288284315510). To incorporate a broad perspective on managing and curating software code, we interviewed individuals who were affiliated and unaffiliated with EPICS and who came from three disciplines. Table 5.1 shows the affiliations of the interviewees.

Results of the Needs Assessment

Both the faculty and students rated each of the 12 DIL competencies on a 5-point scale according to how important it was for graduate students to master the competency. The rating results by our six participants are presented in Figure 5.1.

TABLE 5.1   *Purdue DIL Team Interviewees by Department and Affiliation*

DIL Interviewee	Academic Discipline	EPICS Affiliation
Faculty #1	Electrical engineering	Affiliated
Faculty #2	Engineering education	Affiliated
Faculty #3	Computer science	Nonaffiliated
Faculty #4	Computer science	Nonaffiliated
Graduate student #1	Electrical engineering	Nonaffiliated
Graduate student #2	Computer science	Nonaffiliated

Among the top DIL competencies for the faculty we interviewed were *data quality and documentation* and *metadata and data description*. It is interesting to note that faculty rated these two competencies much higher than the graduate students did, demonstrating a disconnect between the attitudes and perceptions of faculty and students in these areas. Furthermore, these two are highly rated within the 12 competencies on average, despite students indicating that they place less importance on them. Faculty recognized data quality and documentation in developing software code as a weakness in students. While students frequently are instructed to document code development, their understanding of what this documentation should consist of and the degree to which quality documentation is necessary are often misunderstood, which leads to high variability in their team's performance and in the quality of the code. Faculty recognized *metadata and data description* as important. However, while faculty were aware of the need for metadata, they reported that they themselves did not have the understanding or skills to apply metadata nor to teach their students about it.

Conversely, graduate students rated *data conversion and interoperability* and *discovery and*

acquisition higher in importance than the faculty. For *data conversion and interoperability*, this is likely due to one faculty member stating that her lab did not engage in converting data, and another stating that this was not a skill that all students needed as long as they had access to someone knowledgeable in this area. Rather, the area of particular interest for both faculty and students within this competency was the prevention of data loss in the conversion process. For the *discovery and acquisition* competency, the faculty indicated that it may not always be crucial to the research being conducted. For example, their projects were not making extensive reuse of software code. However, the graduate students stated that they will search for existing code that performs similar functions to the code that they were generating, which may explain their rating of this competency as more important than the faculty's. Interestingly, we found that the primary means of locating existing code for the graduate students and faculty we interviewed is a literature search of conference proceedings. A literature search is then followed by a Web search to find the project or author's website where the code may be available.

On the basis of the interviews, our environmental scan, and our knowledge of EPICS, we

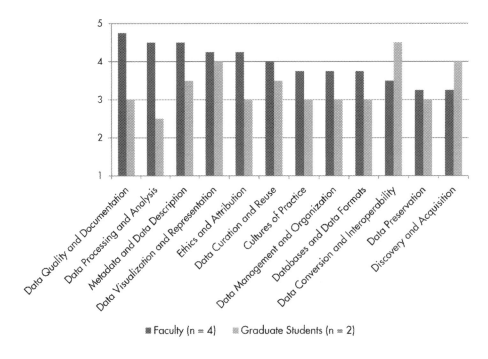

Figure 5.1 The average ratings of importance for each of the 12 data competencies for faculty and students interviewed.

developed and built the educational intervention around the *data quality and documentation* and the *metadata and data description* competencies. Our intended audiences were the graduate student TAs and their undergraduate team members in the EPICS program.

OVERVIEW OF THE EPICS ENVIRONMENT

The EPICS curriculum develops engineering design and professional skills in an environment intended to be a bridge to the students' professional careers. EPICS is a highly structured and intense environment as students must take on a fair amount of work in new and unfamiliar areas and are held to high standards of professionalism by their instructors.

This environment requires students to take initiative in developing their assigned projects independently but with the knowledge that their instructors will evaluate their work and performance. Consequently, students receive rubrics that will be used for evaluations so that they better understand what is expected of them. Students also learn the design life cycle, a framework for developing and executing their projects (Lima & Oakes, 2006). Students map their work to the stages of the design life cycle as they progress through the course. The work is performed in teams, and within each team students assume particular roles, such as team leader or as primary contact for the project partner (see Table 5.2).

EPICS uses a number of different approaches to develop these skills. Typically, at the beginning of the semester, EPICS holds introductory lectures for students that include distribution of

TABLE 5.2 *Defined Team Roles in the EPICS Curriculum*

Role	Responsibility	Faculty, Graduate, or Undergraduate (F/G/U)
Team leader	Team member responsible for overseeing all projects conducted by team in a given semester	U
Project leader/ manager	Team member responsible for overseeing work on a single project for a given semester	U
Project partner liaison	Team member responsible for initiating and maintaining communication with community partner	U
Advisor	Faculty member assigned to oversee the student team for a given semester	F
Graduate teaching assistant	Graduate student responsible for providing resources, holding team accountable, and grading	G

the rubrics that will evaluate their performance. Next, students participate in a series of skill sessions to teach them some of the fundamentals they will need to know to be successful, such as programming languages, team building skills, and appropriate use of laboratory resources. All students meet for weekly lab sessions during the semester, where they discuss their progress and the challenges they have encountered while working with their team. As the semester progresses, students present their work in two separate design review sessions, which often include a representative from the project partner organization and professional engineers. There, students receive feedback and suggestions on their work and the quality of their presentations.

In EPICS, students are expected to produce documentation that describes their own work as well as the decisions and actions taken by the team to accompany their coding files. Students organize their data sets using multiple techniques. The primary sources of project-level documentation are the design notebooks or blogs required for completion of the EPICS

class. Students store their notebooks in a physical location near the lab meeting place or on a server in their digital form. The internal project management documents and the external or user documentation are in a variety of Microsoft Office files and are located on a server, wikis, or Subversion (SVN). Teams manage and store the code itself using SVN. They write code using software languages such as C++ and JavaScript as well as utilizing the Android and Apple mobile platform development tools. Depending upon the team, there may be several software code data sets under development at any given time.

Within the EPICS environment, it is very important to be able to share code both within a team and outside of it. As projects typically span multiple semesters, students will transition in and out of the team over the life of a project. As such, a need within EPICS is that the resulting code and code structure be readily apparent, logical, and "human readable" to facilitate the transition between developers on each project. Another consideration is that the software code has real-world application outside of the educational realm. The code is designed for practical use by nonprofit agencies in the local community. It is therefore very important that the code be designed and delivered in ways that support its ongoing use and maintenance over time. More information about EPICS can be found on its website (https://engineering.purdue.edu/EPICS).

The challenge for the DIL team involved supporting the development of useful software code products, which was a complex endeavor made more complicated by the high rate of turnover among team members between semesters. TAs are asked to hold their undergraduate student team members accountable for the quality of their code during the grading process. However, it was evident from the interviews that the TAs did not have the experience, comfort level, or tools to grade the quality of the code and the documentation that the students were submitting, and ultimately they had difficulty holding the team members accountable.

EPICS as a whole did not have a cohesive, clearly articulated culture of practice regarding the management and documentation of code. Some teams agreed to naming conventions for files and variables or developed other "local" standards, but this was left up to the individual teams to decide. Generally, the code writers looked to more experienced teammates to provide them with standards, rather than developing standards among the group by consensus. A few faculty advisors provided expectations for code documentation, but it was not a standard across EPICS and happened infrequently.

A variety of development tools were used as needed by individual teams that supported creating documentation for code, such as JavaDocs (http://www.oracle.com/technetwork/java/javase/documentation/index-jsp-135444.html) and Yii (http://www.yiiframework.com/). TAs

supervised more than one team, which meant that the TAs had to familiarize themselves with the tools that each team was using. On some of the teams new students went through multiple weeks of training to teach them how to use the tools as well as introductory coding skills. TAs provided guidance during this process and one-on-one instruction for student coders who were having difficulty.

Faculty advisors generally agreed that the level of oversight for student coding projects was insufficient. The TAs indicated that part of the difficulty in providing oversight was a subjective measure of quality for the coding. Although EPICS faculty and TAs raised documentation, organization, and transferability of the software code as serious issues, they had not yet developed supporting materials or strong cultures of practice in these areas within EPICS. Therefore the DIL team saw an opportunity to support the work of the TAs, who in turn supported the education of undergraduates in the EPICS program, through developing resources and providing a framework for good software code documentation practices.

AN EMBEDDED LIBRARIAN APPROACH TO ADDRESSING DATA INFORMATION LITERACY NEEDS

The DIL team developed goals and learning objectives for educational programs based on the results of the interviews, environmental scans, and previous knowledge of EPICS. They had three overarching goals:

1. To raise the students' awareness of the need to generate quality documentation and description of the software code they generated

TABLE 5.3 *Learning Objectives for Students and Teaching Assistants in EPICS*

Target Audience	Learning Objectives
Undergraduate students who are a part of software development EPICS teams will:	Recognize that documentation and description are integral components of developing software code (and are not simply "busy work") in order to hold oneself and team members accountable for producing quality documentation and description in a timely manner
	Document own code and methods in developing the code in ways that enable the reproduction of work by others in order to ensure the smooth transfer of work to other students and the EPICS project partner
	Create and communicate standard operating procedures for managing, organizing, and documenting code and project work within the team in order to develop consistent practice and to facilitate clear communication amongst team members
Teaching assistants who lead software development EPICS teams will:	Identify characteristics of well-written software documentation in order to recognize well-written project and software documentation
	Evaluate project and software documentation in order to identify both positive and negative data practices
	Critique project and software documentation in order to assess quality and assign grades

2. To provide students and graduate TAs with the knowledge and tools to generate quality documentation and description for software code

3. To develop a shared cultural practice in EPICS based on disciplinary values in data management issues, particularly issues in quality, documentation, and the description of data and software code

Table 5.3 lists the specific learning objectives for the two target audiences.

Given the structured nature of EPICS and the intensity of the work, the DIL team found that the students had little time for "additional" learning activities or events. So we decided to take an "embedded librarian" approach to developing and delivering a DIL educational program that connected with the EPICS structure and culture. Embedded librarianship can be defined as the process of presenting information literacy content as a part of course curricula in ways that are directly relevant to student outcomes for the course (Schulte, 2012). Embedded librarianship is a particularly promising method for implementing information literacy instruction due to the presentation of information literacy competencies in an immediately relevant manner (Tumbleson & Burke, 2010). Given the project-based nature of the course, an embedded librarianship approach appeared to best integrate with the course design and content that already existed within the EPICS program.

To implement our embedded librarian approach, in the fall of 2012 we focused on three groups within EPICS. Each of these groups had at least one faculty advisor, a graduate student TA, and multiple teams of students that each worked on a particular project. Our approach for implementing our educational programming was to forge connections with the faculty advisors, graduate TAs, and students in EPICS by taking advantage of built-in opportunities to interact with each group. This included

- developing an evaluation rubric for TAs to apply to student work;
- offering a skills-based session on documenting code and project work;
- attending lab sessions and observing team meetings;
- participating as reviewers in the students' design review sessions.

To create this educational program, we first returned to the literature review, particularly the sources that described criteria for developing "clean code," to identify relevant best practices and documentation guidance for software developers. Next, using the existing rubrics developed by EPICS as a guide, we crafted two rubrics (Appendix A to this chapter) that the graduate TAs could use to evaluate both the code and the documentation created by their students. We also distributed a one-page document (Appendix B to this chapter) to team leaders that explained the expectations for quality code and described why documentation of code is important. Finally, we shared our work with the TAs and made some adjustments based on their feedback. Table 5.4 shows the full schedule.

We held the skills session on documenting and organizing code during the third week of the semester. The focus was on helping the team leaders in EPICS recognize what constituted quality, professional practice in documenting and organizing code, and the need for students to internalize these practices. The session comprised three modules (see the complete lesson plan in Appendix C to this chapter). In the first module we presented quotes from articles written by several prominent coders that described the attributes of "clean code." We then distributed three examples of code that had been generated by previous EPICS teams. We asked the class to identify the strengths and weaknesses of the code from the perspective of documentation and organization. We closed this module with a discussion of what constitutes good code versus poor code. In the next module we discussed why writing well-documented and well-organized code matters. We emphasized that writing software code is inherently a collaborative activity as the majority of code will be used by others, both as a product and also as something edited and maintained by other coders (future EPICS students in this case). We then introduced a coding skills inventory (see Table C.1 in Appendix C to this chapter), a list of 12 skills to facilitate good coding habits in EPICS teams. In the last module, the team leaders picked one of the skills on the coding skills inventory list that they saw as a high priority for their team and designed a short learning activity that would address this skill. We provided the team leaders with activities that could support such an intervention (see the list in Appendix D to this chapter). We recognized that the teams were at different stages in the software development process, so we mapped our list of activities to the stages of the design life cycle to facilitate this process. Finally, each team leader shared a selected skill and activity with the group and defined the measure of success for the activity.

Unfortunately the skills session was voluntary and there was a poor turnout. While all team leaders and project leaders were invited, only five students attended from four teams. We found that this introduction to DIL skills was not pervasive enough to introduce and instill a foundation of good practice.

As the semester progressed we made frequent visits to the EPICS labs. Early in the semester we attended a lab for each of the three teams we were working with and introduced ourselves to the students. We distributed the documentation

TABLE 5.4 *Embedded Librarian Engagement Activities*

Semester Timeslot	Activity	Description
Week 2	Introduction	Initial visit to the EPICS weekly lab session to introduce the DIL team and distribute rubric materials to all students
Week 3	Voluntary skills session on documenting and organizing code	This session was offered to team leaders in EPICS and covered the following: Module 1—What is good coding? Module 2—Why is it important?—EPICs as a stakeholder—appeal for coding may not be as relevant—professional—take a poll Module 3—How to foster good coding practices in your team
Weeks 4–6	Embedded librarianship	Observations and consultations in weekly lab sessions
Week 7	Design review #1	First round of feedback and suggestions for student work in documenting their code and their projects
Weeks 8–13	Embedded librarianship	Observations and consultations in weekly lab sessions
Week 14	Design review #2	Second round of feedback and suggestions for student work in documenting their code and their projects
Post-semester	Assessment	Collected and reviewed student lab notebooks

rubric that we had developed. Subsequently, we each attended multiple lab sessions for each of the three groups over the course of the semester. These interactions gave us the opportunity to observe how students were developing their work and to interact with them (though in a limited fashion as lab sessions covered many aspects not related to the DIL project). We also attended both of the design reviews (7 weeks and 14 weeks into the semester) and were able to provide some suggestions for their work in documenting their code and their projects.

Our approach in assessing this work has been twofold. First, we met individually with two of the three TAs for the teams (the third was unavailable) and two of the faculty advisors at the end of the fall 2012 semester. We asked about any changes in student behavior they

observed, changes in their perceptions of these topics, and possible next steps for our work with EPICS. Although the feedback we received was generally positive, no one reported a substantial change in student activities in writing code and documenting their work. They encouraged the DIL team to keep working with EPICS, and as a result of these conversations, developed some ideas for the future as described in the "Discussion" section. Second, we reviewed the lab notebooks that students in one of the groups we had worked with had written during the fall semester. The DIL team developed a coding schema to evaluate student knowledge and skills in documenting their work effectively. This analysis will enable us to better pinpoint areas of need and will inform our work in developing more targeted responses.

DISCUSSION

The opportunity to embed within a highly structured, multiple section class provided this Purdue DIL team a broad range of insights for actionable next steps, future research, and recommendations to the EPICS leadership team.

First, we identified that the team leader and project leader roles are key to the dissemination of good data management planning and practice within any given team. We identified this early through interviews and attempted to address this via a one-shot skill session aimed at the student project and team leaders. Given the low level of turnout and lack of observed knowledge/skill transfer from the session, we needed to develop a more embedded approach to data management skills building.

The current approach of having students share the responsibility of documentation and description instead of designating a member of the team to have direct ownership of these tasks is a major cause of the low-quality documentation and difficulties in the transfer of work.

Another differentiating aspect of the EPICS environment is the assignment of specific roles to students within their groups. Teams in EPICS select their project and team leaders early in the semester, along with more specific roles such as the webmasters, project partner liaisons, and financial officers, among others. Despite the near ubiquity of teams encountering issues with the documentation done by previous students, teams do not acknowledge this issue in their meetings or do much to address it formally. A defined role for a student member of a team might ensure that code documentation and description of the project were carried out efficiently and in ways that ensured a smooth transition from semester to semester, as well as from EPICS to the community agency when the project is done. The current approach of having students share the responsibility of documentation and description instead of designating a member of the team to have direct ownership of these tasks is a major cause of the low-quality documentation and difficulties in the transfer of work.

Therefore, the DIL team proposed a pilot project for the fall of 2013 to define and implement a project archivist role within selected EPICS teams. The purpose is to integrate fully the oversight of documentation formally within the team structure by creating a specific team role. We envision the project archivist's role as taking a big picture approach toward capturing the description and documentation of the project, including the design constraints, decision-making processes, and design implementations for each team. As a result, the EPICS teams might see smoother transitions of the project to future team members, graduate teaching assistants, faculty advisors, EPICS administrators and project partners. We will be working with a continuing lecturer and an EPICS advisor to further define, implement, and assess the impact of the project archivist role.

Second, while the rubrics for evaluating software code and documentation that we developed are a good start, there is a need for further curricular development to integrate the rubric into the EPICS workflow for the semester. A high priority will be to address the individual and team documentation templates used by EPICS. Currently, these templates do not highlight the need for excellent coding practices and data management. Working with the EPICS administrative team, we hope to create a template or other workflow that highlights the need for well-designed and well-written code while providing a structure for individual and team-level accountability. These resources will support the TA's role as a mentor to EPICS students, using a train-the-trainer approach.

Another need that the DIL team identified was a central reference solution that enables students (both undergraduate and graduate) to learn needed data skills at their point of need, while working either independently or in a laboratory setting. We feel that a library of short videos (perhaps hosted on a YouTube channel) that covers software and data management topics would be highly useful to EPICS. The EPICS curriculum is built around the idea of working independently to write code that is then brought back to the group for further development. It is important that students have instruction on clean coding, creating excellent documentation, and project management planning that is available to them outside of class. Similarly, graduate students frequently work independently, submitting code to their supervisor for comment and review. A YouTube library would create a ready reference for those needs that arise while the students are practicing or expanding their skill sets.

Finally, we noted that the depth and quality of project documentation and reflection captured in the team members' lab notebooks varied widely. The highest order of learning skills according to Bloom's taxonomy (Bloom, 1956)—evaluation and analysis—were not often present within the EPICS notebooks, even as the students were engaging in a creative process. Evaluation and analysis are at the heart of excellent data management skills; by looking at the long-term life span of the project, students identified the immediate worth of clean code not only for themselves but also for future EPICS team members, project partners, clients, and users. Working with the EPICS

administrators, we hope to emphasize the reflective practice of code writing, particularly for software and hardware engineering disciplines.

CONCLUSION

This approach toward developing and implementing a DIL educational program was to embed into the structure and environment of EPICS. Embedded librarianship was a natural choice given the highly structured nature of the EPICS program and engineering disciplines. This approach allowed us to reach a relatively large number of students (40 approximately) in ways that aligned with their current practices. However, employing an embedded librarian approach in our program took a great deal of planning and investment for the DIL team to set up and carry out.

Several interrelated factors should be addressed in this type of DIL model. First, the embedded librarian approach requires that librarians build solid relationships with the people running the program. When a librarian is embedded in a course, this may include just the faculty instructor and his or her teaching assistant. We decided to partner with a service-learning center and to focus our efforts on three groups and their graduate student TAs overseeing the work of multiple teams of students. This structure required us to build connections with the faculty advisors, the graduate student TAs, the EPICS administration, the student team leaders, and others. Sapp Nelson's prior experience aided our relationships in working with EPICS, as did Carlson's previous interactions with one of the faculty advisors. Nevertheless, our approach still required multiple meetings to introduce ourselves, explain what we were trying to do, and establish contact with a great number of people. We recommend that librarians who wish to launch a DIL program plan to cultivate and maintain relationships as a part of their program development.

Second, we worked hard to align our efforts to fit into the structure of our partner. EPICS has a very structured way of doing things that did not allow for a great deal of deviation. Therefore, we had to identify these structures early on and then determine how best to integrate ourselves to reach students in meaningful ways. We took advantage of opportunities to reach students, such as holding a voluntary skill session early in the semester and attending design reviews at the midpoint and end of the semester. However, we also had to create additional ways of connecting with students within the EPICS structure. Our approach was to align our instruction and interactions as best we could with current practices. We did this by creating a rubric for evaluating student documentation and organization practices and making ourselves available during some lab sessions.

Learning the context and gaining an understanding of the setting were as important to our program as defining our terms. This was very much an iterative process.

Third, the embedded librarian approach required a fairly significant time commitment. In addition to the time that we invested in identifying which of the DIL competencies to address and in developing the knowledge to design an educational program to respond, the DIL team put in many hours attending lab sessions and design reviews, offering the skill session, developing resources, and meeting with faculty advisors and TAs affiliated with EPICS. We believe that the in-person contact was worth the effort as it definitely helped make an impact, forge relationships, and better understand the EPICS environment. However, it was occasionally difficult to find the time to devote to making these personal appearances given our other responsibilities and because we followed EPICS's schedule rather than our own. The time commitment continues as we review the content of team lab notebooks to better determine the impact the DIL program had on students and to observe where their DIL competencies strengths and weaknesses lie. Here too, we believe that the time commitment in assessing student work will pay off as we continue to develop our partnership with EPICS.

Beyond the lessons learned from developing the program itself, we gained a better understanding of the 12 DIL competencies from the interviews. We decided to focus on only 2 of the 12 competencies for our work with EPICS on the basis of its needs and our ability to respond to those needs. However, the needs expressed were many and may provide additional opportunities for follow up. In particular both the faculty and the students we interviewed indicated that competency with *data visualization and representation* was important. In addition to the breadth of needs expressed in the interviews, we observed wide variations in baseline skills of students working with EPICS. For this project, we deliberately kept the definitions of the competencies loose, as we wanted interviewees to express their opinions and perspectives on the competencies with little direction or interference from us. For our work with EPICS on *data quality and documentation,* it was clear that its success is very much specifically oriented on a particular skill in that competency: "Documents data sufficiently enough to enable the reproduction of the research results and the data by others." However, we needed to define what this statement really meant for EPICS and how it was (or was not) understood by the students, TAs, faculty advisors, and EPICS administration to be able to respond effectively. Learning the context and gaining an understanding of the setting were as important to our program as defining our terms. This was very much an iterative process.

NOTE

This case study is available online at http://dx.doi.org.10.5703/1288284315477.

REFERENCES

Ali, N., Gueheneuc, Y. G., & Antoniol, G. (2011). Trust-based requirements traceability. In *Program Comprehension (ICPC), 2011 IEEE 19th International Conference on* (pp. 111–120) [IEEE Xplore Digital Library version]. http://dx.doi.org/10.1109/ICPC.2011.42

Bashir, M. F., & Qadir, M. A. (2006). Traceability techniques: A critical study. In *Multitopic Conference, 2006. INMIC '06. IEEE* (pp. 265–268) [IEEE Xplore Digital Library version]. http://dx.doi.org/10.1109/INMIC.2006.358175

Bettenburg, N., Adams, B., Hassan, A. E., & Smidt, M. (2011). A lightweight approach to uncover technical artifacts in unstructured data. In *Program Comprehension (ICPC), 2011 IEEE 19th International Conference on* (pp. 185–188) [IEEE Xplore Digital Library version]. http://dx.doi.org/10.1109/ICPC.2011.36

Bloom, B. S. (1956). *Taxonomy of educational objectives, Handbook I: The cognitive domain.* New York: David McKay Co. Inc.

Chen, S. (2001). The paradox of digital preservation. *Computer, 34*(3), 24–28. http://dx.doi.org/10.1109/2.910890

Crowston, K., Annabi, H., & Howison, J. (2003). Defining open source software project success. In *ICIS 2003 Proceedings* (Paper 28; pp. 327–340). Retrieved from AIS Electronic Library: http://aisel.aisnet.org/icis2003/28/

Doxygen. (n.d.). Generate documentation from source code. Retrieved from http://www.stack.nl/~dimitri/doxygen/index.html

Grechanik, M., Fu, C., Xie, Q., McMillan, C., Poshyvanyk, D., & Cumby, C. (2010). Exemplar: EXEcutable exaMPLes ARchive. In *Proceedings of the 32nd ACM/IEEE International Conference on Software Engineering, Vol. 2* (pp. 259–262) [ACM Digital Library version]. http://dx.doi.org/10.1145/1810295.1810347

Halloran, T. J., & Scherlis, W. L. (2002). *High quality and open source software practices.* Paper presented at Meeting Challenges and Surviving Success: 2nd Workshop on Open Source Software Engineering, Orlando, FL. Retrieved from http://flosshub.org/system/files/HalloranScherlis.pdf

Hasan, M., Stroulia, E., Barbosa, D., & Alalfi, M. (2010). Analyzing natural-language artifacts of the software process. In *Software Maintenance (ICSM), 2010 IEEE International Conference on* (pp. 1–5) [IEEE Xplore Digital Library version]. http://dx.doi.org/10.1109/ICSM.2010.5609680

Knuth, D. E. (1984). Literate programming. *Computer Journal, 27*(2), 97–111. http://dx.doi.org/10.1093/comjnl/27.2.97

Lethbridge, T. C., Singer, J., & Forward, A. (2003). How software engineers use documentation: The state of the practice. *IEEE Software, 20*(6), 35–39. http://dx.doi.org/10.1109/MS.2003.1241364

Lima, M., & Oakes, W. (2006). *Service-learning: Engineering in your community* (1st ed.). Okemos, MI: Great Lakes Press.

Marcus, A., & Menzies, T. (2010). Software is data too. In *Proceedings of the FSE/SDP Workshop on the Future of Software Engineering Research* (pp. 229–231) [ACM Digital Library version]. http://dx.doi.org/10.1145/1882362.1882410

Martin, R. C. (2008). *Clean code: A handbook of agile software craftsmanship.* Upper Saddle River, NJ: Prentice Hall.

Matthews, B., Shaon, A., Bicarregui, J., & Jones, C. (2010). A framework for software preservation. *The International Journal of Digital Curation, 5*(1), 91–105. http://dx.doi.org/10.2218/ijdc.v5i1.145

Menzies, T., & Di Stefano, J. S. (2003). More success and failure factors in software reuse. *IEEE Transactions on Software Engineering, 29*(5), 474–477. http://dx.doi.org/10.1109/TSE.2003.1199076

Sapp Nelson, M. (2009). Teaching interview skills to undergraduate engineers: An emerging area of library instruction. *Issues in Science & Technology Librarianship,* (58). http://dx.doi.org/10.5062/F4ZK5DMK

Sapp Nelson, M. (2013). Find the real need: Understanding the task. In M. Fosmire & D. Radcliffe (Eds.), *Integrating information into engineering design* (pp. 87–99). West Lafayette, IN: Purdue University.

Schulte, S. J. (2012). Embedded academic librarianship: A review of the literature. *Evidence Based Library & Information Practice, 7*(4), 122–138.

Sojer, M., & Henkel, J. (2010). Code reuse in open source software development: Quantitative evidence, drivers, and impediments. *Economic Policy, 11*(12), 868–901.

Tumbleson, B. E., & Burke, J. J. (2010). Embedded librarianship is job one: Building on instructional synergies. *Public Services Quarterly, 6*(2–3), 225–236. http://dx.doi.org/10.1080/15228959.2010.497457

Von Krogh, G., Spaeth, S., & Haefliger, S. (2005). Knowledge reuse in open source software: An exploratory study of 15 open source projects. In *Proceedings of the 38th Annual Hawaii International Conference on System Sciences (HICSS'05)—Track 7* (Vol 7, p. 198b) [CS Digital Library version]. http://dx.doi.org/10.1109/HICSS.2005.378

APPENDIX A: Rubrics for Evaluating Software Code and Documentation Produced in the Purdue University EPICS Program

EPICS SOFTWARE CODE RUBRIC			
Outcome	Expected	Acceptable	Unacceptable
The code performs as intended	The code produces the desired performance in a timely, straightforward, consistent, concise, simple, and logical manner without extraneous elements	The code produces the desired performance, but includes elements that add to processing time, adds unnecessary complexity, unnecessarily lengthens the code, contains inconsistencies, or obscures logic	Code fails to perform
The code is human readable	The code itself and corresponding documentation are easily understood by a person with a basic understanding of the coding language used. The code is straightforward and intuitive	The code and documentation are easily understood in most places. In some places coding is convoluted or wordier than is necessary.	The code and documentation are generally not easily understandable. The code includes esoteric coding strategies
The code contains meaningful names	Meaningful names—names that clearly convey the distinct purpose, behavior, or intent of a particular element of the code—are used in all facets of the code, including variables, procedures, functions, classes, and objects. Names should be distinct, descriptive, non-redundant, and technically correct.	Meaningful names are used in most of the facets of the code, including variables, procedures, functions, classes, and objects	Meaningful names are used only occasionally in the facets of the code, including variables, procedures, functions, classes, and objects
The code is consistent	The code follows standardized rules, conventions, or a consistent logical pattern in its structure, format, and use of names	The code generally follows standardized rules, conventions, or consistent logical patterns in its structure, format, and use of names	The code occasionally or rarely follows standardized rules, conventions, or consistent logical patterns in its structure, format, and use of names

Continued

Outcome	Expected	Acceptable	Unacceptable
The structure and layout of the code is appropriate and logical	The structure and layout of the code consistently follows a logical order that conveys meaning to the reader. Variables are always placed in close proximity to their use	The structure and layout of the code generally follows a logical order that conveys meaning to the reader. Variables are often placed in close proximity to their use.	The structure and layout of the code does not follow a logical order that conveys meaning to the reader. Variables are not placed in close proximity to their use
The code makes appropriate use of comments	Comments in the code are consistently clear, concise, and informative and consistently explain intent or assumptions made by the author as needed. Comments in the code always contain appropriate information about the code and do not duplicate other sources of documentation. Comments appear as close to the part of the code they refer to as possible. Comments reflect the current state of the code and have been updated when the code was updated	Comments in the code are usually clear, concise, informative, and sufficient in explaining intent or assumptions made by the author. Comments in the code generally contain appropriate information about the code, but may duplicate other sources of documentation. Comments often appear close to the part of the code they refer to. Comments generally reflect the current state of the code	Comments in the code are occasionally clear, concise, and informative and do not really explain intent or assumptions made by the author. Comments in the code do not generally contain appropriate information about the code, or often duplicate other sources of documentation. Comments do not appear close to the part of the code they refer to. Comments are outdated and do not reflect the current state of the code

EPICS SOFTWARE DOCUMENTATION RUBRIC

Outcome	Expected	Acceptable	Unacceptable
Documentation describes functionality of code	The documentation includes clear information on the purpose of the code and what the code does	The documentation only partially describes the purpose and functionality of the code, and is at times unclear to non–team members. Documentation omits minor details	The documentation fails to describe the purpose and functionality of the code in a way that is understandable to non–team members. Documentation omits multiple and/or important details
Documentation describes the composition of the software package	All constituent parts of the software code and accompanying hardware/documentation are identified, and interrelationships between the parts are clearly identified	Most constituent parts of the software code and accompanying hardware/documentation are identified, and most interrelationships between the parts are clearly identified. Documentation omits minor details	Significant numbers of constituent parts are not identified and/or the interrelationships are not adequately identified to enable non–team members to orient themselves to the software package. Documentation omits multiple and/or important details

Continued

Outcome	Expected	Acceptable	Unacceptable
Documentation accounts for significant changes and tracks versions of the code	Changes are tracked via a versioning system; ownership of changes is clearly noted in the documentation so that future team members can retrieve background information from blogs/notebooks	The majority of changes are tracked; ownership of changes is not always identified	Changes aren't recorded and responsibility for those changes is not recorded consistently. Documentation omits multiple and/or important details
Documentation describes human-centered design decisions	All interfaces and human interaction points with the software are documented, along with the software designer's decision-making process for those interactions	Interfaces are identified, but it is not clear to future team members why or how those decisions were made. Documentation omits minor details	Interfaces are not identified. Neither are decisions identified. Documentation omits multiple and/or important details. The future team member must make assumptions or create a backstory for code decisions made
Documentation describes the software environment	All hardware, operating systems, programming languages, compilers, software libraries, other software packages, and peripherals necessary for using/understanding the code have been identified	There have been oversights in listing component systems and languages. Documentation omits minor details	Little or no attempt has been made to collocate the components the software design and programming relies upon. Documentation omits multiple and/or important details
Documentation describes software architecture decisions	In the case of databases and apps, decisions on the architecture (backups, client/server operations, or peer-to-peer interactions) have been fully explained in the documentation	The system architecture is understood, but requires research in the code in order to identify the underlying architecture fully. Documentation omits minor details	The documentation does not have enough information for the underlying architecture of the system to be easily understood and the code does not make it clear. Documentation omits multiple and/or important details
Documentation is updated in a timely and consistent manner	Documentation is up to date for all changes to that point in the semester. Documentation is digitally signed by the code author and dated	Documentation is somewhat behind the current state of the code. Documentation is digitally signed by the code author and dated	Documentation is completely out of date and/or has not been signed and dated by the code author

APPENDIX B: One-Page Handout for EPICS Graduate TAs Introducing the Project

Software Coding and Documentation Practices for EPICS

While researching the coding and documentation practices of electrical and computer engineering and computer science programmers, we noticed consistent gaps in the coding and documentation practices of previous EPICS teams. With feedback from advisors and TAs, we developed rubrics to hold software creators and their teams accountable for producing quality software and documentation.

Why is this important?

As you know, EPICS teams continue from semester to semester. It is very challenging for new team members to join a project team when the documentation, comments, and quality of the code produced by previous teams are difficult or impossible to understand. Existing team members may or may not be available to explain how design decisions were made. Regardless, poor coding and documentation practices needlessly slow down the project and require that the delivery be pushed back as teams second guess or are forced to recreate decisions. Most professional positions will be situated in a team environment and will develop components of software code across multiple teams. Therefore, gaining an understanding of good documentation skills and being able to demonstrate these skills in one's code are critical skills for EPICs students.

What are the expectations for quality code?

The following questions help define expectations for quality code:

- Does the code work as it was designed?
- Can a non–team member easily understand what the code is doing?
- Are the names chosen in the code meaningful to an outside code reader or user?
- Is the code internally consistent in naming and other conventions?
- Do the structure and layout of the code assist a non–team member in understanding the code?
- Do the comments assist a non–team member in reading and understanding the code?
- Does the documentation identify all major decision points, relationships, components, and operational features of the code?

Is this extra work?

Yes and no. This is a grading structure for existing deliverables, including the design documentation and individual blogs/notebooks. Your team might already be doing these things on a routine basis. However, if you have not been coding with these criteria in mind, then you will need to take some action to ensure that they are included in your workflow.

Do you have questions? Contact Megan [Megan's e-mail] or Jake [Jake's e-mail].

APPENDIX C: Skills Session Lesson Plan for Week 3 of the EPICS Data Information Literacy Intervention

Organizing, Managing, and Documenting Software Code

Objectives
Recognize desired coding habits of software professors and companies to internalize the need for good code habits.
1. Articulate observable differences between poor coding product and good human readable code product to identify practices that support or denigrate code products.
2. Identify ways that good coding facilitates quality outcomes and facilitates the completion of the EPICS project to build a case for developing strong coding habits.
3. Determine your expectations and define what resources and tools your team will need to carry out these expectations to foster a work environment that supports a culture of good coding practices.

Module Themes
The skills session will be presented in three modules:

- Module 1—What is good coding?
- Module 2—Why is good coding important?—EPICS as a stakeholder—appeal for coding may not be as relevant—professional—take a poll.
- Module 3—How to foster good coding practices in your team.

Curriculum Methods
Module 1
Lecture—Goal 1: Introduction.
Visual—Goal 1: Convey desired coding habits quotes from interviews.
Needed resources: Computer; projector; PowerPoint; quotes regarding coding habits.
Quotes from *Clean Code* book on what clean code is (in page number order).[*]

- Grady Booch, page 8
- "Big" Dave Thomas, page 9
- Ward Cunningham, page 11
- Bjarne Stroustrup, page 7

Hands-on lab—Goal 1: compare examples of code snippets generated from previous EPICS teams as groups of two to three working together with a TA.

---

[*] See Martin, R. C. (2008). *Clean code: A handbook of agile software craftsmanship* (Vol. 1, p. 464). Retrieved from http://dl.acm.org/citation.cfm?id=1388398

Needed resources: Examples of code snippets in print or electronic form.

Group report back—Goal 1: Using the examples, identify as a group what the differences are between poor and good code.

Needed resources: Whiteboard and dry erase markers, eraser.

Module 2

Group reflection/discussion—Goal 2: Why does writing good code matter? How does it support quality outcomes? (Responding to the question: If the code does what is needed, why does it matter?)

- Code will be used by more than just its author(s).
- Code needs to have a shelf life beyond its immediate purpose/context (your grade).

Needed resources: Whiteboard and dry erase markers, eraser.

Coding Skills Inventory Worksheet—Goal 2: What skills are needed to facilitate good code habits among your teams? Review and discuss briefly (and if necessary, solicit additional skills to add to this list).

Needed resources: Worksheet (below) composed of a list of potential skills that students need to have.

CODING SKILLS INVENTORY WORKSHEET FOR MODULE 2

Coding Skills Inventory

Evaluating code quality	Establishing and following team standards in developing documentation
Establishing norms and consistencies in the structure and organization of the code	Developing code and documentation that can be easily understood and used by project partner and stakeholders
Version control/tracking changes/synchronization of the code (group editing)	
Transferring/inheriting code to and from other project teams (maintaining continuity and avoiding loss of knowledge)	Processes and structure for managing and maintaining the code and documentation as it is being developed
Ensuring the sustainability of the code	Review and testing the code to ensure quality and usability
Ensuring that documentation is updated in a timely manner and accurately reflects the current state of the code	Understanding/documenting the relationship between project components (e.g., code, documentation) and the software environment as a whole
	Documentation of the decisions/actions/processes taken by teams

Module 3

Hands-on lab—Goal 3: As a team of two to three people, pick one of the skills listed on the coding skills inventory worksheet as a high-priority need for your team. Using the list of activities provided as a starting point, plan a short (5–10 min.) intervention for your team members that will address this need.

Needed resources: Coding skills inventory worksheets; activities handout.

Small team reflection/discussion—Goal 3: How will you know if your intervention has worked? How will you know if your team members "got it"? What will you be able to observe that shows that the code quality is improving?

Group reflection/discussion—Goals 3 and 4: What intervention did you plan? How will you know that it is successful?

Needed resources: Computer; Microsoft Word.

[*Instructor notes:* Create a transcript of proposed ideas and assessments. Distribute to all participants/keep as a part of the assessment of the skill session.]

APPENDIX D: Design Process–Centered Activities for Documentation and Organization

We have developed ideas for possible activities that would help students gain an understanding of documentation and organization practices for software code and for projects more generally. These activities are organized according to the phases in the design cycle as depicted in "The Engineering Design Method for Service-Learning."[**] Each stage in this life cycle has a learning objective attached to it that pertains to the documentation/organization of software code or the project itself. The activities listed beneath the learning objective are possible ways to teach these objectives to your students/team members.

Please contact us if you have any questions or if you would like our assistance in further developing or running these discussions or activities.

Megan Sapp Nelson, Subject Liaison for Engineering—[Megan's e-mail]

Jake Carlson, Data Services Specialist—[Jake's e-mail]

Phase 1. Problem Identification
Activity: Environmental Scan

What existing technologies are being used with which your new code must interact? How do they function? What interaction is there between your code and that existing code? What conventions are used in coding the existing software? What languages are used? What are the key structures of the code that will impact your new software?

Discuss your conclusions with your project team. How do these observations change your understanding of the problem identified by the project partner?

Activity: Skills Identification Inventory

Complete the skills identification inventory. Which skills do individuals have on the team? What are the strengths of each individual? What weaknesses does the project team have? Create a plan to build capacity in areas of team weakness. Create a plan to divide tasks on the basis of individual strengths.

Activity: Infrastructure Setup

Set up backups and versioning software. Make sure that everyone on the team has access to appropriate directories and understands how to access them.

Phase 2. Specification Development
Activity: Personas

Create personas for the end users who will be using the delivered final product. Who are they? Why are they interacting with the software? How do they interact with the software and documentation? Are all of their needs met within the current specifications? Who is maintaining this software? What are they responsible for? Capture the personas in the project documentation.

[**] Lima, M., & Oakes, W. (2006). *Service-learning: Engineering in your community.* Okemos, MI: Great Lakes Press.

Activity: Project Partner Interview

Create a list of questions to ask the project partner. In your questions emphasize who the users of the software are, the level of expertise of users, plans for maintenance, and situational infrastructure that could have an impact on your software design.

Resources: SharePoint, skill sessions, project partner interview worksheet.

Activity: Design Matrix

Create a design matrix identifying the most important specifications the team identified during the project partner interview. Consider implications for coding and documentation as you discuss these specifications.

Phase 3. Conceptual Design
Activity: Discussion

Hold a discussion with the aim of reaching a consensus on the following issues:

- Standards for formatting the code covering issues such as indentation, line lengths, use of comments, and so forth.
- Naming conventions and/or controlled vocabulary for variables, procedures, functions, classes and objects used in the code.
- How and to what extent the code will be reviewed and tested to ensure that it functions as expected.

If applicable, the team should make use of existing standards such as Sun's Java Code Conventions or tools such as JavaDoc. However, teams should not adopt standards or tools without reviewing them and knowing how they could or should be applied in the EPICS context. It is important that teams take ownership of the documentation convention they adopt or develop.

Outcomes should be written up, shared, and used in practice. The key decision points should also be captured and stored in a place where it is easily accessible to the team. Team members should be held accountable for following the decisions for documenting their code and other project deliverables.

Activity: Team Covenant

Create a team covenant. Include the following in the discussion: standards for formatting indentation, line lengths, use of comments, naming conventions, functions, classes, and objects. The covenant should be written up, shared, and used in team coding.

Activity: Software Tool Selection

Select a tool for the project team to use to create documentation as code is developed. JavaDoc is one such tool. Ask your TA or advisor for further input in the use of tools that will facilitate team coding and documentation.

Activity: "Living" Wire Frame

Identify the various components that need to be built into the code and diagram how the code and the functionality of the code map onto each other. Make this a living document for the team that changes as further code is added and the code is redesigned.

Phase 4. Detailed Design
Activity: Functional Design Outline

Create a diagram showing the functional design of the code, including human interaction points and area that will potentially require ongoing maintenance. Discuss these interaction points, putting yourselves in the position of the project stakeholders.

- What information will each of the stakeholders need to know about the interaction points to understand and make use of the code effectively upon delivery?
- What information will each of the stakeholders need to know about the interaction points to maintain the code?

Document the key decision points and the decisions that are made. Assign individuals to write up more substantive descriptions in the project documentation.

Activity: Team Coding

Have members of the team "exchange" code they have written and clearly indicate to the author areas of code that are not human readable as written. Are the standards that were agreed upon earlier in the semester being followed? Are the names clear? Are the functions identifiable? Revise the code and exchange with yet another member of the team. Continue until the code is human readable.

Activity: Code Synopsis

Create a brief document that synthesizes the coding decisions that you have made. Use it for a design review and ask for feedback from design reviewers. Make changes based on the feedback you received and enter the document into the team documentation.

Phase 5. Production
Activity: Software Code Peer Review

Team up with another project team involved in generating code. Have each team attempt to use the code generated by the other team, review the documentation of the other team's code, assign a rating to the quality of the other team's code using the EPICS software documentation rubric, and make recommendations as to how the code could be improved and deliver these recommendations to the other team in writing.

Activity: Testing Plan

Ask your TA for guidance in developing a testing plan for your software that focuses on exception testing. Develop and implement the testing plan. Consider bringing in people from outside the team to have them test the software. Record your testing plan and any major changes that are implemented as a result.

Activity: Usability Testing

Create a structured usability test. Have representative users (see the personas activity above) test the interface. Are they interacting with the interface as anticipated? Are there any changes that should be made in light of the discussion? Document any observations and resulting changes.

Phase 6. Delivery/Transfer
Activity: Transfer Role-Play

Role-play the process of transferring responsibility. Recruit team leaders, TAs, or EPICS administrators to play the role of the client or the next team leader for the project.

The situation is that a meeting has been called to transfer the deliverables of the project from the project team to the client or to the team leader for the next project team. The student(s) are to prepare for this meeting by identifying what the client will need to know to understand, implement, and use the deliverables, or what the next team leader will need to know to continue the project with a minimal amount of disruption. The student will then need to identify how and where this information is documented to ensure a smooth transfer.

An alternative approach would be to reduce the scale of this activity from a focus on the overall project to a focus on the code or a portion of the code. The questions would then shift to "What does the client/future team leader need to understand about the code to implement and use it?" and "How and where is this information documented?"

Activity: Peer Review of Documentation

Create a sample "transfer package" of materials (based on an actual project to the extent possible) and have students review and evaluate the contents paying special attention to the stated needs of the client or the likely needs of future project teams. Have them answer either of the following questions:

1. What will the client need to know to understand, implement, and use the deliverables, and how and where is this information included and conveyed in the transfer package?
2. What will the next project team need to know to continue the project, and how and where is this information documented?

Phase 7. Service/Maintenance
Activity: Maintenance Documentation

Have students create an annotated inventory version of the project documentation that indexes the sources of the information needed to maintain and/or service the project.

- What will people need to know to maintain or service the project?
- Where is this information documented, and who is response for drafting and maintaining this documentation?
- How complete is this documentation? Are there any gaps that need to be filled?

As a precursor to this exercise, students could be given a sample annotated inventory to critique.

Activity: Code Synopsis

Create an outline of the code that points back to files, .svn versions, and other necessary documentation. Test this document on students who are not affiliated with the project. Can they quickly find necessary information to understand the existing code?

CHAPTER **6**

TEACHING DATA INFORMATION LITERACY SKILLS IN A LIBRARY WORKSHOP SETTING

A Case Study in Agricultural and Biological Engineering

INTRODUCTION

This Data Information Literacy (DIL) project team worked with two faculty members in a hydrology lab in the Department of Agricultural and Biological Engineering at Purdue University; this was one of two Purdue University teams participating in the DIL project. The data produced by the lab include field-based observations, remote sensing, and hydrology models to help understand land-atmosphere interactions and the hydrologic cycle. Interviews with the faculty and graduate students in the research group indicated that data management standards were their primary concern. These Purdue researchers were neither aware of nor using disciplinary-developed data standards for storage, sharing, reuse, or description of data. Data standards would allow their data to be interoperable with other data generated by researchers in their field and would prevent them from "reinventing the wheel" each time data must be shared. Additionally, they were very interested in contributing to disciplinary standards since they believed that standards developed by the community had a better chance of being adopted. Over the course of the project, one of the participants became the campus representative to a national data repository, which gave our program a greater urgency: current and future students who worked in their labs must be trained in and use these standards.

Through user assessment, the DIL team members determined that the most important DIL areas to address through instruction were creating standard operating procedure documents for collecting the lab's data, finding external data, and creating metadata. With regard to operating procedures, the research group indicated that they had some instructions for data management listed on their wiki, but students did not follow them very often.

The DIL team determined that the students had not internalized the need to manage and document data for their own work and to share with other members of the group. The wiki procedures were not specific enough to give students direction to successfully manage their data. Students also needed to incorporate external data—for example, using weather/climate data as inputs in their simulations. Locating, understanding, cleaning, and formatting those data is not a trivial process, and students can save significant time if the data are in a format that is usable by or easily importable into their programs. Finally, metadata was the key to effectively organizing, managing, and disseminating data. The more one knows about the contents of a data set, the more likely one can make the right choice about whether to use it. So, a well-documented data set will be more visible, comprehensible, and potentially useful to the research community at large.

We determined that the most effective approach to teach these skills within the time constraints of the research group was to conduct three instruction sessions over 3 months during the lab's normally scheduled meetings. Embedding the instruction within the lab's meeting schedule emphasized (1) how important the data skills were to the faculty members, and (2) that there was an urgent need to embed community standards for data management and curation into everyday practice. Overall, this approach to instruction was to present a contextualized program, grounded in the actual activities and procedures of the group, to reinforce the practical need for DIL skills and attitudes and increase buy-in from the lab group members.

We developed a different assessment for each module, appropriate for the range of learning objectives. The results of the assessment revealed that applying the content presented to real-life research workflows is a real challenge for students. Even though they clearly understood the material presented—and even recognized its importance—students did not incorporate data management practices into their everyday workflow. Future plans include collaborating with the faculty and students to incorporate these skills into standard lab practices.

LITERATURE REVIEW AND ENVIRONMENTAL SCAN OF DATA MANAGEMENT BEST PRACTICES

The literature review focused primarily on water and hydrology disciplinary data management resources, though the interdisciplinary nature of the lab's work led us to include ecological and biological research resources as well. The literature showed that students had little experience with creating metadata (Hernandez, Mayernik, Murphy-Mariscal, & Allen, 2012).

The most useful information for our background review came from the Consortium of Universities for the Advancement of Hydrological Science, Inc. (CUAHSI) organization (http://www.cuahsi.org/). Created in 2001 by the National Science Foundation, CUAHSI is the water-science community response to "the need to organize and extend the national and international research portfolio, particularly to develop shared infrastructure for investigating the behavior and effects of water in large and complex environmental systems" (CUAHSI, 2010). The consortium lists a number of points in its mission statement that are crucial to addressing better access to data, including creating and supporting research infrastructure and increasing access to data and information. Its strategic plan lists four data access goals, which demonstrate the forward thinking of the organization:

1. Develop and maintain search services for diverse sources of data and the underlying metadata catalogs (building on and extending from the Hydrologic Information System—HIS), including an access portal and coordination with providers of water-related information
2. Develop a mechanism for citation and use tracking to provide professional recognition for contributions to community data archives
3. Solicit community input on emerging data needs and facilitate access to new types of data
4. Coordinate development, promotion, and adoption of metadata standards between universities, governmental agencies, and the private sector for interpreted data products (e.g., potentiometric surfaces, areal estimation of precipitation, and input-output budgets). (CUAHSI, 2010, p.18)

Perhaps the most interesting area to note in the CUAHSI strategic plan is its continued development of metadata standards. CUAHSI recognizes the need for a shared language for both researchers and information systems to communicate to other researchers and information systems. To this end, the consortium is expanding the CUAHSI Hydrologic Information System (HIS), a Web-based portal for accessing and sharing water data (CUAHSI, 2013). The HIS operates with two important metadata standards: the Water Metadata Language (OGC, 2013), which is an open metadata schema created by the San Diego Supercomputing Center for hydrological time series and synoptic data, and the Federal Geographic Data Commission (FGDC) metadata schema (FGDC, 1998) created for geographic information system (GIS) and spatial data. Other metadata and data practices include the well-developed schema of the Ecological Metadata Language (EML), originally developed by the Ecological Society of America for ecology and related disciplines (Knowledge Network for Biocomplexity, n.d.b). Although not specifically created for hydrology, the EML metadata standard uses similar descriptions and requires an understanding of geospatial needs that are specific to the hydrology discipline, more so than more general standards such as Dublin Core (Dublin Core Metadata Initiative, 2013). Additionally, this Purdue DIL team consulted very useful EML tools, such as the Morpho data management application, a downloadable metadata entry template (Knowledge Network for Biocomplexity, n.d.a), when creating a metadata exercise for the graduate students.

Since the greatest needs for our research group focused on metadata and laboratory standard operating procedures for data management, we consulted Qin and D'Ignazio (2010), who provided details of a metadata-focused scientific data course of study. Stanton (2011) described the duties of practicing e-science professionals, which provided a foundation in actual tasks that scientists undertook in the course of managing data. Finally, the EPA (2007) provided a solid introduction to the purpose and process of creating standard operating procedures, which were applied to the student activities.

CASE STUDY OF GRADUATE STUDENT DATA INFORMATION LITERACY NEEDS IN AGRICULTURAL AND BIOLOGICAL SCIENCES

The hydrology research groups consisted of two faculty members who focused on the integration of field-based observations, remote sensing, and hydrology models to increase understanding of land-atmosphere interactions and the hydrologic cycle. Their work requires the acquisition of different kinds of data and the ability to convert data to ensure interoperability. The primary faculty member understood the importance and significance of good data practices, but still struggled with achieving high-quality data management in the research groups. The data collected in the lab ran the gamut of data types. On the one hand, the lab manually collected water samples and analyzed the results; tracking their processes with print lab notebooks that were later scanned into electronic formats. On the other hand, the group also downloaded remote sensing data from external sources, which were fed into computer models that created large data files in the process. Managing these three types of data—field samples, (external) remote sensing data, and computer simulations—provided constant challenges, especially as the students gathering or processing each different kind of data communicated their results with each other.

To understand the needs of the graduate students, the Purdue DIL team conducted six interviews between April and June of 2012. We used the DIL interview protocol (available for download at http://dx.doi.org/10.5703 /1288284315510). This is a semi-structured interview instrument that allows for follow-up and clarification questions. The Purdue DIL team interviewed the primary faculty member (Faculty A), from the Department of Agricultural and Biological Engineering (ABE). We then interviewed five ABE graduate students (a mix of master's and PhD students) working in this faculty member's research group. (Note: A second faculty member [Faculty B] and other graduate students working on their research team could not be reached for interviews but were included in the educational program. This second faculty member was included in all subsequent actions and discussions in creating instructional content and assessments.)

One reason that our team approached Faculty A to be part of this project was because he had already expressed concern about teaching data management and data literacy skills to graduate students for the educating, acculturation, and training process of graduate school. He was familiar with many data literacy skills already, generally from the absence of good practices. These resulted in data loss by students due to the lack of proper backup, poor description, and poor organization of files. For example, he described:

> I have been slowly developing a data management plan after our conversations over the last couple of years, . . . [but one] that's more in my head. . . . But I think just the general conversation has clarified in my head that rather than just repeating over and over again to my students what they should be doing, having a written statement certainly helps. And then when they get in trouble, like the student who was saving everything on their external USB hard drive, I [can] point back to the data management plan that says [they] weren't allowed to do that.

He further described:

> I tried to establish a naming convention, but nobody ever listens to the naming conventions, so next thing you know you've got five files labeled "Final 1", "Final 2", "Final A", "Final C." So we keep running into this problem with stuff that people who have left, right? So what is this file? We've got three files that look identical except for the "Final" variation name. Which one is it?

Faculty A also experienced difficulties with understanding or obtaining the lab's data from students after their graduation. He explained:

> I had a student in my first couple of years who [collected] field data for me, and I didn't have a written plan. He didn't follow my [verbal] plan, and so he left with all of the material. . . . I've had a couple of people ask me about that data and what was available and it's like, well, I've never actually seen it.

Faculty A offers a class on environmental informatics. Most of the skills in the course are not taught to graduate students generally prior to their entering the lab unless they are picked up informally from other advisors or students. The class included general best practices for research, but many discipline-specific items were covered as well. Even so, one of Faculty A's primary concerns was that students were not receiving any data training outside of his lab or in their course work. Additionally, all his research group students were in the ABE department studying some aspect of hydrology but from a variety of angles: using field or observed data, using remote sensing data, or creating models. This meant that it was difficult to create and enforce a one-size-fits-all approach to a written DMP. Faculty A stated:

> So I think if you have a lab-based kind of group, then they probably have some methodology that they lay out in a lab book, but it's harder when it's—you know—a small group and people are doing different things. This is the dilemma for me. I've got one graduate student who's doing mostly remote sensing work. I've got a couple of grad students who are going to do more observational work. And then most of them are doing modeling work. . . . [I]t becomes more individualized, right? It's harder to invest the time to come up with the documentation [for data management] because it's [for] one or two people. But

the problem is that those one or two people become somebody else [grad students replacing current] or maybe multiple people at some point, right? So we need to be capturing this.

To help with this problem, Faculty A had introduced students to some general data management policies on a wiki site once they started in his lab. When interviewed, students all displayed some awareness that there were formal data management policies in place within the research group. However, they also all expressed varying degrees of compliance, sometimes because they were not sure they applied to their specific data situation. One graduate student said:

Yes we have a wiki site. [The faculty advisor] lists all of the procedures that we need to follow. . . . (Laughs) But I think I do not follow that, because my data is too large and it's very difficult to ask Purdue to extend my space.

In addition to our interview results in the DIL project, our interview included ratings of the DIL competences. Here, both the faculty and the graduate students interviewed rated most of the DIL facets as important (see Figure 6.1). The highest rated concepts by the students were *discovery and acquisition, data processing and analysis,* and *data management and organization,* with *ethics and attribution, data visualization and representation,* and *metadata and data description* very highly rated as well.

A MULTI-SESSION INSTRUCTION APPROACH TO DATA INFORMATION LITERACY SKILLS

In developing our DIL program, we discussed with both of the faculty members the nature and extent of instruction needed by their students. The discussion centered on the highest priority skills needed by the students, which skills would best be facilitated by librarian partners, and which skills, if successfully learned, would have the greatest impact on the research group overall. We also discussed how much time would realistically be available for face-to-face instruction, so that we could make the best use of the research groups' time. With a total of 2 faculty members and 13 students, each with their own academic schedule, the faculty found it challenging to find dates and times for even an hour-long group meeting a week.

We settled on a three-part instructional strategy that included some prep work prior to the face-to-face session and homework for the students to complete following the session. Given the time constraints, the DIL team felt that we should concentrate on just the most important and directly applicable DIL skills for which the librarians had unique expertise. Consequently, we decided to focus our instruction on *discovery and acquisition, data management and organization, ethics and attribution,* and *metadata and data description* as the remaining high-impact fundamental areas from the survey. While additional topics such as *data visualization and representation* and *data processing and analysis* were important, they might best be taught by the faculty members themselves.

It became apparent that, while the research group had a preliminary set of data management policies, these policies were not well understood or adhered to by the graduate students. Thus, we determined that one way to provide a scaffold for the DIL topics would be to develop standard practices for handling data in the research group. From the literature review and environmental scan, we concluded that these standards must be developed collaboratively to ensure maximum adoption by the group. In short, our goal was to help the group establish its own community standards.

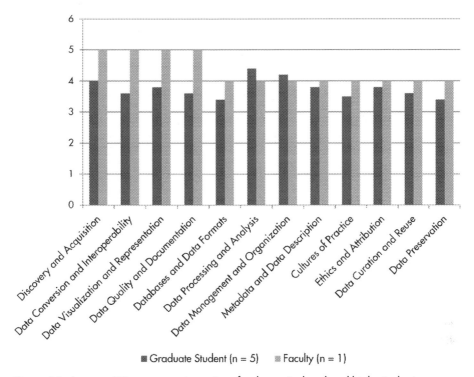

Figure 6.1 Average DIL competencies ratings for the agricultural and biological sciences case study. Ratings based on a 5-point Likert scale: 5 = essential; 4 = very important; 3 = important; 2 = somewhat important; 1 = not important.

To increase the authenticity of the exercises, each of the instructional activities focused on students tackling the actual problems of their group using the content presented in class.

RESULTS OF THE FALL 2012 INSTRUCTION SESSIONS

On the basis of our findings, our team decided to give three presentations to the combined research group over a 3- to 4-month period in the fall of 2012. Our approach was to fold the instruction into the regular meeting schedule to make the DIL material part of their workflow, rather than as something extra or outside of what they would have to do as a group anyway. Faculty A and Faculty B's research groups met together biweekly, so our team worked

with them at every other meeting, or roughly once a month, starting in September, for a total of three sessions.

The topics for the three sessions included (1) developing a data checklist modeled on a standard operations procedures or laboratory protocol format, (2) searching for data in external databases, and (3) creating metadata. The learning objectives for each session are listed in Table 6.1 and the following sections detail the sessions.

Session 1: Data Checklist/Standard Operating Procedures

The aim of Session 1 was to teach the students to articulate the relevant components of a standard operating procedure and to apply those components when creating the actual procedures for the research group. In earlier

TABLE 6.1   *Learning Objectives of the Fall 2012 Library Instruction Sessions*

Session #	Topic	Learning Outcomes
Session 1	Data checklist/ standard operating procedures	Students are able to articulate the relevant components of a standard operating procedure and apply those components to create an actual procedure for the research group
Session 2	Searching for external data	Increased student appreciation for the value of metadata in locating data from external sources, and as a corollary, the importance of applying metadata to their own data sets so others can find (and cite) them in their own research
Session 3	Creating metadata	Students are able to analyze their own data sets and determine appropriate metadata to describe those sets. Students would then be able to curate their data within the structure of Purdue's data repository

discussions with Faculty A, he mentioned that something as simple and straightforward as a checklist for the kinds of data that might be collected would be a good approach. This could outline all the types of data needed, while providing an overview of the data in this outline. Faculty A created an initial checklist for the three categories of data collected: field observation data, remote sensing data, and model simulation data. Each category was unique and therefore had a different checklist governing its organization. Initially, each checklist contained 7 to 15 elements. For example, the field observation data checklist included the following information and data elements for organization and management:

- Field notebooks—scanned copies of all pages related to activities
- Digitized notes and measurements from field notebooks
- Raw files downloaded from field equipment
- Changes to sample control program (text file)
- Photos of sample sites

- IDs associated with physical samples, if collected
- Lab analysis results for all physical samples

The original checklist was meant to be a step-by-step list of things that a student might do to properly capture and describe all the data gathered in an instance of field observation. However, after discussions with the faculty collaborators, we determined that the checklists gave insufficient or ambiguous directions, which was why students did not find the checklists useful.

The DIL team started the session by having students recall when they started in the group and what information they would have liked to have about the data they were working with from the previous students. We brainstormed the attributes that were important to them (e.g., units, weather conditions, analysis techniques, calibration information) and used that to set the stage for determining how they could provide that information about the data they were collecting or producing. We also introduced some examples of best practices in standard operating procedures to show students how to translate their needs for information into an actual set of steps/activities that would lead to the production of that information.

The team followed up the instruction with an exercise using these checklists. To have the students gain ownership of the checklists, the team asked students which elements were missing. This generated some initial suggestions, and then we broke the students into three groups based on which of the three checklists matched most closely with the type of work they did within the research group. Some students matched with two or even all three areas, so they self-selected which group they wanted to join based on their interest or to help balance the group sizes. The faculty members each joined one of the groups. The groups were then asked to work with their assigned checklist in more depth, adding to it and documenting the most realistic way it could be implemented in current workflows. Their homework was to finish their checklist and share their work with the group in 2 weeks. Each group took a slightly different approach; the two groups with the professors as members were more thorough than the third group. The third group possibly lacked the pressure, the focus, and the expertise of having their instructor as a member of their work group.

The three resulting checklists are in Appendix A to this chapter, and the entire research group continues to work toward incorporating the data checklists into their regular workflow. Overall, the team found that the final, community-driven checklists were greatly improved over the faculty member's original draft. They exhibited more detail and less ambiguity, and they showed that students could transfer the content of the instructional session to documentation that was directly relevant to their lab.

Session 2: Searching for External Data

For the second session, the goal was to increase student appreciation for the value of metadata in locating data from external sources, and as a corollary, the importance of applying metadata to their own data sets so that others can find (and cite) them. After debriefing the checklist homework from the first session, which provided reinforcement of the core concepts of standard operating procedures, the second class introduced the Ecological Metadata Language or EML, and Morpho, the tool for describing data sets using EML. Although the Water Metadata Language (WML) at first seemed to be the best fit with the hydrology group, and may prove to be in the long run, the WML tools were not yet as fully developed nor as user-friendly as those provided for EML. The DIL team began the discussion with the "peanut butter sandwich exercise" (i.e., to write down the instructions to make a peanut butter sandwich and then have someone else carry out those instructions explicitly). This demonstrated how description can make a difference in how well individuals understand procedural processes and to illustrate the need to be explicit and complete when describing something.

Next, we drew parallels of the description exercise to metadata. Here we discussed how well-documented metadata could help someone else understand a data set—from how it was gathered to how it was analyzed—and its greater meaning in the context of other data. Students were divided into small groups and asked to search the Knowledge Network for Biocomplexity (KNB) data registry using Morpho to find a data set that might be relevant to them. This was challenging for many students: the keywords that they used were very specific and often unsuccessful while very general keywords such as "water" succeeded. The general "water" records were quite illustrative of how helpful more precise and in-depth descriptions would have been for the searcher.

In the end-of-class assessment, we asked students what they learned, what they will begin to incorporate into their own work, and what was still unclear (see Appendix B to this chapter for the assessment tool). Almost all students responded that they had a deeper understanding of how important metadata could be in describing their data to others and as a way for others to locate their data. They also appreciated the need to be explicit in their own descriptions of their data so that searchers can determine if and how the data might be useful to them. The results of these self-assessments, reinforced by the instructors' observations of the students while searching for external data, aligned very well with the learning outcomes. The students saw clearly that poor description could make another researcher's data difficult, if not impossible, to reuse, and this set the stage for what they would learn in Session 3, creating their own metadata.

Session 3: Creating Metadata

We designed the third session for students to be able to analyze their own data sets and determine appropriate metadata to describe those sets within the structure of an online repository. To demonstrate this, students were asked to submit their own data to our institutional data repository, the Purdue University Research Repository (PURR), and to create a brief metadata record to describe it. We asked students to bring a sample of their data to this session. A data scientist introduced the students to PURR and described the basic principles of what a repository could do for their submitted data. After a brief walk-through on the mechanics of getting started, which included creating an

account in PURR, each student and the two faculty members created a project space. The PURR project space allows users to designate individuals with various roles such as "collaborators" or "owners," and allows owners of the project space to provide access to the materials in their project space to selected individuals. Each participant then uploaded his or her data file to the project space.

For each file uploaded, PURR requires very basic metadata, based on the Dublin Core metadata standard (http://dublincore.org), for description. Because the metadata that is asked for by PURR is so general in nature, we decided to add a more sophisticated metadata assignment to the class that was discipline appropriate. For this assignment, the libraries' metadata librarian created a Web-based form based on EML (see Appendix C to this chapter) and asked students to fill out and include with their data submission to PURR. The 15-field metadata form included subject-based items such as geographic coordinates, temporal coverage, methods, and sampling units, as well as more general items like keywords, abstract, data owners, and data contacts. This information automatically populated an Excel file that could be repurposed as a supplementary document for the data deposited into PURR. Unfortunately, at the time PURR did not accommodate custom metadata fields as a part of its metadata registry. So the metadata had to be downloaded as a separate text file for a potential user of the data to take full advantage of the EML information provided by the author. The metadata, if properly qualified, could also be inserted into a bibliographic data repository, such as the KNB data registry, using their metadata software, Morpho. However, the students were not asked to take that extra step due to time constraints.

This exercise required students to think about how best to describe their data for anyone other than themselves. This required them to capture their tacit knowledge and internalized assumptions about a data set—knowledge that must also be passed along to another individual, even someone they may be working closely with, in order for them to understand the data. DIL team members reviewed the students' metadata submissions and offered suggestions for improvement. Although students were reluctant to do additional metadata entry when depositing their data, the convenience and straightforwardness of the online form improved students' willingness and confidence to complete this task successfully. In the future, as the use of WML continues to increase and as it becomes more robust, we recommend using an online metadata form with fields from WML, or a blend of EML and WML, if that would be appropriate, for a broader audience of data submitters.

Although students said that they understood the need for good descriptive metadata, they were not quick to fill out the metadata template that we provided. Students were prompted several times to complete the form, and 10 out of 12 finally submitted the form. When filling out the forms, students succeeded in writing descriptive methods, study extent, and sampling procedures, and to a lesser extent, in providing keywords (perhaps because completing these tasks are already a familiar exercise when writing papers for journals). Additionally, they were very thorough in describing geographic coverage. This may not be surprising given the geographic focus of their research. Students were less successful when listing data owners, contacts, and affiliated parties, even though this was covered in class. Understanding who owns the data and what roles they "officially" play in creating the data

was a complicated aspect of describing data. This is an area that the team intends to cover more fully in future sessions. Overall, the team will need to find ways to work with the faculty members to insert the metadata template into an existing workflow, so that students do not see this merely as something externally imposed and extra work.

DISCUSSION

The integrated lab-meeting approach was generally successful and contained elements that could be replicable for a wider audience. The exercise of creating checklists to address *data management and organization* skills, though the results here are specific for these research groups, is a general approach that could be used by other labs or researchers. Any lab or work group can generate the detailed list of items that need to be captured or addressed in the data gathering process. Also, with the faculty-student-librarian team approach used in the DIL project, this list can be developed so that there is a feeling of shared ownership and responsibility, each bringing unique skills and responsibilities to the task. Faculty provide the domain expertise and an understanding of what information

Contextualize the DIL model to the needs of the target audience and highlight specific benefits of data management skills for each research group.

absolutely has to be collected. Students bring an operational perspective of how the data are incorporated into the data collection; they are often the ones performing the collection tasks and can identify ways to streamline the process. Finally, librarians bring the DIL expertise to facilitate the discussion between faculty and students as well as to optimize the accessibility, internal consistency, and organization of the data.

Even before the DIL project began, the disciplinary faculty member believed that metadata, or some description of the data, was critical. He had experienced too many instances where one student's data could not be understood, by himself or by others, due to inadequate description. Sometimes this was reparable after many hours spent trying to reconstruct what the data represented; other times the data were simply lost or unusable due to the fact that the description could not be recovered or the student had graduated and taken the data. Our instruction sessions covering the importance of good data description and specific metadata tools positively impacted the students' understanding of the issue. In their assignments the students demonstrated their understanding of how poor metadata could make a data set useless to anyone other than the creator. They applied this knowledge when creating better metadata for their own data descriptions meant for a broader audience.

Despite this appreciation, the students still needed metadata tools to guide this process if they were to be successful. Creating the online tool for entering modified EML metadata increased the likelihood that they would actually adopt this new step in the data management process. The DIL team would like to make the metadata more usable, so that others might take advantage of the work that the students put into describing their data. Currently, saving the EML metadata as an Excel file does not take full advantage of the power of the descriptive language; therefore developing a more robust online entry form and/or brokering the metadata to disciplinary-specific repositories will help stu-

Getting the students to adopt these practices into their everyday workflow was a challenge.

dents appreciate the value of their work. Ultimately, search tools that take advantage of the descriptive metadata can lead to greater reuse of the data by others.

However, getting the students to adopt these practices into their everyday workflow was a challenge, and we had limited success with this during the project. In hindsight, recognizing adoption as one of the greatest barriers, we might have worked with the students from the beginning to incorporate these practices into their research workflows. In tandem, we might have worked more closely with the faculty to create a structure, higher expectations, and a process for implementing the DMP within the lab. However, the adoption of these new practices might simply take time. It could be that regular use of the practices will eventually become habit. Additionally, asking the faculty partners to enforce the new practices through regular and frequent monitoring will likely pay off in the long run with regard to adoption. As these practices become "business as usual" they will transfer easily to new students as they cycle into the research groups and formal training for one student becomes peer-to-peer learning for the next.

CONCLUSION

Overall, this DIL team felt that the program was very successful in communicating DIL concepts and impressing upon graduate students the importance of good data practices. Implementation is still a work in progress, as the faculty researchers are in the best position to address accountability in order to embrace the practices that the group has developed. That said, there have been robust conversations within the research group about the need for improving data management, and all of the members of the group are speaking from a higher level of understanding than they had previous to the project. The DIL model works best when contextualized to the needs of the target audience. Hands-on activities aligned with the goals of the research group extended what they were already doing or trying to do, which gave them more tools and concepts to apply to their research environment. At the end of the instructional program, students had tangible results that included standard operating procedures for the lab and data sets submitted to a repository.

As we reflect on the activities, *data management and organization* (standard operating procedures) and *metadata and data description* (describing and depositing data sets into a repository) jump out as the areas that found the most traction within the research group, and might be the driving principles for a more general DIL model in this discipline. Also, while library and information science professionals may focus on the need to share data and make it openly available, the focus among researchers is shifted more toward sharing data and making it accessible mainly within the research group. Therefore, when stressing the value of data management skills, highlighting the benefit to the research group is key.

In the course of the activities, we discovered that much of the data in distributed repositories is not well described, so locating and using that data is a continuing challenge. As a result, researchers may gravitate toward centralized, well-stewarded data—for example, such as that produced by government agencies. For many "small science" areas, the lack of quality knowledge management systems provides challenges for the successful interoperability and sharing of data among research groups. The lack of good metadata limits progress in this area, as there are few examples of best practices in action in the disciplinary data repositories for their community.

Finally, this case study found that graduate students have no trouble grasping the concepts of DIL when the concepts are presented to them. However, getting students to change current practices, whether on their own or in a group setting, is an ongoing challenge. It is unclear whether this is due to the lack of emphasis on data management in the lab, because faculty are not stressing the need, or that students are not comfortable nor knowledgeable about how to adjust current practice. The important conclusion is that our educational approach of modules was not enough to ensure implementation of best practices. Further research and development is needed to address how students and faculty can not only learn the skills involved with DIL, but implement the DIL best practices as well.

ACKNOWLEDGMENTS

Thanks to C. C. Miller, who contributed to the initial stages of our Purdue DIL team project.

NOTE

This case study is available online at http://dx.doi.org.10.5703/1288284315478.

REFERENCES

CUAHSI. (2010). *Water in a dynamic planet: A five-year strategic plan for water science.* Retrieved from https://www.cuahsi.org/Posts/Entry/115292

CUAHSI. (2013). The CUAHSI hydrologic information system. Retrieved from http://his.cuahsi.org/

Dublin Core Metadata Initiative. (2013). The Dublin Core Metadata Initiative. Retrieved from http://dublincore.org/

Environmental Protection Agency. (2007). *Guidance for preparing standard operating procedures (SOPs)*. Retrieved from http://www.epa.gov/quality/qs-docs/g6-final.pdf

Federal Geographic Data Committee. (1998). *Content standard for digital geospatial metadata workbook, Version 2.0*. Retrieved from http://www.fgdc.gov/metadata/documents/workbook_0501_bmk.pdf

Hernandez, R. R., Mayernik, M. S., Murphy-Mariscal, M., & Allen, M. F. (2012). Advanced technologies and data management practices in environmental science: Lessons from academia. *Bioscience, 62*(12), 1067–1076. http://dx.doi.org/10.1525/bio.2012.62.12.8

Knowledge Network for Biocomplexity. (n.d.a).

Morpho data management application. Retrieved from https://knb.ecoinformatics.org/morphoportal.jsp

Knowledge Network for Biocomplexity. (n.d.b). Ecological metadata language (EML). Retrieved from https://knb.ecoinformatics.org/#external//emlparser/docs/index.html

OGC. (2013). OGC WaterML. Retrieved from http://www.opengeospatial.org/standards/waterml

Qin, J., & D'Ignazio, J. (2010). The central role of metadata in a science data literacy course. *Journal of Library Metadata, 10*(2–3), 188–204. http://dx.doi.org/10.1080/19386389.2010.506379

Stanton, J. M. (2011). Education for escience professionals. *Journal of Education for Library and Information Science, (2)*, 79–94.

APPENDIX A: Data Archiving Checklists for Session 1 of the Agricultural and Biological Sciences Case Study

These checklists were generated by the students and faculty in the Agricultural and Biological Sciences case study of the DIL project. They include checklists for handling the three types of data generated by the research group: (1) Field Observation Data, (2) Remote Sensing Data, and (3) Simulation Model Data.

Data Archiving Checklist
Field Observation Data

Field notebooks—scanned copies of all pages related to activities
 Date scanned:
 Date scanned:
 Date scanned:
Digitized notes and measurements from field notebooks
 Date scanned:
 Date scanned:
 Date scanned:
Raw files downloaded from field equipment
 Date downloaded:
 Date downloaded:
 Date downloaded:
Changes to sample control program (text file)
 Text file name:
 Photos of sample sites
 Photo files stored:
IDs associated with physical samples, if collected
 ID:
 ID:
 ID:
Lab analysis results for all physical samples
 Files stored:
 Files stored:
 Files stored:
Associated remote sensing data?
 Notes:
Associated simulation data?
 Notes:

Processed Files

Name of file:

Quality control program:

Outside data sources:

Photographs of samples:

Writing/compiling data:

Order of Processing:

Formats, fields, missing data, processing, units, time, how collected, where collected, weather conditions

Simulation data: inputs, sim software used (version), size/resolution/scale, format, fields, units

Remote sensing: resolution-temporal, spatial; when collected; name of sensor; cloud/weather, calibration, projection, file type—raster/shape

Metadata file: Data dictionary

Data Archiving Checklist
Remote Sensing Data

Remote sensing platform(s) and sensor(s) used, and status

Platform/sensor/status:

Platform/sensor/status:

Platform/sensor/status:

Raw remote sensing files (DNs)

DN file:

DN file:

DN file:

Atmospheric conditions, including radiosonde or other vertical profile data; output from data assimilation models; weather maps—collect all available data

Notes:

All files/information required to georegister imagery

Files stored:

Files stored:

Files stored:

Radiance files, not georegistered

Files stored:

Files stored:

Radiance files, georegistered

Files stored:

Files stored:

Final imagery analysis products

Files stored:

Files stored:

Documentation of all steps taken in processing remote sensing images to final form
    Atmospheric corrections
    Emissivity corrections
    Georegistration process
    Classification or analysis methods
Associated field observation data?
    Notes:
    Associated simulation data?
    Notes:
Data dictionary

Data Archiving Checklist
Model Simulation Data

Model inputs (all inputs should be for simulations used in analysis)
    Meteorology
        File stored:
    Vegetation
        File stored:
    Soils
        File stored:
    Global control file
        File stored:
    Streamflow routing model input files
        File stored:
        File stored:
        File stored:
Model evaluation data
    Observed streamflow
        File stored:
    Other observation types
        Observation type/file stored:
        Observation type/file stored:
Model version
    Hydrology model source code as used in the simulations
        Source code file stored:
    Routing model source code
        Source code file stored:
    Source code from other models used
        Source code file stored:
        Source code file stored:
    Model analysis products

Raw model simulation output
  For very large data sets, a filename should be provided and a location on fortress
    File stored:
  For smaller data sets, all output files should be migrated into HDF5 or tarred into a
    single file
    File stored:
Files that have been developed from the raw model output and that were the basis of
  analysis (e.g., output from the HDF5 summary statistics program), especially if they
  contain additional information not used in the final published product but could be
  used for additional analysis
  File stored:
  File stored:
All data files used to develop graphics or tabular data
  File stored:
  File stored:
  File stored:
Scripts used to develop published graphics or tabular data
  Script:
  Script:
  Script:
High-quality EPS (preferred since they can be edited for minor changes), PNG (figures),
  or JPEG (pictures) files of published figures.
  EPS file:
  PNG file:
  JPEG:
Associated field observation data
  Notes:
Associated remote sensing data?
  Notes:
What not to do format/units
Metadata document/data dictionary

APPENDIX B: Assessment Tool for Session 2 of the Agricultural and Biological Sciences Case Study

The Data Information Literacy (DIL) team used the following tool to assess the students' response to each of our three sessions.

1. Briefly describe what you learned in today's session:
2. List one thing that you will definitely incorporate into your own data gathering/description/management after today:
3. Briefly describe anything that was discussed today that is still unclear for you:

APPENDIX C: Metadata Form for Session 3—Data Package Metadata

Enter the title of the data package. The title field provides a description of the data that is long enough to differentiate it from other similar data.

Title:*

Enter an abstract that describes the data package. The abstract is a paragraph or more that describes the particular data that are being documented. You may want to describe the objectives, key aspects, design, or methods of the study.

Abstract:*

Enter the keywords. A data package may have multiple keywords associated with it to enable easy searching and categorization. In addition, one or more keywords may be associated with a keyword thesaurus, taxonomy, ontology, or controlled vocabulary, which allows the association of a data package with an authoritative description definition. Authoritative keywords may also be used for internal categorization. An example of an authoritative thesaurus is the National Agricultural Library Thesaurus: http://agclass.nal.usda.gov/dne/search.shtml

Authoritative keyword source. If an authority was used for the keywords, identify by name the authority source.

Keywords (separate with commas):*

Enter information about the owners of the data. This is information about the persons or organizations certified as data owners (e.g., principal investigator for a project). The list of data owners should include all people and organizations who should be cited for the data. Minimally include full name, organization name, owner address, and e-mail.

Data Owners:*

Enter information about the contacts. This is information about the people or organizations that should be contacted with questions about the use or interpretation of your data package. Minimally include full name, organization name, contact address, and e-mail.

Contacts:*

Enter associated parties' information. These are persons or organizations functionally associated with the data set. Enter the relationship. For example, the person who maintains the data has an associated function of "custodian." Minimally include functional role, full name, organization name, party address, and e-mail.

Associated Party:

Is your data set part of a larger umbrella project? Data may be collected as part of a larger research program with many subprojects, or they may be associated with a single, independent investigation. For example, a large NFS grant may provide funds for several primary investigators to collect data at various locations.

If part of a larger project, identify by name the project. If applicable, include funding agency and project ID.

Enter a paragraph that describes the intended usage rights of the data package. Specifically, include any restrictions (scientific, technical, ethical) to sharing the data set with the public scientific domain.

Usage rights:*

Enter a description of the geographic coverage. Enter a general description of the geographic coverage in which the data were collected. This can be a simple name (e.g., West Lafayette, Indiana) or a fuller description.

Geographic coverage:*

Set the geographic coordinate s which bound the cove rage or a single point. Latitude and longitude values are used to create a "bounding box" containing the region of interest (e.g., degrees/minutes/seconds N/S/E/W) or a single point.

Bounding box or point:

Enter information about temporal coverage. Temporal coverage can be specified as a single point in time, multiple points in time, or a range thereof.

Temporal Coverage:*

Enter method step description. Method steps describe a single step in the implementation of a methodology for an experiment. Include method title, method description, and instrumentation.

Methods:

Study extent description. Describe the temporal, spatial, and taxonomic extent of the study. This information supplements the coverage information you may have provided.

Study extent:

Sampling description. Describe the sampling design of the study. For example, you might describe the way in which treatments were assigned to sampling units.

Sampling:

*Required fields

CHAPTER **7**

TEACHING CIVIL ENGINEERING DATA INFORMATION LITERACY SKILLS

An E-Learning Approach

Lisa R. Johnston, University of Minnesota
Jon Jeffryes, University of Minnesota

INTRODUCTION

The University of Minnesota (UMN) team collaborated with a civil engineering lab researching the structural integrity of bridges, experimentally and within the state of Minnesota, to identify the data information literacy (DIL) skills that graduate students in that discipline needed to be successful researchers. In-depth interviews with the civil engineering group found that graduate students lacked DIL skills, particularly *metadata and data description, ethics and attribution,* and *digital preservation.* The absence of these skills negatively impacted the students' abilities to effectively pass their data sets on to the next graduate student on the project.

Based on these findings, in the fall of 2012 the authors launched an instructional response to address the DIL skills absent from the curriculum. This instructional approach utilized a modularized e-learning format to reach busy graduate students (Brenton, 2008) through an extracurricular Data Management Course. The DIL team created a seven-module non-credit online course (http://z.umn.edu/datamgmt) using Google Sites, Screenflow, and YouTube. The self-paced course allowed students to complete the requirements outside of their formal course work and research activity. As a component of the course, each student wrote a draft data management plan (DMP) for creating, documenting, sharing, and preserving his or her data using a template offered by the instructors that aligned with each of the seven modules. The instructors offered this online course to all structural engineering graduate students in the fall of 2012 (11 students enrolled), giving students the whole semester to complete the requirements, and then opened up the course to any science, technology, engineering, or mathematics (STEM) graduate student in the spring

of 2013. Forty-seven students enrolled in the spring semester (for a total of 58 students overall). Five students from the fall semester completed the course (three out of these five choose to defer their participation to the spring semester when they expected to work with research data) and six additional students completed the course in the spring. The results of an assessment survey sent to students immediately after completing the course, iterative feedback on their completed DMP, and a follow-up survey on how they implemented the DMP 6 months after taking the course were positive. Results from this course informed the development of a "flipped classroom" version of the course in the fall of 2013.

DATA MANAGEMENT TRAINING AND PRACTICE IN THE CIVIL ENGINEERING DISCIPLINE

Currently civil engineering poorly defines its disciplinary expectations regarding teaching data management to its students. The topic of data literacy can only be inferred into existing learning outcomes or other standards that touch upon data tangentially, usually under outcomes that focus on the overall experimentation process.

The American Society of Civil Engineers' engineering curriculum, *Civil Engineering Body of Knowledge for the 21st Century: Preparing the Civil Engineer for the Future* (BOK 2) (ASCE, 2008), does not address data literacy explicitly. Currently the integration of these skills into the graduate-level curriculum remains completely voluntary. Students graduating have no guarantee of receiving formal education in the best practices of data management. Many students learn through informal instruction or address the problem when they suffer their own data loss.

A report produced between iterations of the BOK, *Development of Civil Engineering Curricula Supporting the Body of Knowledge for Professional Practice,* found room for improvement in the depth of students' engagement with data, citing one example where "students are not able to take an open-ended real world situation and design the experiments that would provide the necessary data to solve the problem" (American Society of Civil Engineers Curriculum Committee, 2006).

Data literacy skills can be inferred in many of the outcomes focused around its seventh outcome group, "Experiments." The relevant outcomes are

- Identify the procedures . . . to conduct civil engineering experiments
- Explain the purpose, procedures . . . of experiments
- Conduct experiments . . . according to established procedures
- Analyze the results of experiments (ASCE, 2008, p. 106)

Data literacy can also be inferred from the outcomes regarding communication (BOK 2, Outcome 16), which call for students to "use appropriate graphical standards in preparing engineering drawings" and "[o]rganize and deliver effective . . . graphical communications" (ASCE, 2008, p. 110). It can be read as part of Outcome 13: Project Management, if the new standard procedure for conducting experiments includes creating a plan to manage data, including organization, security, and preservation (now mandated by some funding agencies).

The engineering field, more widely, shares this opacity of expectation with regard to data

management. The outcomes suggested in the BOK 2 echo those already implemented by the Accreditation Board for Engineering and Technology (ABET) in their outcome, "an ability to design and conduct experiments, as well as to analyze and interpret the data" (ABET, 2012, General Criterion 3[b]).

Locally, UMN students and faculty receive somewhat varied and inconsistent DIL training. For example, the university requires all principal investigators (PIs) of grants to complete one of two Web-based instructional modules on the "best practices of research integrity" (University of Minnesota Research Education and Oversight, 2014). These modules cover some aspects of data control and intellectual property concerns. However, these responsible conduct of research (RCR) modules are only required for PIs and are not well described or discoverable to those looking for just-in-time data management education. Beginning in 2010, researchers could supplement that training with workshops taught by the libraries on "Creating a Data Management Plan for Your Grant Application" or "Introduction to Data Management for Scientists and Engineers," available as drop-in library workshops and online video recordings (University of Minnesota Libraries, 2014). The former workshop reached more than 300 faculty members and is offered for RCR continuing education credit (Johnston, Lafferty, & Petsan, 2012). However, both RCR training and library-led workshops were designed specifically for faculty PIs and therefore do not target the graduate student population.

It is possible that data management skills are being addressed, along with other information literacy competencies, in student research experiences such as undergraduate research opportunities programs, research assistantships, or cooperative educational programs, but the literature on information literacy has focused primarily on information retrieval skills (Jeffryes & Lafferty, 2012). One student in our study mentioned receiving some data management skills in an introductory research methods class, but considered it too early in her student career to be useful to her current research project. The current integration of data management skills into the graduate curriculum is neither constant nor at the point of need.

The DIL team also investigated the current data management best practices used by the discipline locally. One of the graduate student subjects worked in the Multi-Axial Subassemblage Testing (MAST) Laboratory, which provided explicit best practices for data management and support for data upload to the national NEEShub data warehouse, a National Science Foundation–funded data repository for earthquake engineering data. The other students in the study population did not receive documented support or management guidance during their research.

Data repositories, examples of curated data, and management protocols exist for some subdisciplines relevant to the work conducted by the research population. The student working with the MAST Laboratory was required to post her data into NEEShub. Although the other researchers were not connected to a specific data repository, Table 7.1 provides examples of metadata schemas and requirements that researchers in structural engineering might encounter.

We discovered documentation and training opportunities provided by these bodies through Internet searches. Overall we found two disciplinary leaders within structural engineering, NEES and NISEE, both of which focus on the curation of earthquake engineering data (NEEShub, 2009; Thyagarajan, 2012; Van Den Einde et al., 2008; Wong & Stojadinovic, 2004).

METHODOLOGY

The UMN team interviewed the members of a structural engineering research group consisting of one faculty member and four graduate students ranging in experience from a first-year graduate student to a student in her final semester. The interview instrument, based on a modified version of the Data Curation Profiles Toolkit instrument (available for download at http://dx.doi.org/10.5703/1288284315510), allowed us to gather detailed information about the practices, limitations, needs, and opportunities for improving DIL practices from the perspective of both the faculty member and graduate students in the subject area. We collected and evaluated relevant documentation, including data set examples and supporting research practices.

The interviews took place between March 13, 2012, and April 20, 2012. These structured, 1- to 2-hour interviews took place in a library conference room using two audio recorders each producing a file that a graduate assistant transcribed for analysis. The interview comprised two components: a worksheet that participants filled out and a list of follow-up questions that were asked of interviewees based on their responses from the worksheet. The data we collected, including the sample of the research data provided by the research group, the interview transcripts and audio files, and the interview worksheets, were anonymized, compiled into a Microsoft Excel file, and analyzed.

RESULTS OF THE NEEDS ASSESSMENT

The interviews provided a snapshot of the DIL skills needed for structural engineering graduate students at UMN. The analysis revealed

TABLE 7.1 *Data Repositories Identified in the Disciplinary Environmental Scan of Civil Engineering*

Repository	Location	URL
NEEShub (earthquake engineering)	Purdue University	http://nees.org
NISEE (earthquake engineering)	University of California, Berkeley	http://nisee2.berkeley.edu
DARPA Center for Seismic Studies	Arlington, Virginia	http://gcmd.nasa.gov/records/GCMD_EARTH_INT_SEIS_CSS_01.html

several needs at various stages throughout the data life cycle. It was clear that the students had no formal training in DIL. Students reported collecting various types of data, but primarily data from sensors placed on the bridges they were evaluating, to study bridge integrity factors. The lab works with and receives funding from national and state agencies to conduct its research projects. These project partnerships have a noticeable effect on the treatment and handling of the data. The student working within NEES was expected to share data via the processes and standards for sharing and curating data developed by the NEES repository. The state agency, on the other hand, claimed ownership over the data and required approval before the data could be shared. Although the work of the lab was influenced by the expectations of its external partners, no formal policies or procedures (for documenting, organizing, or maintaining data) existed in the lab itself. As a result, individual students approached data storage and management in different ways. The faculty researcher expressed concern about students' abilities to understand and track issues affecting the quality of the data, to transfer the data from their custody to the custody of the lab when they graduated, and to take steps to maintain the value and utility of the data over time: "The skills that

they need are many, and they don't necessarily have it and they don't necessarily acquire it in the time of the project, especially if they're a Master's student, because they're here for such a short period of time."

We asked the participating faculty and students to indicate the importance for graduate students to become knowledgeable in each of the 12 competencies of DIL, by using a 5-point Likert scale, and then to explain their choices. Interviewees identified additional skill sets they saw as important for graduate students to acquire (see Figure 7.1).

In the course of interviewing the graduate students, certain steps in the data life cycle were present regardless of the research project, though the students did not use a consistent vocabulary when describing these steps (see Table 7.2).

To analyze the skills and needs described in the interviews, we reviewed the results in the context of each of the stages of the data life cycle. Although the students did not explicitly identify preservation as a step in their data life cycle, they mentioned critical aspects of this topic throughout the results phase. These observations provided a foundation for a generalized approach to understanding the data interactions of structural engineering graduate students in a research group.

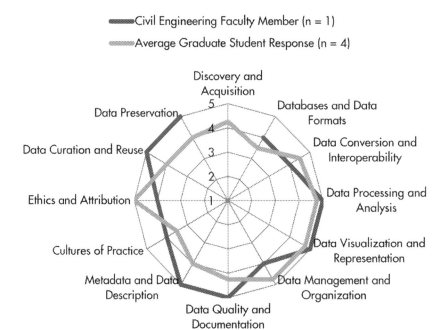

Figure 7.1 The rating of DIL skills by the UMN faculty member and the average graduate student response. Scale: 5 = essential; 4 = very important; 3 = important; 2 = somewhat important; 1 = not important. (NOTE: The faculty member did not rate Discovery and Acquisition.)

Stage 1: Raw Data

In the first module of the interview we asked the graduate students to describe the type of data with which they worked. All graduate students reported using sensor data as the crux of their research projects. Three out of the four graduate students collected data for projects that generated real-time sensor data to monitor the performance of local bridges, while one graduate student generated experimental data and simulations on concrete column performance in simulated earthquake conditions.

Although the expectations of their external partners influenced the work of the lab, the lab itself did not have formal policies or procedures in place for documenting, organizing, or maintaining their data. As a result, individual students approached data storage and management in different ways. The faculty researcher expressed concern about his students' abilities to

understand and track issues affecting the quality of the data, to transfer the data from their custody to the custody of the lab upon graduation, and to take steps to maintain the value and utility of the data over time. For example, the faculty interview highlighted the need for students to understand the potential hazards of collecting "bad" data. The faculty member thought that having a better understanding of how sensors collect data might help. Several students mentioned knowing about potentially disruptive elements such as temperature conditions or scheduled construction/testing that might impact their data; however, their processes and documentation did not merge these events with the data they collected.

Stage 2: Collection and Organization

In discussions regarding data collection and organization, more trends emerged:

TABLE 7.2   *Data Life Cycle Stages as Described by the Case Study Graduate Students*

Student	Student Response				
	Initial	Second	Third	Fourth	Fifth
Grad #1	Raw sensor data	Processed data	Processed with figures	Comparison (with other research)	Share the data (stages 1 and 2)
Grad #2	Raw	Excel 1	Excel 2	Stress calculation/ force and moment calculation	Final Excel file
Grad #3	Raw numbers	Organization	Analysis and conclusion		
Grad #4	Data download from a website	Organize data into test folders and regular activity of bridge folder	Analyze data	Create alarms to warn of potential problems on the bridge	
	Data Stage				
	1. Raw data	2. Collection and organization	3. Processing and analysis	4. Results	5. Sharing and archiving

- Students used date-based file-naming structures, even when they weren't familiar with the concept of a file-naming structure. As one student remarked: "I've never even heard of a file naming system."
- Students did not consider data security an issue and felt that they had adequate protections in place.
- Backup of their data was often sporadic or nonexistent. Two of the students displayed some confusion about the concept of data backup versus data redundancy. For example, one student described her backup process as copying files to a separate folder on her desktop (which would not protect against theft or computer damage).

- Students agreed that they had no formal DIL instruction but had to rely on their peers, family, and previous experience for direction. As one student described: "I've had many projects with Excel files and stuff that I've needed to save, and I guess I learned [data management] just out of habit, mainly."

Students used formal and informal documentation practices to record the data collection process, and changes made to the data were ad hoc and varied. For example, while some students labeled columns in Excel, additional information, such as the bridge sensor locations, were in multiple locations and separate from the data files (e.g., in e-mail correspondence or schematic drawings). Most of the students did not have an understanding of the concept of metadata. Only one of the graduate students was familiar with the term, and when asked to define it the student replied, "It means data captured and saved during the test." The other students all responded negatively when asked if they were familiar with the term. Regardless, all of the students provided some level of metadata to the data they were working with, but the majority were not collecting or applying it in an intentional or formal manner.

When asked if they had any means of documenting the steps for someone else to repeat, the students described the inefficiencies of their own system. One student admitted, "I guess if I were to repeat [the research project], I would probably do it in a different way. I could probably document what I've done and I probably will do so, but then I'll also suggest maybe keeping things a little less complicated."

Stage 3: Processing/Analysis

Each of the graduate students described a process for analyzing, visualizing, and making conversions of the data beyond the original raw data stage. The majority of the graduate students spoke of a process of converting ASCII text files into Excel for further manipulation and sense making. One graduate student used a proprietary sensor program that allowed for data manipulation within her Web-based software. Regardless of format, they described a process of further manipulation of the data, such as removing "bad" data (i.e., bridge sensor readings contaminated due to noise during construction), synthesizing the rough data using equations, and creating graphical representations of the data ("plotting"), all to better communicate findings.

The faculty member held the graduate students' facility with Excel and MATLAB in high esteem, but had some concern that students weren't receiving all the support they needed in more advanced data analysis, saying:

> It's the relational databases . . . and their capabilities for statistical analysis that are a little weak. And there are courses they can take on campus for the statistical and the relational databases, so maybe it's something that we should be requiring. The problem is that if they're going to do a Master's thesis, they take only seven courses.

He echoed the sentiment for further development of student skills in this area by noting that students would benefit from further education on the strategy behind data plotting. His ideal would be for graduate students to demonstrate an "ability to take the data and come up with a way of conveying it so that the reader can pick it up very quickly." Indeed one student described his process of creating data visualizations in Excel as "mostly trial and error."

The faculty member also specifically called out the need for students to be able to identify and track the quality of the data they were collecting when it may have been compromised by outside forces, such as with construction on the bridge where they collected sensor data. The professor commented that the students weren't currently tracking this aspect of their data analysis in the documentation, but "it would be nice, especially when they're collecting huge amounts of data, if we could somehow get measures of the quality of the data, statistically. And if we could use these measures to keep track of getting good data and when we're not getting good data."

Stage 4: Results

During discussions about ensuring long-term access to the data collected, numerous preservation concerns arose. Several issues were not addressed in the research group, such as physical storage (e.g., desktop computers used by graduate students would eventually be recycled) and file migration (e.g., use of a proprietary and future incompatible version of Excel) for data stored in the lab.

Students were unclear about whose responsibility it was to preserve the data for long-term access. Additionally, they were unclear about how to preserve data for 20 to 50 years, or the life of the bridge. For example, one student suggested that the contracting state agency held the responsibility for preserving the data and that the agency would keep the data "forever." When asked to identify the steps needed to preserve the data and if the state currently implemented those steps, the student responded: "I think that's just sort of what they do. . . . [B]ecause they've had issues in the past where people have completed projects and then others have wanted to repeat them or go more into depth with them and then haven't been able to find any of the original data for it, . . . I think that's kind of just their policy." When asked for steps to preserve the data set the graduate student responded, "Just putting [it] onto that hard drive and making sure it doesn't melt I guess."

In our conversation with the faculty member, the issue of data versioning for long-term access and preservation arose. Along with identifying and implementing steps to preserve and store data for the long term, researchers must choose which versions of their data should be preserved for future use and authenticity. The professor responded to the issue of versions:

> This is an interesting problem. There are actually multiple stages and multiple things that you do [to the data], and so how many data sets do you store? Clearly, you want the raw data. That's the purest form. And clearly you want the data that you think has been completely digested as you think it needs to be. But how many of the intermediate stages do you want to keep?

Stage 5: *Sharing and Archiving*

Each of the four students shared his or her data results in some way. One student shared her data in a formal process through the mandatory data archiving protocol of the NEEShub program, while the other students shared their data with state contractors, their advisor, and the graduate students continuing the project.

Although students had little to no experience with data citation, when asked their thoughts on its importance, they reported an understanding of the value of this practice. A student explained: "Because you need to know where this data is coming from, and obviously if it's not your own, then I feel like it's important to make other people aware that it is not data that you actually collected yourself."

As to the potential for other researchers to reuse their data, only one student felt that his analyzed data was unique and therefore of potential value. The other students had a harder time imagining how their data might be useful to researchers outside of their specific project. The graduate students demonstrated little to no knowledge of data repositories in their field or experience using another researcher's data from outside their lab. One student mentioned that looking at another researcher's data in the literature review led to his experiment, but he found the data by chance and the repository was not a standard destination.

The graduate students did not see the value in archiving similar data sets together in a subject-based repository structure. Referencing the Interstate 35W bridge in Minneapolis, which was rebuilt after the tragic 2007 collapse with sensors measuring strain in a similar way to the data obtained by our interviewee, the student noted, "Unless you could come up with some good way to compare the two sets of data, I don't know really what use it would be to collect them all into one place." The student did see the value of data repositories to save on space, however, so that "there aren't 50 external hard drives floating around."

Issues around privacy and confidentiality were a complex topic for students working on a state-contracted project analyzing bridge sensor data. Students knew to contact their advisor with requests to share the data owned by the state agency. One student described her caution with presenting the state-funded data results at a conference: "I had to get permission from [the state contractor] first before I could even do that." However, the reasons beyond "ownership" were unclear. The faculty member was able to explain the sensitive nature of the data when asked if the state agency had any specific interests in sharing this data beyond the agency. The professor replied:

> That's a really good question. They would like to share data, as long as they can protect their interests. And I don't mean any advantage in having that data. What they're afraid of is this data represents measurements that are taken off of real bridges, and that can very easily be misinterpreted and used to undermine a bridge that's actually not in bad shape, and then present a bloated and incorrect scenario about how bad the bridge problem is. Or the claim that a bridge is in great condition, when in fact it needs to be replaced. For that reason, they are very, very, very unwilling to have anything like open access.

All Stages

With our findings, the UMN team developed a list of skills needed by graduate students in this discipline. These are detailed in Appendix A to this chapter.

E-LEARNING APPROACH TO TEACHING DATA INFORMATION LITERACY SKILLS TO GRADUATE STUDENTS

The benefits of taking an e-learning approach to educating graduate students are enumerated in the literature reviews and discussions of many studies (Gikandi, Morrow, & Davis, 2011; Safar, 2012). The U.S. Department of Education (2010) in its meta-analysis of the literature found that "students in online conditions performed modestly better, on average, than those learning the same material through traditional face-to-face instruction" (p. xiv). Gikandi, Morrow, and Davis's review of formative assessment in online learning, citing the influence of Oosterhof, Conrad, & Ely (2008), posited that online learning benefitted students by providing instructors "many additional opportunities to dynamically interact with and assess learners" (p. 2333). Gruca (2010) nicely outlined benefits of libraries' adopting e-learning platforms to deliver their instruction. Most resonant with our experience was her assertion that "e-courses are equally accessible for full-time and remote students and may be a step towards inclusion for disabled students" (Gruca, 2010, p. 20). We wanted our instruction to be as accessible as possible to graduate students who carried a full course load as well as a time-intensive research schedule. Although Gruca (2010) never explicitly used the phrase, many of the benefits of e-learning she listed support the scalability of instruction inherent in an e-learning platform. Gruca stated that e-learning "saves teachers' and students' time" and "[o]nce published, an e-course may be improved and used many times" (p. 20). The ability to scale would be integral to ensuring expansion of our work at a university where we support tens of thousands of students.

Learning Objectives and Assessment Plan

Conceptualization and creation of the course took place over the summer of 2012. Table 7.3 shows the learning outcomes for each module of the course.

In the course design phase of the project, we met with the faculty partner to vet the learning outcomes and strategize on connecting students to our course content. Because the graduate-level curriculum was already quite full, the approach had to be a voluntary, extracurricular program for students. The online, e-learning format was clearly a good fit. In addition, modularized video lessons would be easy to download and watch on any device that matched the busy graduate student lifestyle. The syllabus is in Appendix B to this chapter.

We thought the course needed a real-world application in which the students might demonstrate or test their newly acquired skills. Therefore, building on our earlier success offering data management training to researchers, we chose to use a DMP template as the framing device for course content delivery and evaluation. Each of the seven course modules mapped to a corresponding section of a DMP template where the student directly applied what he or she learned in the course. (See Appendix C to this chapter for a DMP template.) The resulting seven course modules became

1. Introduction to Data Management
2. Data to be Managed
3. Organization and Documentation Methods
4. Data Access and Ownership

5. Data Sharing and Reuse
6. Data Preservation Techniques
7. Completing Your DMP

Although data analysis and visualization skills came up in our interviews with faculty and students, we chose not to include them because the librarians did not have the expertise to teach them. As an alternative we added a page to our course website pointing students to local and freely available resources and training.

At the outset of our course design we decided that our guiding principle for creating online instructional modules would be to "utilize preexisting content." With that philosophy in mind our first step was to find content openly available for reuse, including video, images, and e-learning tools that covered any of our data management topics. A library science practicum student helped review relevant content. We discovered many sources labeled for reuse, including professional library-generated tutorials such as MANTRA (http://datalib.edina .ac.uk/mantra), a UK-based data management skills support initiative, as well as informal YouTube videos and cartoons. We embedded several of these through the modules after receiving permission from the authors. In addition, we customized content from the in-person data management workshops that the UMN libraries have offered to focus on the particular needs of structural engineering graduate students.

To create the modules we wrote scripts, created slides, and recorded videos for each of the seven topics. The scripts were written to incorporate a logical flow of the information and to set up the student to respond to each learning outcome. Next, we built a slide deck in Microsoft PowerPoint and then captured the screencast presentation with voiceover using ScreenFlow (http://www.telestream.net/screenflow/overview .htm), an Apple-based video recording software.

TABLE 7.3 *Descriptions and Learning Outcomes of the Seven Modules in the UMN Data Management Course*

Course Module	Brief Description	Learning Outcomes (Students will . . .)
1. Introduction to Data Management	In this module we introduce the concept of data management using an example from the academic discipline	Describe the benefits of data management to explicitly understand the benefits of participating in the course Articulate what they will get out of this program to reinforce the learning outcomes of the curriculum
2. Data to Be Managed	This module helps students define what information will be managed, document the data collection process, and create a plan to store, back up, and securely house these data	Create a data inventory for their research project (e.g., data, project files, documentation) to not overlook any aspects of their DMP Write a backup and storage plan to avoid potential loss of data
3. Organization and Documentation Methods	This module helps students plan for how to organize their data, track versions, create metadata, and document data collection for reuse	Plan an organizational structure for their data using a file naming system and directory structure that is well-documented and interoperable with other data sets to decrease versioning issues and data duplication Articulate a plan to collect and share the supplementary data points of their research to assist other researchers in making sense of their data Fill out a metadata schema example for their data to model ideal metadata practices
4. Data Access and Ownership	In this module we illustrate some of the intellectual property and access concerns that researchers face when sharing their data with others	Name the stakeholders of their data to understand the potential intellectual property and ownership concerns with releasing their data to a broader audience Report potential access concerns with their data to plan for the appropriate access controls Identify potential access controls to secure their data prior to release
5. Data Sharing and Reuse	In this module we describe the benefits of data sharing and potential for reuse as well as introduce students to the concept of data publishing and citation	Name the audience for whom the data will be shared to customize the documentation and format for potential reuse Explain an approach they will use to share the data to instill best practices for their future data sharing Cite their data in a properly structured format in accordance with emerging standards to prepare them to ethically reuse data in the future

Continued

TABLE 7.3 *Descriptions and Learning Outcomes of the Seven Modules in the UMN Data Management Course—cont'd*

Course Module	Brief Description	Learning Outcomes (Students will . . .)
6. Presevation Techniques	In this module we introduce the preservation and curation techniques used by information professionals who manage digital information for long-term access	Explain the life span of potential use for their data to recognize the long-term value of their data Identify the relevant preservation-friendly file format for their research data to ensure long-term access to their digital information
7. Complete Your DMP	This final module instructs students on how to complete and implement their DMP within their lab, research group, or future project	Map out an implementation plan to put their DMP into action. Identify the components of a DMP to repeat the process with future research activities

ScreenFlow was chosen because it allowed us to capture and edit existing YouTube videos that we embedded in PowerPoint presentations and included in our modules. ScreenFlow also presented a relatively easy-to-learn editing interface over alternative software such as Apple iMovie or Adobe Captivate. After creating the videos, we uploaded them to a YouTube channel to allow us to link or embed them into content platforms. YouTube also facilitated closed captioning of the videos, making them more accessible to a variety of learners.

The video content was organized on a Google Site as the course home page at http://z.umn.edu/datamgmt (see Figure 7.2). The Google Site allowed us to create separate Web pages for each module, which includes the following components:

- Text descriptions of each module's learning outcomes
- Instructional video (embedded from YouTube)
- Assignment (links to the student's DMP template)

- Links to additional resources (if applicable)
- Cartoon illustration of a relevant data management concept

The course site is open to the public. We choose Google Sites over other campus e-learning tools due to the ease of creation, discoverability, and potential for one-click "cloning" if the library adapts the course in future semesters or for disciplinary sections beyond civil engineering.

Beta testing of the e-course revealed several minor errors and inconsistencies with the video modules and website. The test users were primarily UMN librarians and members of the DIL grant project. ScreenFlow allowed for quick video edits and insertions while the written-out scripts proved easy to edit and rerecord.

To assess the success of the instructional intervention we used a three-pronged assessment plan including formative and summative assessment techniques. Throughout the course students would take the information covered in the individual modules and apply it

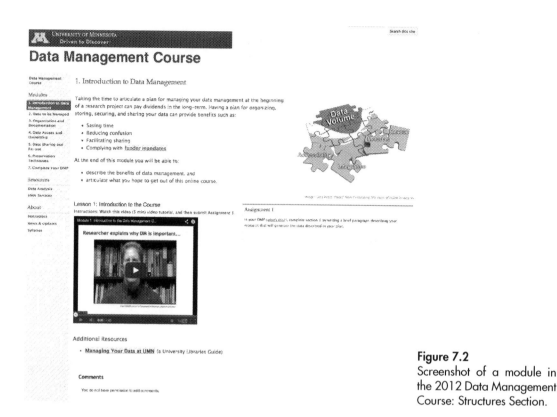

Figure 7.2
Screenshot of a module in the 2012 Data Management Course: Structures Section.

directly to their own research project through the creation of a DMP. The instructors created a unique copy of a DMP template that they shared with students via Google Drive (see Appendix C to this chapter) upon their enrollment in the course. We used the completion of the DMP template as a formative assessment throughout the course. Oosterhof, Conrad, and Ely (2008) described formative assessment as "those [assessments] that occur *during* learning," analogous to "what a mentor does continuously when working with an apprentice" (p. 7). The different modules strategically mirrored the DMP template. This design made it easy for students to create a real-world application. Since the students' DMP document was shared with the two instructors via Google Drive, we could check on the students' understanding periodically and provide feedback via the "Comment" feature. This form of assessment allowed us to gauge

student understanding in an organic way that would seem relevant to the students.

For the second prong of our assessment plan, we sent a course satisfaction survey immediately to students who had completed the course (see Appendix D to this chapter). These responses provided a summative view of each student's experience in the course. The instructors learned which aspects of the instructional approach were effective, and which needed further improvement.

The third prong measured the long-term impact of the course via an online survey that we sent out 6 months after the completion of the online course (see Appendix E to this chapter). This assessment was to show us whether completing the course impacted students' practice of managing research data. This form of assessment showed us whether the students successfully moved through the "hierarchical order of the different classes of

Figure 7.3 Announcement and e-mail invitation to participate in the 2013 spring Data Management Course.

objectives" found in Bloom's taxonomy, from knowledge, to comprehension, to application, to analysis, to synthesis (Bloom, 1956, p. 18). As Bransford, Brown, and Cocking (1999) stated in a report on the science of learning, "It is essential for a learner to develop a sense of *when* what has been learned can be used—the conditions of application" (p. xiii).

Results of the Fall 2012 and Spring 2013 Course

At the end of the first week of the fall 2012 semester the two library instructors discussed the data management course during the Civil Engineering Structures Seminar, a required course for all the graduate students in the "structures" track (around 20 students). We focused on why data management is important. At the end of the session the students completed a "1-minute paper" explaining how they thought a DMP would benefit their research. Subsequently, 11 students enrolled. The students controlled their own progress through the

course. The instructors sent e-mails three times throughout the semester to nudge students to participate: once at the semester's midpoint, once a week before the course deadline (the last Friday of classes), and on the day of the deadline of the course. The instructors periodically reviewed the DMPs of the enrolled students in Google Drive to provide feedback. There was no progress on the templates until late in the semester.

In the spring semester, we scaled the course to reach other researchers across our campus. We built the course so it would be relatively easy to replace the discipline-specific content with that of other research areas. In the spring of 2013, the instructors sought the help of 6 subject librarians, liaisons to the engineering and other science disciplines on campus. With their help, we opened the course to graduate students from other engineering and science disciplines (see Figure 7.3). There were 47 enrollees from 14 departments. No introductory session was offered in person as it had been in the fall due to the wide variety of students.

The spring course was similar to the fall semester course, except that liaison librarians, not the original course authors, sent periodic e-mail reminders to engage the students. Midway through the course, we offered an in-person 2-hour workshop that delivered all of the course material in a single, collaborative environment. Instead of working through the seven Web-based modules on their own, students could attend the workshop and ask questions and get feedback in class. They could learn from peers and discuss the practical application of data management with them. Thirteen students attended this session.

Course completion included not only watching the video modules (or attending the in-person session) but also completing a DMP. The plan had to be submitted to instructors for feedback before the course could be considered complete. At the end of the fall semester only 2 out of 11 students had completed the DMP template. Five students asked for extensions or permission to defer their enrollment into the next semester. The reasons for postponing included heavy workloads and lack of an actual data set to apply the principles covered in the videos. Three of those 5 students who chose to defer successfully completed the course in the spring, bringing the fall course completion rate to 5 students (a 45% completion rate). In the spring, 6 out of the 47 students who signed up successfully completed the course by turning in a written data management plan (13% completion rate). Overall, we ended the 2012–13 academic year with a total of 11 graduate students completing the course. This is a 19% completion rate for an online, non-required class—higher than that for most MOOCs (massive open online courses), which according to Parr (2013) is about 7%.

We sent a four-question survey to all 11 students once they finished the course, along with a certificate of completion for their UMN training history. Seven students (64%) completed the survey and demonstrated a high level of satisfaction. One student summed up the course:

> This course gave me good techniques which I will not only be able to implement in my current research in addition to what I have already been doing, but also use them in the rest of my career.

We received five (45%) responses to the 6-month follow-up survey. The questions mirrored the seven module topics of the course and the primary learning objects for each module. Overall the results and comments were very positive. Comments also demonstrated understanding of some of the primary learning objectives of the course—for example file naming and metadata schemas as illustrated by this comment:

> Some forethought on naming and metadata conventions goes a long way when managing data. This aspect of the course was very important and I have tried to employ it as often as possible. I sense that many students and possibly some researchers/professors don't commonly use a clear naming structure or metadata schema.

Comments also highlighted some surprising aspects of the course that students did not find relevant. For example, data ownership and access:

> This aspect of the class was also very thought provoking but isn't quite as relevant to my data. However, I am involved with many projects that have multiple organizations with interest in common data and so, some

forethought on data ownership will help clarify who is in charge of this data and how to process/pass it along.

DISCUSSION: LESSONS LEARNED FROM THE E-LEARNING APPROACH

Our two semesters proved to be learning experiences in the presentation of this course. We applied key lessons from the first iterations of the e-learning approach, which included connecting to actual student data sets and providing generic simulations, as well as incentivizing the course to ensure completion.

Connection to Actual Data Sets

We attempted to make this course applicable by tying course content to the actual work students were doing in their labs. Therefore, students had to have their own research data to make the course useful. But many of the students interested in the course were not far enough along in their program to have started collecting data for their project. In the in-person workshop we included an example of a completed DMP that provided students with a data set and a model they could follow when constructing their own plans. An approach to consider for students who do not have a research project is to provide a generic simulation to which students could apply the principles addressed in the video modules.

Ensuring Completion

Although a large number of students enrolled in the course, the completion rate was low. In the first iteration of the course a certificate of completion was used as a prompt for completion (on the advisement of our faculty partner), but only 2 of 11 students completed the course

(though 5 more asked to defer their completion). We are considering promoting the course through principal investigators and lab advisors.

• • •

We learned many lessons from implementing an online instruction model for teaching DIL. For example, we believed that our approach would allow busy graduate students to engage in supplementary materials on their own time. However, setting aside time to self-educate proved to be a major hurdle for students. The response to the optional workshop showed that students were willing to attend training in person because it provided a structure for completion. As one student stated: "I really liked the in-person lecture. Made it easy to set aside one block of time to go through all the information and have staff on-hand to answer questions."

We applied key lessons from the first iterations of the e-learning approach that included connecting to actual student data sets and providing generic simulations, as well as incentivizing the course to ensure completion.

Therefore, in response to these findings we changed the pedagogy of the course in fall 2013 to a "flipped course." Participants in the workshops met for 1-hour sessions once a week for 5 weeks. Students watched an online video before attending the corresponding hour-long hands-on workshop. In class we used fictional data scenarios from a wide range of disciplines to introduce students to practical aspects. To encourage completion, we offered participants who attended all five data management workshops a certificate of data management training for their UMN training records. Developing a written DMP was optional.

The first offering of the flipped course was a success. To accommodate the number of students interested in attending, the library offered two classes for each of the five sessions. Eighty-three students enrolled in at least one of the five sessions. Attendance was a little over 50% on average for the series. Sixteen students (33% of attendees) completed all five sessions and received a certificate of data management in their UMN training history.

CONCLUSION

The results of this case study have been used to develop and implement several variations of online and flipped classroom instructional interventions. The UMN DIL team drafted a set of learning outcomes targeting the perceived greatest needs of graduate students that arose in the interviews. The partnering civil engineering faculty member vetted these outcomes and provided suggestions for involving students with the topic. Incorporating content from existing sources and tying instruction to federal requirements for data management, we developed a seven-module online course over three semesters.

The UMN librarians applied their expertise in organizing and managing information to the curation of research data. The civil engineering faculty member provided a reality check to ensure that the skills would speak to the students' experiences and fit within disciplinary norms. This partnership proved mutually beneficial, since the faculty could address a skill gap without creating the content to fill that gap. It gave the librarians a new way to engage with students and to introduce ourselves as resources for managing and sharing data.

This case study has been a starting point in the conversation of disciplinary norms. A replication or adaptation of this process administered more widely would gauge the DIL needs of students across institutions in the civil engineering field. Once the educational gaps have been identified, the ASCE's BOK should be updated to address these skills.

Because the course lives online in a modular package, we were able to repurpose the pedagogy and teach the course in a way that better met student needs. Moreover, students can revisit the course material online and continue to develop their DMP through the openly accessible materials.

The course provides a framework for other librarians who hope to learn more about data management themselves or want to build learning objects for their institutions. Through the promotion of the DIL website, social media presence, and presentations at conferences, we have been in correspondence with librarians interested in examining what we are offering.

On our campus we've seen a hunger for guidance on these issues from both faculty and researchers. This is a natural extension of classic library services, including information classification and organization as well as information literacy instruction. DIL is a key component in the librarian's role on campus.

NOTES

Portions of this case study are reprinted with permission from Johnston, L., & Jeffryes, J. (2013, February 13). Data management skills needed by structural engineering students: A case study at the University of Minnesota. *Journal of Professional Issues in Engineering Education and Practice.* http://dx.doi.org/10.1061/(ASCE)EI.1943-5541.0000154; and Jeffryes, J., & Johnston, L. (2013). *An e-learning approach to data information literacy education.* Paper presented at the 2013 ASEE Annual Conference, Atlanta, GA. Available at http://purl.umn.edu/156951.

This case study is available online at http://dx.doi.org.10.5703/1288284315479.

REFERENCES

Accreditation Board for Engineering and Technology (ABET). (2012). *Criteria for accrediting engineering programs, 2012–2013*. Retrieved from http://www.abet.org/DisplayTemplates/Docs Handbook.aspx?id=3143

American Society of Civil Engineers (ASCE). (2008). *Civil engineering body of knowledge for the 21st century: Preparing the civil engineer for the future* (2nd ed.). Reston, VA: American Society of Civil Engineers.

American Society of Civil Engineers Curriculum Committee. (2006). *Development of civil engineering curricula supporting the body of knowledge for professional practice* [Report]. Retrieved from http://www.asce.org/uploadedFiles/Committees _-_New/curriculacommreportdec2006.pdf

Bloom, B. S. (Ed.). (1956). *Taxonomy of educational objectives: The classification of educational goals; Handbook 1: Cognitive domain*. New York, NY: Longman, Green and Co.

Bransford, J., Brown, A. L., & Cocking, R. R. (Eds.). (1999). *How people learn brain, mind, experience, and school*. Washington, DC: National Academy Press.

Brenton, S. (2008). E-learning—An introduction. In H. Fry, S. Ketteridge, & S. Marshall, S. (Eds.). (2008). *A handbook for teaching and learning in higher education: Enhancing academic practice*. London, UK: Routledge.

Gikandi, J. W., Morrow, D., & Davis, N. E. (2011). Online formative assessment in higher education: A review of the literature. *Computers & Education, 57*(4), 2333–2351. http://dx.doi .org/10.1016/j.compedu.2011.06.004

Gruca, A. N. (2010). E-learning in academic libraries. *New Review of Information Network-ing, 15*(1), 16–28. http://dx.doi.org/10.1080 /13614571003741395

Jeffryes, J., & Lafferty, M. (2012). Gauging workplace readiness: Assessing the information needs of engineering co-op students. *Issues in Science and Technology Librarianship*, (69). http:// dx.doi.org/10.5062/F4X34VDR

Johnston, L., Lafferty, M., & Petsan, B. (2012). Training researchers on research data management: A scalable cross-disciplinary approach. *Journal of eScience Librarianship, 1*(2), Article 2. http://dx.doi.org/10.7191/jeslib.2012.1012

National Science Foundation (NSF) (2010). Scientists seeking NSF funding will soon be required to submit data management plans (Press release 10-077). Retrieved from http://www.nsf.gov/news /news_summ.jsp?cntn_id=116928&org=NSF

NEEShub (2009). NEES curation. Retrieved from http://nees.org/topics/NEESCuration

Oosterhof, A., Conrad, R., & Ely, D. P. (2008). *Assessing learners online*. Upper Saddle River, NJ: Pearson/Merrill Prentice Hall.

Parr, C. (2013, May 10). Not staying the course. *Inside Higher Ed.* http://www.insidehighered .com/news/2013/05/10/new-study-low-mooc -completion-rates.

Safar, A. H. (2012). The students' perspectives of online training at Kuwait University. *College Student Journal, 46*(2), 436–458.

Stebbins, M. (2013). Expanding public access to the results of federally funded research. Retrieved from Office of Science and Technology Policy, the White House website: http://www .whitehouse.gov/blog/2013/02/22/expanding -public-access-results-federally-funded-research

Thyagarajan, R. (2012). NEEShub boot camp webinar—Data upload tools—January 2012. Retrieved from NEEShub website: http://nees.org /resources/4047

University of Minnesota Libraries. (2014). Managing your data. Retrieved from https://www.lib .umn.edu/datamanagement

University of Minnesota Research Education and Oversight. (2014). Core curriculum. Retrieved from http://research.umn.edu/reo/education/core.html#.Utr0zGTnYnU

U.S. Department of Education. (2010). *Evaluation of evidence-based practices in online learning: A meta-analysis and review of online learning studies* [Report]. Retrieved from http://www2.ed.gov/rschstat/eval/tech/evidence-based-practices/finalreport.pdf

Van Den Einde, L., Fowler, K., Krishnan, S., Rowley, J., Bhatia, K., Baru, C., & Elgamal, A. (2008). *The NEES data model and NEES central data repository: A framework for data collaboration in support of earthquake engineering research.* Paper presented at the Fourteenth World Conference on Earthquake Engineering, Beijing, China, October 12–17. Retrieved from http://www.iitk.ac.in/nicee/wcee/article/14_11-0168.pdf

Wong, J. M., & Stojadinovic, B. (2004, August). *Structural sensor data repository: Metadata and Web-based user interface.* Paper presented at the 13th World Conference on Earthquake Engineering, Vancouver, Canada. Retrieved from http://www.iitk.ac.in/nicee/wcee/article/13_956.pdf

APPENDIX A: Data Information Literacy Skills Needed by Graduate Students in Civil Engineering

We identified the following skills as important educational needs for graduate students participating in structural engineering advanced degree programs.

Data Stage	DIL Skills Needed by Civil Engineering Graduate Students
1. Raw data generation	**All students** Understand how sensors work and respond to physical phenomenon Download sensor log files securely Understand privacy issues associated with data (i.e., real-time bridge sensor data) Track external events and understand how these affect raw data generation (e.g., temperature, weather, maintenance) Determine the best way to manage data collected over time (i.e., DMP) **Some students** Write a work plan/experimental design Create/read schematic representation of sensor locations on physical bridge Work with experimental laboratory personnel Troubleshoot issues with sensor hardware attached to structures Find/reuse existing data
2. Collection and organization	**All students** Organize data with temporal component (i.e., 15 min. increments) Collect/organize data from multiple sensor sources into a single file Track multiple versions of a data file shared with multiple people Create documentation about data collection Back up data appropriately Co-locate metadata and processing actions with organized data Create a custom file naming schema that can be easily understood by others E-mail documents securely/efficiently (so not to make multiple versions) Track versions of the data and maintain authority control Be aware of university security policies (using laptop for remote data collection) Understand how to separate out data that was affected by external events **Some students** Manage media files generated by MAST instrument (video, images)
3. Processing and analysis	**All students** Create documentation of analysis steps for future graduate student or data reuse Use known engineering theories to process data (temperature, age) Apply equations to transform data into results (e.g., sensor frequencies into stresses) Compare data to simulation results Identify trends Generate graphs and plots to visualize the data **Some students** Understand how to find, use standards and code books Utilize programming tools such as MATLAB to create simulation data Analyze data in instrument-specific software program

DMP, data management plan; *MAST*, Multi-Axial Subassemblage Testing; *NSF*, National Science Foundation; *NEES*, Network for Earthquake Engineering Simulation.

Continued

Data Stage	DIL Skills Needed by Civil Engineering Graduate Students—*cont'd*
4. Results	**All students** Report results of data analysis Explain trends in the data Create/plot graphs that accurately convey meaning of data **Some students** Report data to funding bodies (NSF, state contracts) Show results in presentation format
5. Sharing and archiving	**All students** Understand the potential for others to reuse data Acknowledge the implications of accessing/sharing data using proprietary software Understand the scientific value of sharing data Archive data in the lab **Some students** Deposit data into discipline repository (NEES) Archive locally on external hard drive
6. Preservation	**All students** Use file formats that allow long-term access Create preservation backup copies Understand the funder requirements for maintaining access to data Understand the issues/problems associated with the preservation of data Co-locate the data and documentation

DMP, data management plan; *MAST*, Multi-Axial Subassemblage Testing; *NSF*, National Science Foundation; *NEES*, Network for Earthquake Engineering Simulation.

APPENDIX B: Syllabus of E-Learning Online Course

Module 1: Introduction to Data Management

In this section we will introduce the concept of data management using an example from an academic researcher.

After completing this module, students will:

- Describe the benefits of data management to explicitly understand the benefits of participating in the course
- Articulate what they will get out of this program to reinforce the learning outcomes of the curriculum

Assignment: Write one paragraph in Section 1, "Introduction," of your DMP describing why data management is important for this project.

Module 2: Data to Be Managed

This module will help students define what information they will be managing, document the data collection process, and plan to store, back up, and securely house these data. After completing this module, students will:

- Create a data inventory for their research project (data, project files, documentation, and so forth) to not overlook any aspects of their DMP
- Write a backup and storage plan to avoid potential loss of data

Assignment: In your DMP, complete Section 2, "Data Types," by describing what data you will manage and including details on how you will store and back up these files.

Module 3: Organization and Documentation Methods

This module will help students plan for how they will organize their data, track versions, create metadata, and prepare their documentation for sharing. After completing this module, students will:

- Plan an organizational structure for their data using a file naming system and directory structure that is well documented and interoperable with other data sets to decrease versioning issues and data duplication
- Articulate a plan to collect and share the supplementary data points of their research to assist other researchers in making sense of their data
- Fill out a metadata schema example for their data to model ideal metadata practices

Assignment: Complete Section 3, "Data Documentation, Organization, and Metadata," of your DMP by describing what standards and documentation will be used in your project or lab. (Optional: Embed video or images to describe your process. Fill in the metadata template to describe your data set.)

Module 4: Data Access and Ownership

This section will illustrate some of the intellectual property and access concerns that researchers face when sharing their data with others. After completing this module, students will:

- Name the stakeholders of their data to understand the potential intellectual property and ownership concerns with releasing their data to a broader audience
- Report potential access concerns with their data to plan for the appropriate access controls
- Identify potential access controls to secure their data prior to release

Assignment: In your DMP, complete Section 4, "Data Access and Ownership," describing any access and ownership considerations your data may have.

Module 5: Data Sharing and Reuse

This section will describe the benefits of data sharing and potential for reuse as well as introduce students to the concept of data publishing and citation. After completing this module, students will:

- Name the audience for whom the data will be shared to customize the documentation and format for potential reuse
- Explain an approach they will use to share the data to instill best practices for their future data sharing
- Cite their data in a properly structured format in accordance with emerging standards to prepare them to ethically reuse data in the future

Assignment: In your DMP, complete Section 4, "Data Sharing and Reuse," describing how your data will be shared for reuse. Update your DMP if data will be deposited in a data repository and include a preferred citation for your data set.

Module 6: Preservation Techniques

This module will introduce the preservation and curation techniques used by information professionals who manage digital information for long-term access. After completing this module, students will:

- Explain the life span of potential use for their data to recognize the long-term value of their data

- Identify the relevant preservation-friendly file format for their research data to ensure long-term access to their digital information

Assignment: In your DMP, complete Section 6, "Data Preservation and Archiving," describing how your data will be preserved for long-term access.

Module 7: Complete Your Data Management Plan

This final module will instruct the students on how to complete and implement their DMP within their lab, research group, or future project. After completing this module, students will:

- Map out an implementation plan to prepare them to immediately apply the information presented in the previous modules
- Identify the components of a DMP to repeat the process with future research activities

Assignment: Compile the final version of your DMP. Write a one-paragraph implementation plan describing how the DMP will be used in your future research. Submit the final DMP (Word doc or PDF) to the instructors for review and feedback.

APPENDIX C: Data Management Plan (DMP) Google Docs Template

DATA MANAGEMENT PLAN

V1 last updated MM-DD-YYYY

Name of student/researcher(s)	Your name
Name of group/project	Project name or research lab (for group plan)
Funding body(ies)	
Partner organizations	
Project duration	Start: MM-DD-YYYY End: MM-DD-YYYY
Date written	MM-DD-YYYY

Table of Contents

1. Introduction
2. Data Types
3. Data Organization, Documentation, and Metadata
4. Data Access and Intellectual Property
5. Data Sharing and Reuse
6. Data Preservation and Archiving

1. Introduction

The research project described in this data management plan (DMP) . . .

2. Data Types

The types of data generated and/or used in this project include . . .

Section 2 Checklist

What type of data will be produced?
How will data be collected? In what formats?
How to document data collection?
Will it be reproducible? What would happen if it got lost or became unusable later?
  • How much data will it be, and at what growth rate? How often will it change?
Are there tools or software needed to create/process/visualize the data?
  • Will you use preexisting data? From where?
Storage and backup strategy?

3. Data Organization, Documentation, and Metadata

The plan for organizing, documenting, and using descriptive metadata to assure quality control and reproducibility of these data includes . . .

Section 3 Checklist

What standards will be used for documentation and metadata?
- Is there good project and data documentation format/standard?
- What directory and file naming convention will be used?

What project and data identifiers will be assigned?

Is there a community standard for metadata sharing/integration?

4. Data Access and Intellectual Property

The data have the following access and ownership concerns . . .

Section 4 Checklist

What steps will be taken to protect privacy, security, confidentiality, intellectual property, or other rights?

Does your data have any access concerns? Describe the process someone would take to access your data.

Who controls it (e.g., principal investigator, student, lab, university, funder)?

Any special privacy or security requirements (e.g., personal data, high-security data)?
- Any embargo periods to uphold?

5. Data Sharing and Reuse

The data will be released for sharing in the following way . . .

Section 5 Checklist

If you allow others to reuse your data, how will the data be discovered and shared?

Any sharing requirements (e.g., funder data sharing policy)?

Audience for reuse? Who will use it now? Who will use it later?

When will I publish it and where?

Tools/software needed to work with data?

6. Data Preservation and Archiving

The data will be preserved and archived in the following ways . . .

Section 6 Checklist

How will the data be archived for preservation and long-term access?
How long should it be retained (e.g., 3–5 years, 10–20 years, permanently)?
What file formats? Are they long-lived?
Are there data archives that my data is appropriate for (subject-based? Or institutional)?
Who will maintain my data for the long-term?

APPENDIX D: Assessment Form 1: Follow-Up Satisfaction Survey

Data Management Course Evaluation

Thank you for completing the Data Management Course (http://z.umn.edu/datamgmt). Your feedback will help us to improve this course.

1. Course content was delivered in a clear manner.
   a. Yes, I strongly agree
   b. Yes, I agree
   c. Neutral, unsure
   d. No, I disagree
   e. No, I strongly disagree
2. Course content was appropriate for my research area/focus.
   a. Yes, I strongly agree
   b. Yes, I agree
   c. Neutral, unsure
   d. No, I disagree
   e. No, I strongly disagree
3. What did you find most useful about the course?
4. How might we improve the course?
5. Please provide any additional comments or suggestions.

APPENDIX E: Assessment Form 2 – 6-Month Follow-Up Survey

Data Management Course: Follow-Up

We're interested to learn if participation in the fall 2012 Data Management Course (z.umn.edu /datamgmt) impacted your data management behavior in the months following your participation.

*Required Question

1. How useful was the storage and back-up plan portion of your data management plan?*
   a. Very useful: I employed the plan in storing my data
   b. Useful: I employed aspects of the plan in storing my data
   c. Not useful: I did not employ this portion of the data management plan in storing my data

   Comments:

2. Which of the following describes your experience with organizing and documenting your data?* Circle all that apply.
   a. I created and employed a file naming structure that is clear and easy to understand
   b. I created and employed a file naming structure that only I can understand
   c. I did not use structured file naming
   d. I employed a metadata schema for my data and applied it consistently during my research
   e. I employed a metadata schema for my data and occasionally applied it during my research
   f. I did not use a metadata schema

   Comments:

3. How useful was thinking about data ownership and access to your data?*
   a. Very useful: This topic came up in my research and it was good to have anticipated the concerns in my plan
   b. Useful: It was worthwhile to consider this in my plan, but the issue never came up
   c. Not useful: This topic never came up during my research

   Comments:

4. How useful did you find planning for data sharing and reuse?*
   a. Very useful: I've made my data available for reuse
   b. Useful: I'm glad to have a plan for sharing, if the request arises
   c. Not useful: I don' t plan to share my data

   Comments:

5. How useful was planning for data preservation and archiving for your data?*
   a. Very useful: I'm archiving my data so that the files will be preserved for future use
   b. Useful: I'm glad to know about data preservation techniques, should I choose to archiving my data
   c. Not useful: I don't plan to archive my data

6. Anything else you would like to tell us about implementing your data management plan?

CHAPTER 8

TEACHING ECOLOGY DATA INFORMATION LITERACY SKILLS TO GRADUATE STUDENTS

A Discussion-Based Approach

Brian Westra, University of Oregon
Dean Walton, University of Oregon

INTRODUCTION

At the University of Oregon, our Data Information Literacy (DIL) team worked with a vegetation ecology research group that was in the final year of a 4-year grant-funded project. The purpose of the project was to study climate change impacts on Pacific Northwest prairie ecosystems. The librarian team consisted of the science data services librarian and the subject specialist for biology, environmental science, and geology. We partnered with a professor in the Department of Landscape Architecture within the School of Architecture and Allied Arts and a co-principal investigator (co-PI) on a climate change impacts (CCI) study. All other members of the team, including the lead investigator for the Department of Energy grant, were in the Institute of Ecology and Evolution within the Department of Biology. The CCI research group composition changed as students completed projects, but at the outset of our work, it consisted of two faculty, two postdoctoral research associates, three graduate students, and one research assistant who had completed an undergraduate degree in ecology.

The CCI team investigated the impacts of increased temperature and precipitation on vegetation ecology in prairie ecosystems. The research used three localities, each with plots where temperature and precipitation were artificially increased above ambient levels, and un-manipulated control plots for comparison. Team members researched a variety of factors, such as growth and reproduction of specific plant populations, transpiration rates, and soil characteristics, with individual projects within this larger context.

LITERATURE AND ENVIRONMENTAL SCAN OF ECOLOGICAL DATA MANAGEMENT BEST PRACTICES

To better understand the data management culture of practice within ecology, as well as current theory and guidance, we examined the literature on research data management (RDM) practices in biology, ecology, and aligned environmental fields, additional generic best practices, and resources.

The literature revealed a robust set of articles on RDM in established ecological and science journals. The ecology and environmental sciences publications were useful not only because of their applicability to the team's needs, but also because sharing such resources from journals in their research domain might lend greater credibility to instructional efforts with the team. Data management, sharing practices, and related topics have been presented in articles, reviews, and columns in journals such as the *Bulletin of the Ecological Society of America* (Borer, Seabloom, Jones, & Schildhauer, 2009; Fegraus, Andelman, Jones, & Schildhauer, 2005), *Trends in Ecology & Evolution* (Madin, Bowers, Schildhauer, & Jones, 2008; Michener & Jones, 2012), *PloS ONE* (Tenopir et al., 2011; Wieczorek et al., 2012), *Global Change Biology* (Wolkovich, Regetz, & O'Connor, 2012), and *Ecological Informatics* (Enke et al., 2012; Madin et al., 2007; Michener, 2006; Michener, Porter, Servilla, & Vanderbilt, 2011; Veen, van Reenen, Sluiter, van Loon, & Bouten, 2012).

These articles make the case for good data management practices and outline specific steps that researchers can take to curate their data. One of the most informative and practical articles was Borer et al. (2009), which we shared with the team as a pre-instruction session reading. The authors provided a list of basic data management steps that could be taken with ecology data, such as

- using scripts to record statistical analyses;
- storing and sharing data in nonproprietary formats;
- archiving original raw data;
- using descriptive file naming;
- creating optimal spreadsheet structure and database schema;
- recording full taxonomic names;
- standardizing date and time formats;
- recording metadata early and frequently.

More recent articles take a similar approach, such as advocating for the publication of biodiversity data (Costello, Michener, Gahegan, Zhang, & Bourne, 2013), and highlighting steps that will make it easier for others to re-use the data one might publish (White et al., 2013).

Data practices in research teams are often not standardized (Borgman, Wallis, & Enyedy, 2007) and vary from one person to another even within research teams under a common faculty member (Akmon, Zimmerman, Daniels, & Hedstrom, 2011).

Science and engineering faculty interviewed at Purdue University and the University of Illinois at Urbana-Champaign wanted graduate students to better understand and implement good metadata practices (Carlson, Fosmire, Miller, & Sapp Nelson, 2011). Metadata standards and usage have been discussed in a number of articles aligned with the CCI team's ecology focus (Fegraus et al., 2005; Jones, Schildhauer, Reichman, & Bowers, 2006; Kunze et al., 2011; Madin et al., 2007, 2008; Michener, 2006; Michener, Brunt, Helly, Kirchner, & Stafford, 1997).

However, some scientists have been reluctant to provide metadata due to the time it would take to create and record it, concerns about misuse of data, and loss of intellectual property rights (Schmidt-Kloiber et al., 2012). Concerns about data ownership may have more to do with "scientific revenue" (Janßen et al., 2011) than intellectual property that would generate income, particularly since these are fields with less potential for monetization of research discoveries through technology transfer. Some posit that a consensus-driven agreement on data ownership is needed to further scientific collaboration and avoid conflict (Fraser et al., 2013). In an attempt to facilitate continuing individual control over data sharing, some proposed an "account-based approach to data property rights management" (Janßen et al., 2011, p. 617). A study of the Center for Embedded Networked Sensing (CENS) noted that data sharing transactions can resemble bartering for goods transactions with other trusted colleagues (Wallis, Rolando, & Borgman, 2013).

There are, however, a growing number of influential proponents for open access to research data (Dryad, 2014; National Evolutionary Synthesis Center, n.d.). Funding agency requirements to share research data (Holdren, 2013) will likely accelerate the transition to practices and services in support of open data. Dryad provides a leading example of a data repository, with Creative Commons Zero (CC0) licensing for all submitted data. This is integrated with the publication review process for a growing number of ecology journals (Dryad, 2014).

INTERVIEWS AND RESULTS

We conducted interviews with several members of the CCI team using the DIL interview protocol (available for download at http://dx.doi .org/10.5703/1288284315510). Our interviews were with the collaborating professor, a postdoctoral fellow, the research assistant, and two graduate students (one completing a master's degree, the other working on a doctorate).

Participants in the interviews provided descriptions of the data life cycles of their research, though data sharing processes and project close-out practices were less clear because they did not yet have experience in those areas.

The team primarily collected and created tabular data, such as manually recorded field observation data that were later transcribed into spreadsheets, and data downloaded from field devices and sensors. At least one graduate student was conducting laboratory analyses of soil samples, but those tests did not commence until a few months later. They compiled tabular data using Excel and usually imported them into statistical programs for analysis (typically SPSS, though PC-ORD and R were also noted). They graphed results for review, analysis, and presentation or publication using programs such as SigmaPlot and GIMP.

Interviewees were aware of the types (including format) and numbers of data files (computer files or data sheets) collected and created in their work at almost all stages of the data life cycle. Interviewees were less aware of the typical size of any given data file, but were also confident that the size and numbers were small compared to the storage space available on a typical laptop computer.

Interviewees were generally comfortable using their data collection and analysis tools, though some were in the process of learning tools such as SigmaPlot. The type of statistical analysis tools varied based on personal preference and previous experience. Data conversions were typically between Excel and .csv file formats. In limited instances, there were reprojections of spatial data sets.

Most group members were familiar with the concept of metadata, if not the actual term. The types of annotations and other descriptive information associated with data collection varied slightly between individuals for their own unique project data. However, all individuals who collected data in the field used data sheets and field notebooks to annotate data collection issues. They backed up field notes by transcribing them from the field notebook to a lab book that did not leave the lab. The degree of detail in these records varied based on descriptions by the interviewees. Team members held differing views on how readily another person could reproduce their research or reuse the data if relying solely on the notebooks and metadata.

There was a lack of consistency across the team in file management practices, from file naming and version control, to storage and backup. All interviewees assumed that they would leave a copy of their data with the faculty, but interestingly, faculty and students both assumed that lab notebooks were the property of the students. Interviewees expressed interest in establishing protocols for handing off work product to the PIs as they completed their respective research projects. Interview responses indicated that the participants were motivated to improve their practices, even as the grant approached its closeout date.

The team members used multiple storage locations, including external hard drives, personal laptops, home computers, and a shared computer in the team's research offices. All team members backed up their data; however, backup intervals differed from person to person.

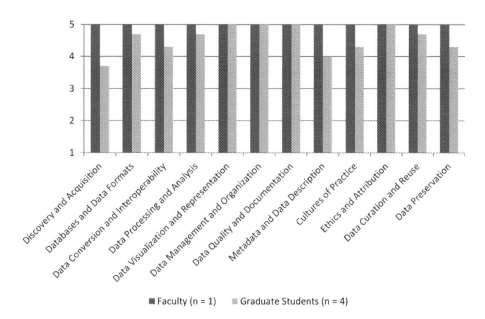

Figure 8.1 Data information literacy competencies as rated by the University of Oregon faculty and graduate students. Ratings based on a 5-point Likert scale: 5 = essential; 4 = very important; 3 = important; 2 = somewhat important; 1 = not important.

Because few, if any, had used external data for their own research, and none had published data, their knowledge of practices and resources in these areas was limited. However, all expressed a willingness to share their data and felt that their data could provide a baseline for other studies on the effect of climate change on plant ecosystems. For this reason they believed that their data would be important for many years. Restrictions that they might impose on data sharing were primarily related to proper acknowledgment of the source. They were aware that some journals required the submission of associated data sets with a manuscript, but they did not know how the data would be annotated, preserved, or shared. Most interviewees reported that they had not received training in dealing with intellectual property and data ethics issues and had a limited understanding of privacy, confidentiality issues, and the university's policies on research.

Educational Needs and Priorities

The faculty member who participated in the interview indicated that all 12 of the data literacy competences were important to the research project. He felt that skills in each of the competencies were needed to do proper research and that both he and the students would benefit from training in these areas (see Figure 8.1).

The rest of the team agreed, at least conceptually, about the importance of these data skills. However, in comparison to the professor, the other team members were not as familiar with each of the concepts. Their ratings of the importance of the competencies ranged from "important" to "essential," with the exception of one "I don't know" because of unfamiliarity with metadata concepts. The team reported that self-teaching (or trial and error), peer-to-peer, and student-to-mentor (whether faculty or postdoc) consultations were the common practice for addressing RDM questions as they arose.

A DISCUSSION-BASED APPROACH TO TEACHING DATA INFORMATION LITERACY SKILLS

We scheduled our instruction for the group to be completed during the fall quarter of 2012, which was also the final quarter of their 4-year grant. Seasonal and weather-dependent field data collection events could not be delayed; the potential data to be collected would be irreproducible. With these pressures on the faculty and the rest of the research team, it was reasonable to expect that our access to the team for instruction would be limited.

We negotiated with the two faculty members to schedule a 1.5-hour session in place of a regular team meeting in October. The session incorporated lecture, group exercises, and discussion. Providing training for a small team of research scientists enabled us to design and present the instruction in an informal, conversational setting.

After reviewing the interviews and the results of our literature review, we developed a data management training session on the following:

- Metadata as it relates to documenting, sharing, finding, and understanding data
- File naming
- Data structure and recording methods
- Data repositories and shared data
- Commonly accepted lab notebook policies
- Data ownership and preservation

We believed it would be unrealistic to expect the team to implement many new practices with only a few months left in the project. However, these topics and resources might be applied when handing off data to the faculty and when publishing research results, and the skills would applicable to future projects. The topics and respective learning outcomes that we generated for our DIL program are displayed in Table 8.1.

To develop a foundational link to cultures of practice, we provided two assigned readings from the research domain prior to the instruction session and then integrated them into the discussions. A third reading was included to highlight typical policies and best practices for research notebooks. The readings were

- "Some Simple Guidelines for Effective Data Management" from the *Bulletin of the Ecological Society of America* (Borer et al., 2009);
- a *Global Change Biology* article on the need for open science and good data management for advancing global change research (Wolkovich, Regetz, & O'Connor, 2012);
- an online chapter on lab notebook policies and practices (Thomson, n.d.).

The research team had some turnover between our interviews and the instruction session. Six people attended the training: two faculty, two postdocs, and two graduate students. Only two of this group had participated in the interviews: our faculty partner and one graduate student.

Instructional Components

We created a session outline which included links to examples presented in the class, additional resources, and references (see Appendix A to this chapter).

We anticipated that the readings we assigned before the team meeting would provide shared understanding and starting points for some of the discussion. The instruction

TABLE 8.1 *Learning Outcomes for the University of Oregon Training Session*

Topics	Learning Outcomes
File formats and conversions	Is aware of and accounts for interoperability issues throughout the data life cycle: considers impacts that proprietary file formats, identifiers, and data access can have on linked data/Semantic Web, and so forth Knows how and why to convert files from one format to another and does so consistently
Publishing data	Knows where to find relevant data repositories and how to evaluate and select where to deposit data, and where to get data Publishing data with *Nature*, other journals, Dryad?
Preservation and archiving	Knows what data preservation is, why it is important, and what it costs; employs some evaluative criteria in choosing what to preserve and for how long Records metadata in the repository so others can find, understand, use, and properly cite the data set Knows how to properly package and hand off the data to the PI at the close of his or her participation in a project
Data citation	Correctly cites data from external sources Knows what a unique identifier is, and its utility for data citation Knows how to publish/share data/identifiers Understands usage permissions issues, and permissions management tools and restrictions such as creative commons, copyright, and data commons

session was a combination of lecture with slides, online resources, hands-on activities, and discussion. Some of the presentation slides were taken from education modules by the DataONE project.

The instruction session began with why data management is important, the risks of poor data practices, and the value of sharing data to the researcher, scientific community, sponsor, and the public.

To direct a discussion of the chapter about lab notebook policies and practices, we asked: (1) What policies or guidelines were new to you? and (2) Is there anything you might change or do differently in light of the guidelines? Here the discussion turned to concerns about the applicability of the notebook practices and policy materials to field research note taking. We highlighted roles and responsibilities for data and notebook stewardship,

indicating that these typically are not the property of graduate students, but remain with the PI as a representative of the institution when projects are completed.

Next we looked at file management, reviewing common file naming conventions outlined on the University of Oregon data management website, followed by data backup considerations and file conversions and transformations. We discussed data structures and used a short exercise to test whether they could identify errors in a spreadsheet. This exercise was based on materials from the DataONE project.

Several members of the group reported in the interviews that they did not use relational databases for data and were not confident with these concepts. To demonstrate some basic structures of relational databases, we created a hands-on exercise using "flat files" (which were titled sheets of paper) that could be organized into relationships of one-to-one, one-to-many, and many-to-one. The participants arranged the files in a manner that represented data similar to what they might collect and that showed the relationships of the files.

We reviewed Dryad and DataONE Mercury as two examples of ecological data repositories. Navigating to and examining data sets in these two resources provided a concrete introduction to data repositories, metadata standards, data set registration, unique identifiers and DOIs, and linking between data and publications. The data sets provided a foundation for a discussion about publishing data and access and use permissions.

Finally we highlighted the most commonly noted parts of a data citation from the literature, and then opened the rest of the session to questions and discussion about topics of interest to the team.

Assessment

We based our assessment of the DIL program on discussions in the training session, information gathered in two post-training surveys, and conversations and e-mail correspondence with the faculty and other team members. (The training feedback survey questions are in Appendix B to this chapter.) We collected the initial feedback via a Google form linked from the instructional materials. Five of the six attendees filled out the form, while two responded to a more detailed Qualtrics survey that we distributed later. The two faculty were also asked for more information several months later. This section summarizes the collected comments and suggestions and our own observations.

The results of our assessment indicated that we had raised awareness of data management issues and positively impacted the team. Some team members reported that the initial

interviews prompted them to think more deeply about how they managed their research data. One researcher reported that since the instructional session the team became more cognizant of data management issues and began to embrace new practices. In particular, the team was more conscientious about providing detailed descriptive information (metadata) in notebooks and electronic records, and the lead faculty member for the project requested that data sets be shared with him in non-proprietary formats to ensure long-term access. Team members reported paying closer attention to data storage, preservation, and sharing issues. More specifically, team members said they planned to

- "do a better job of planning for data management at the onset of a project";
- "explore my options for online backups of my data";
- "save long-term data in a .csv format and provide metadata for that file."

One of the faculty reported that the training had "brought me up to date with growing expectations for sharing of data . . . gave me deeper impetus to apply sound meta practices so that future users could understand how and why data was developed and processed the way it was." The sessions "changed the degree to which we systematically apply protocols for data management across all aspects of the project. They also gave us useful insight into the resources available for data curation."

The team valued guidance that was either very closely aligned with the team's data acquisition practices or easily translated into their workflow and publication processes. Several respondents said they appreciated the open discussion on specific needs and questions that occurred at the end of the session. Several said they would have rather spent more time in interactive work with an immediate application to their current research and data management tasks, and less time on overview and basic instruction.

The article by Borer and colleagues (2009) that provided data management guidelines was particularly well received and provided a useful introduction to a number of practices that were at the heart of the session. The article by Wolkovich, Regetz, and O'Connor (2012) was not mentioned as often in the assessment, but it provided a strong case for data sharing in the multidisciplinary field of global change research, the very topic of the CCI project. Though not its primary focus, the article included a useful table listing some of the actions and skills needed for data and code sharing, as well as supporting website links. We included the chapter by Thompson on lab notebooks in our DIL Program as it had been used by a faculty member in the Department of Human Physiology to introduce good notebook practices to new graduate students. However, the chapter elicited several surprisingly strong negative comments from other participants. One of the faculty and at least one postdoc in the CCI group believed it had no application to their research workflow. Admittedly, the guidelines were established for a research laboratory setting more typical of biochemistry than ecology, but we had believed readers could interpret and apply the recordkeeping guidelines to other forms of research documentation.

DISCUSSION

One of the strengths of the DIL model is that the structured interviews provide librarians with a detailed understanding of the RDM practices, skills, and priorities of a particular person or team. That information and the

literature translate to targeted instructional interventions. Training can be tailored to the specific needs of the research group, though the amount of content will be determined by the length and number of sessions that can be accommodated by the research team's schedules and faculty prerogatives.

The interview process can open new lines of communication and opportunities to provide RDM services to research faculty, graduate students, postdocs, and research assistants. The interviews and associated conversations raise awareness of library services for research scientists. For the librarians, these experiences can provide insight into the needs of graduate students, and enable librarians to expand their understanding of the research domains they serve.

The instruction session included conceptual information for the competencies and examples of applied RDM principles. The CCI group clearly favored context-based applied learning and application exercises for their instruction. We incorporated some lecture and slides to provide context for some of the DIL competencies. In retrospect, the Borer article was well received and might have sufficed since it grounded the topics in an ecology research ethos. The lecture was not as productive nor well received in this small group setting. In the future we plan to put much more emphasis on localized use cases, applied practices, and open discussion.

Faculty buy-in is critical and should be kept in mind when selecting faculty partners and research teams for the significant investment that the DIL model requires.

Developing specific and relevant DIL programs can be time consuming, but it will result in a more engaged group that can adopt new skills toward implementation of better RDM practices. To be effective DIL programs have to respond to the needs of researchers within the environment they inhabit. Researchers are under pressure, particularly when time-sensitive field work is on the line. They also want more efficient workflows so they can increase their productivity. This is reflected in a desire to have more immediate application outcomes, through both streamlined and timely instruction and demonstrable improvements in RDM practices. Librarians can gain support for training by connecting learning outcomes to potetially lower risk of data loss, higher research impact, more collaborations, more competitive funding proposals, and more efficient data organization and search and discovery.

There are several considerations in applying the DIL model to smaller research teams. Even with small groups consisting of PIs, research associates and postdocs, and graduate students, there may be a high degree of variability in skills across the team, and individuals may be engaged in highly differentiated projects of their own with unique workflows and data management concerns. This will need to be addressed in planning the instruction, and probably acknowledged at the outset of any training. Highly stratified skill sets might be accommodated by distributing this expertise across groups if the team is large enough. In our case the climate change project provided a unifying theme and data sources, and there was some uniformity due to shared project management and logistics, as well as common research methods and workflows across the group.

The DIL project may ultimately highlight skills that should be integrated into the curriculum for all STEM students.

Should we work with another group that relies on field data collection, we will focus instruction on field notes and documentation methods, and fill in any gaps about policy application, rather than providing laboratory notebook guidance. Clearly several members of the team were looking for materials specific to the form and content of documentation they were using in the field.

In most of the data librarian's discussions with researchers about RDM, faculty typically preferred that we speak directly with the graduate students and postdocs who were conducting research. Faculty were reluctant to unilaterally impose RDM practices on the team. However, faculty buy-in is critical, and a professor can exert a lot of influence on the DIL process, whether through the degree of librarian access to the students, or via the values and attitudes they impart to the team regarding data sharing and funding agency requirements. This should be kept in mind as librarians select faculty partners and research teams for the significant investment that the DIL model requires. Similarly, creating and nurturing a good working relationship with the team is important and can lead to other collaborations and support opportunities after the initial instruction has been provided.

There are other considerations to be made in selecting groups to participate in implementing the DIL model. The academic calendar and grant cycle must be considered when thinking about optimal timing for scheduling interviews and instruction events. These factors may unduly compress the window of opportunity for interactions with the students. The number of master's students and PhD candidates who are on the team and at what stage they are in their program may influence the type and timing of instruction you can implement.

The educational experiences of the team members may sometimes lead to unforeseen ideas. We were working with a relatively small research group and chose to expand our

ADVANTAGES

- Deeper understanding of specialized RDM practices
- More communication with faculty, grad students, postdocs, research assistants
- New opportunities to provide RDM services

LESSONS LEARNED

- Use contextual applications
- Streamline instruction
- Provide instruction at point-of-need
- Consider highly variable skill levels
- Work with faculty who have RDM "buy-in"
- Create and nurture good relationships with research team
- Consider academic calendar and grant project timing in scheduling interviews and instruction
- A 1.5-hour training session is an effective vehicle for developing DIL competencies

investigation of the team's practices by including a postdoc and a research assistant in the interviews. The research assistant, who had not yet started a graduate program, received what we considered to be excellent training in recording metadata as an undergraduate student. She had worked at a field station previously, where students are required to document field work with metadata and pass reviews of their field notes before they could begin their own projects. Data sets from the students' field projects were deposited for public access. This type of experiential learning, integrated directly with and reinforced by reviews of ongoing research practice, is a model that we plan to explore further.

The DIL project may ultimately highlight skills that should be integrated into the curriculum for all STEM students. Within the CCI team a few specific components of DIL are addressed to varying degrees. For instance, our faculty partner in this project remarked that training in information presentation and graphics is a required aspect of the curriculum for students in his department (landscape architecture). In contrast, typical biology students learned data visualization on their own or tangentially through exposure to graphing in foundational statistics courses.

CONCLUSIONS

The DIL model was a very useful tool in developing DIL training for graduate students. The process provides a useful categorization of RDM skills through which research faculty can articulate areas of concern and priorities for skill development for themselves and their graduate students. Structured interviews of the students enabled us to identify the data management skills and perspectives of graduate students conducting research on vegetation ecology, and to prepare, present, and assess an instructional session with the team.

Research teams do not always have time for long-term instructional interventions, particularly when grant deadlines are looming. In these situations, shorter, discussion-based sessions focused on specific local DIL issues can yield a measurable positive impact on graduate student RDM skills and attitudes.

It would be risky to assume that the needs and learning outcomes from this particular team were the same as those from other ecology research teams. Taken with care, however, the literature and lessons we learned about RDM practices and DIL instruction through working with this team provided us with a good foundation for working with other graduate students who conduct field research in the biological sciences.

Our results also informed the model by showing that a 1.5-hour training session can be an effective way of supporting and developing graduate student DIL competencies. However, there are caveats to the method. A short window for instruction significantly limits the number of topics and degree of detail to be covered. Various aspects of the training may gain more support if they are previewed or negotiated with the faculty partner(s). There are many factors that will affect uptake, but active, context-based learning activities and discussions carry the potential to help graduate students understand these skills and integrate them into their research practices.

Finally, positive and supportive interactions with graduate students can set the stage for further instructional efforts and other RDM services by librarians.

NOTE

This case study is available online at http://dx.doi.org.10.5703/1288284315480.

REFERENCES

Akmon, D., Zimmerman, A., Daniels, M., & Hedstrom, M. (2011). The application of archival concepts to a data-intensive environment: Working with scientists to understand data management and preservation needs. *Archival Science, 11*(3–4), 329–348. http://dx.doi.org/10.1007/s10502-011-9151-4

Borer, E. T., Seabloom, E. W., Jones, M. B., & Schildhauer, M. (2009). Some simple guidelines for effective data management. *Bulletin of the Ecological Society of America, 90*(2): 205–214. http://dx.doi.org/10.1890/0012-9623-90.2.205

Borgman, C. L., Wallis, J. C., & Enyedy, N. (2007). Little science confronts the data deluge: habitat ecology, embedded sensor networks, and digital libraries. *International Journal on Digital Libraries, 7*(1–2), 17–30. http://dx.doi.org/10.1007/s00799-007-0022-9

Carlson, J., Fosmire, M., Miller, C. C., & Sapp Nelson, M. (2011). Determining data information literacy needs: A study of students and research faculty. *portal: Libraries & the Academy, 11*(2), 629–657. http://dx.doi.org/10.1353/pla.2011.0022

Costello, M. J., Michener, W. K., Gahegan, M., Zhang, Z.-Q., & Bourne, P. E. (2013). Biodiversity data should be published, cited, and peer reviewed. *Trends in Ecology & Evolution, 28*(8), 454–461. http://dx.doi.org/10.1016/j.tree.2013.05.002

DataONE (n.d.). DataONE education module: Data entry and manipulation. http://www.dataone.org/education-modules

Dryad. (n.d.). DRYAD. http://www.datadryad.org/repo/

Dryad. (2014). Joint data archiving policy (JDAP). Retrieved from http://datadryad.org/pages/jdap

Enke, N., Thessen, A., Bach, K., Bendix, J., Seeger, B., & Gemeinholzer, B. (2012). The user's view on biodiversity data sharing—Investigating facts of acceptance and requirements to realize a sustainable use of research data. *Ecological Informatics, 11*, 25–33. http://dx.doi.org/10.1016/j.ecoinf.2012.03.004

Fegraus, E. H., Andelman, S., Jones, M. B., & Schildhauer, M. (2005). Maximizing the value of ecological data with structured metadata: An introduction to ecological metadata language (EML) and principles for metadata creation. *Bulletin of the Ecological Society of America, 86*(3): 158–168. http://dx.doi.org/10.1890/0012-9623(2005)86[158:MTVOED]2.0.CO;2

Fraser, L. H., Henry, H. A., Carlyle, C. N., White, S. R., Beierkuhnlein, C., Cahill, J. F., Jr., . . . Turkington, R. (2013). Coordinated distributed experiments: An emerging tool for testing global hypotheses in ecology and environmental science. *Frontiers in Ecology and the Environment, 11*(3), 147–155. http://dx.doi.org/10.1890/110279

Holdren, J. P. (2013). *Increasing access to the results of federally funded scientific research* (Executive Office of the President, Office of Science and Technology Policy, memorandum for the heads of executive departments and agencies). Retrieved from http://www.whitehouse.gov/sites/default/files/microsites/ostp/ostp_public_access_memo_2013.pdf

Janßen, T., Schmidt, M., Dressler, S., Hahn, K., Hien, M., Konaté, S., . . . Zizka, G. (2011). Addressing data property rights concerns and providing incentives for collaborative data pooling: The West African vegetation database approach. *Journal of Vegetation Science, 22*(4), 614–620. http://dx.doi.org/10.1111/j.1654-1103.2011.01271.x

Jones, M. B., Schildhauer, M. P., Reichman, O. J., & Bowers, S. (2006). The new bioinformatics: Integrating ecological data from the gene to the biosphere. *Annual Review of Ecology Evolution and Systematics, 37*(1), 519–544. http://dx.doi.org/10.1146/annurev.ecolsys.37.091305.110031

Kunze, J. A., Cruse, P., Hu, R., Abrams, S., Hastings, K., Mitchell, C., & Schiff, L. R. (2011). Practices, trends, and recommendations in technical appendix usage for selected data-intensive disciplines [Report]. Retrieved from eScholarship University of California website: http://escholarship.org/uc/item/9jw4964t#page-1

Madin, J., Bowers, S., Schildhauer, M., Krivov, S., Pennington, D., & Villa, F. (2007). An ontology for describing and synthesizing ecological observation data. *Ecological Informatics, 2*(3), 279–296. http://dx.doi.org/10.1016/j.ecoinf.2007.05.004

Madin, J. S., Bowers, S., Schildhauer, M. P., & Jones, M. B. (2008). Advancing ecological research with ontologies. *Trends in Ecology & Evolution, 23*(3), 159–168. http://dx.doi.org/10.1016/j.tree.2007.11.007

Michener, W. K., & Jones, M. B. (2012). Ecoinformatics: Supporting ecology as a data-intensive science. *Trends in Ecology & Evolution, 27*(2), 85–93. http://dx.doi.org/10.1016/j.tree.2011.11.016

Michener, W. K., Porter, J., Servilla, M., & Vanderbilt, K. (2011). Long term ecological research and information management. *Ecological Informatics, 6*(1), 13–24. http://dx.doi.org/10.1016/j.ecoinf.2010.11.005

Michener, W. K., Brunt, J. W., Helly, J. J., Kirchner, T. B., & Stafford, S. G. (1997). Nongeospatial metadata for the ecological sciences. *Ecological Applications, 7*(1), 330–342. http://dx.doi.org/10.1890/1051-0761(1997)007[0330:NMFTES]2.0.CO;2

Michener, W. K. (2006). Meta-information concepts for ecological data management. *Ecological Informatics, 1*(1), 3–7. http://dx.doi.org/10.1016/j.ecoinf.2005.08.004

National Evolutionary Synthesis Center (n.d.). *NESCent data, software and publication policy.* Retrieved from http://www.nescent.org/public_documents/Informatics_Policy/Data_and_Software_Policy.pdf

Schmidt-Kloiber, A., Moe, S. J., Dudley, B., Strackbein, J., & Vogl, R. (2012). The WISER metadatabase: The key to more than 100 ecological datasets from European rivers, lakes and coastal waters. *Hydrobiologia, 704*(1), 29–38. http://dx.doi.org/10.1007/s10750-012-1295-6

Tenopir, C., Allard, S., Douglass, K., Aydinoglu, A. U., Wu, L., Read, E., . . . Frame, M. (2011). Data sharing by scientists: Practices and perceptions. *PLoS ONE, 6*(6), e21101. http://dx.doi.org/10.1371/journal.pone.0021101

Thomson, J. A. (2007). How to start–and keep–a laboratory notebook: Policy and practical guidelines. In A. Krattiger, R. T. Mahoney, & L. Nelson (Eds.), *Intellectual property management in health and agricultural innovation: A handbook of best practices* (Chapter 8.2). Oxford, UK: MIHR. Retrieved from http://www.iphandbook.org/handbook/ch08/p02/

Veen, L. E., van Reenen, G. B. A., Sluiter, F. P., van Loon, E. E., & Bouten, W. (2012). A semantically integrated, user-friendly data model for species observation data. *Ecological Informatics, 8,* 1–9. http://dx.doi.org/10.1016/j.ecoinf.2011.11.002

Wallis, J. C., Rolando, E., & Borgman, C. L. (2013). If we share data, will anyone use them? Data sharing and reuse in the long tail of science and technology. *PLoS ONE, 8*(7), e67332. http://dx.doi.org/10.1371/journal.pone.0067332

White, E. P., Baldridge, E., Brym, Z. T., Locey, K. J., Mcglinn, D. J., & Supp, S. R. (2013). Nine simple ways to make it easier to (re)use your data. *PeerJ PrePrints, 1,* e7v2. http://dx.doi.org/10.7287/peerj.preprints.7v2

Wieczorek, J., Bloom, D., Guralnick, R., Blum, S., Döring, M., Giovanni, R., . . . Vieglais, D. (2012). Darwin Core: An evolving community-developed biodiversity data standard. *PloS ONE, 7*(1): e29715. http://dx.doi.org/10.1371/journal.pone.0029715

Wolkovich, E. M., Regetz, J., & O'Connor, M. I. (2012). Advances in global change research require open science by individual researchers. *Global Change Biology, 18*(7), 2102–2110. http://dx.doi.org/10.1111/j.1365-2486.2012.02693.x

APPENDIX A: Data Information Literacy Workshop

Readings

Borer, E. T., Seabloom, E. W., Jones, M. B., & Schildhauer, M. (2009). Some simple guidelines for effective data management. *Bulletin of the Ecological Society of America, 90*(2), 205–214. http://dx.doi.org/10.1890/0012-9623-90.2.205

Thomson, J. A. (2007). How to start—and keep—a laboratory notebook: Policy and practical guidelines. In A. Krattiger, R. T. Mahoney, & L. Nelson (Eds.), *Intellectual property management in health and agricultural innovation: A handbook of best practices* (Chapter 8.2). Oxford: MIHR. Retrieved from http://www.iphandbook.org/handbook/ch08/p02/

Wolkovich, E. M., Regetz, J., & O'Connor, M. I. (2012). Advances in global change research require open science by individual researchers. *Global Change Biology, 18*(7), 2102–2110. http://dx.doi.org/10.1111/j.1365-2486.2012.02693.x

Why Manage Research Data?

First, what is data management?

1. Taking good care of data throughout the data life cycle
2. Some basic aspects of data management: http://library.uoregon.edu/datamanagement/index.html

Why is it important?

1. Efficiency: It's easier to collaborate, review, and share data when they are well organized and described
2. Protects the investment of time, money, and intellectual effort
3. Protects unique data that cannot be duplicated
4. Improves capacity to share data
   a. Some research funders require data sharing
   b. Journals and associations increasingly require data sharing
      i. Current Ecological Society of America (ESA) editorial policy on data sharing: The editors and publisher of this journal expect authors to make the data underlying published articles available
      ii. Dryad associations/journals: http://datadryad.org/pages/jdap
      iii. *Nature:* http://www.nature.com/authors/policies/availability.html
   c. Benefits of data sharing[1]
      i. Encourages scientific enquiry and debate
      ii. Promotes innovation and potential new data uses
      iii. Leads to new collaborations between data users and data creators

iv. Maximizes transparency and accountability
v.   Enables scrutiny of research findings
vi. Encourages the improvement and validation of research methods
vii. Reduces the cost of duplicating data collection
viii. Increases the impact and visibility of research
ix. Promotes the research that created the data and their outcomes
x.   Can provide a direct credit to the researcher as a research output in its own right
xi. Provides important resources for education and training
xii. Sharing data leads to increased citation[2–5]

Lab Notebook Guidelines[6]

1. What policies or guidelines were new to you?
2. Is there anything you might change or do differently in light of the guidelines?

File Naming and Organization

1. Things to consider: Informative names, hierarchical searching, and stage in the data life cycles
2. Attributes of appropriate names: Year-month-day, creator, and stage of data analysis (the term *draft* may be too ambiguous), post R, PreJohnsonReview (using Camelcaps)

Backups and Archiving[7]: Comparing Backups to Archives

1. Backups
   a. Used to take periodic snapshots of data in case the current version is destroyed or lost
   b. Backups are copies of files stored for short or near long term
   c. Often performed on a somewhat frequent schedule
2. Archiving
   a. Used to preserve data for historical reference or potentially during disasters
   b. Archives are usually the final version, stored long term, and generally not copied over
   c. Often performed at the end of a project or during major milestones
   d. National Science Foundation (NSF) data management plan (DMP) guidelines mention "archives" for data; they mean an open/accessible archive for sharing the data, not unshared storage
3. Why back up data?
   a. Limit or negate loss of data, some of which may not be reproducible
   b. Save time, money, productivity
   c. Help prepare for disasters
   d. In case of accidental deletions
   e. In case of fires, natural disasters
   f. In case of software bugs, hardware failures
   g. Reproduce results of past

     h. Procedures (if they were based on older files)

     i. Respond to data requests

4. Other considerations

    a. How often should you do backups?

       i. Continually? Daily? Weekly? Monthly?

       ii. Cost versus benefit

    b. What kind of backups should you perform?

       i. Partial: Backing up only those files that have changed since the last backup

       ii. Full: Backing up all files

       iii. How often and what kind will depend upon what kind of data you have and how important it is

    c. What about non-digital files (such as papers)?

       i. Consider digitizing files

    d. Keep backups in different location than source data

    e. Keep the following in mind

       i. What does not need to be backed up?

       ii. How long should you keep backups?

       iii. How do you pay for the storage space?

       iv. What is the plan for when the grant ends/funding runs out?

    f. Check backups on a regular basis

    g. Meet with your IT support and set up a backup plan

File Types, Conversions, Transformations

1. Workflow: How are the data handled, changed, refined, and analyzed?

    a. Use tools that employ and record scripts

2. Terminology

    a. Conversion: From one format to another, such as Excel to .csv, or .bmp to .jpg

    b. Transformation: Changing the structure of the data, from spreadsheets to a relational database, or statistical meaning (i.e., applying a log function)

    c. The file type, the software, the computer operating system and hardware can all influence what data are available and what might be lost during conversion and transformation processes

Data Structures and Cleanup

1. Spreadsheets versus databases

    a. Spreadsheets are great for calculating changes in data

    b. Databases are better for organizing and standardizing data

       i. Easy to see the full lists of variable

       ii. Can be queried

       iii. Allow for easy detection of variations in variable names

      iv. Allow for easy update of variable names or additions

      v. Control the data entry process to prevent wrong entries

      vi. Minimize redundant data

      vii. Minimize redundant data entry

2. DataUp—try it out on one of your spreadsheets: http://dataup.cdlib.org/

Data Repositories and Records

1. Examples of data repositories
   a. Dryad: http://datadryad.org/
   b. LTER: https://metacat.lternet.edu/das/lter/index.jsp
   c. DataONE: https://cn.dataone.org/onemercury/
   d. GenBank: http://www.ncbi.nlm.nih.gov/genbank/
   e. TreeBase: http://treebase.org/treebase-web/home.html
   f. EcoTrends: http://www.ecotrends.info/
   g. Ecological Archives: http://esapubs.org/archive/default.htm
   h. ESA Data Registry and Archive: http://data.esa.org/esa/style/skins/esa/index.jsp
   i. Knowledge Network for Biocomplexity (KNB): https://knb.ecoinformatics.org/index.jsp
   j. NCEAS: https://knb.ecoinformatics.org/knb/style/skins/nceas/
   k. See also: http://library.uoregon.edu/datamanagement/repositories.html
2. What does a shared data set look like?
   a. Examine the following two examples of data records
      i. Dryad: http://dx.doi.org/10.5061/dryad.d2c619hd for Stanton-Geddes, J., Tiffin, P., Shaw, R. G. (2012) Role of climate and competitors in limiting fitness across range edges of an annual plant. *Ecology, 93*(7): 1604–1613. http://dx.doi.org/10.1890/11-1701.1
      ii. DataONE:https://cn.dataone.org/onemercury/send/xsltText2?pid=scimeta_472.xml&fileURL=https://cn-orc-1.dataone.org/cn/v1/resolve/scimeta_472.xml&full_datasource=ORNL%20DAAC&full_queryString=%20(%20text%20:%20oregon%20)%20OR%20%20(%20text%20:%20climate%20)%20AND%20has%20data&ds_id=#top

Metadata

1. Exercise: Look at the data sets and describe five things you would you want to know in order to use these data
   a. What are the data gaps?
   b. What processes were used for creating the data?
   c. Are there any fees associated with the data?
   d. In what scale were the data created?
   e. What do the values in the tables mean?
   f. What software do I need in order to read the data?

    g. What projection are the data in?

    h. Can I give these data to someone else?

2. Is this information different than the information you would want to include if you were sharing your data?

    a. Why were the data created?

    b. What limitations, if any, do the data have?

    c. What do the data mean?

    d. How should the data set be cited if it is reused in a new study?

    e. How would you cite the data?

    f. Why include a unique identifier (to cite) the data?

3. Metadata defined: The information about the data set that helps you and other people

    a. Discover

    b. Comply with permissions

    c. Download

    d. Open

    e. Understand/interpret

    f. Cite

4. Only data that can be found is useful. Metadata is what is needed to find and understand the data

    a. *Who* created the data?

    b. *What* is the content of the data?

    c. *When* were the data created?

    d. *How* were the data developed?

    e. *Why* were the data developed?[7]

5. Where might metadata be recorded?

    a. Internal to the file

        i.   Embedded in file header (image files,[8] MP3s)

        ii. Added to the file (column names, keys)

        iii. Within the file name

    b. External to the file

        i.   Indexes

        ii. Separate metadata files

        iii. Readme.txt

    c. Any of these sources of information could be altered or lost if care is not taken when files are edited or converted

6. NSF DMP guidelines refer to "metadata standards." What does this mean?

    a. An agreed-upon information structure in which the metadata is stored, often XML

        i.   Facilitates computer exchange and linking, sorting, searching

            (a) EML—ecological metadata language (structure): http://knb.ecoinformatics .org/#tools/eml and Morpho (tool) https://knb.ecoinformatics.org/morpho portal.jsp

            (b) Dryad: uses Dublin Core metadata for basic information

b. A shared set of terms and definitions. Ontologies are still poorly developed, but are useful[9-11]

Concerns and Permissions

1. What are some concerns about sharing data?
2. How can metadata help address those concerns?
   a. Guide to Open Data Licensing: http://opendefinition.org/guide/data/
   b. Creative Commons and Data: http://wiki.creativecommons.org/Data
3. How can publishing the data itself address some of those concerns?
   a. Be first
   b. Same rigor of review and enforcement as for articles and other works

Depositing Data/Publishing Data

1. Typically associated with and at the same time as a publication or dissertation, but doesn't have to be
2. Embargoes
   a. In some cases, an embargo can be established, such as for dissertations, for up to 2 years
3. Unique identifiers
   a. For citation and other reasons, deposited data should be associated with a unique identifier; that is, it should be registered
   b. UO Data repository (Scholars' Bank) and many other data repositories now use DataCite to register data sets and create DOIs for them
4. Data deposit example
   a. Dryad: http://www.datadryad.org/pages/faq#depositing and video http://www.youtube.com/watch?v=RP33cl8tL28&feature=youtu.be
   b. Ecological monographs example: http://dx.doi.org/10.1890/11-1446.1
   c. See "Data Availability" at end of full text: links to Dryad (http://dx.doi.org/10.5061/dryad.gd856)

Citing Data

1. What are the components of a citation?[12-15]
   a. Responsible party (i.e., study principal investigator [PI], sample collector, government agency)
   b. Name of table, map, or data set with any applicable unique IDs
   c. Name of data center, repository, and/or publication
   d. Analysis software, if required
   e. Date accessed

    f.   URL and/or DOI/DOI link or other persistent link

    g.   See also: http://library.uoregon.edu/datamanagement/citingdata.html

  2. Feedback: https://docs.google.com/spreadsheet/embeddedform?formkey=dHNxdDRXW mhmaGl1cHhFWW12eGF1Vmc6MQ

References

1. Van den Eynden, V., Corti, L., Woollard, M., Bishop, L., & Horton, L. (2011). *Managing and sharing data: Best practice for researchers* (3rd ed.) [UK Data Archive version]. Retrieved from http://www.data-archive.ac.uk/media/2894/managingsharing.pdf

2. Piwowar, H. A., Day, R. S., & Fridsma, D. B. (2007). Sharing detailed research data is associated with increased citation rate. *PLoS ONE, 2*(3), e308. http://dx.doi.org/10.1371/journal.pone.0000308

3. Henneken, E. A., & Accomazzi, A. (2012). Linking to data: Effect on citation rates in astronomy. In Ballester, P. (Ed.), *Astronomical data analysis software and systems XXI* (Vol. 461, pp. 763–766) [Astronomical Society of the Pacific Conference Series open access version]. Retrieved from http://aspbooks.org/custom/publications/paper/461-0763.html

4. Sears, J. (2011, December). *Data sharing effect on article citation rate in paleoceanography.* Paper presented at the Fall Meeting of the American Geophysical Union, San Francisco, CA.

5. Gaulé, P., & Maystre, N. (2011). Getting cited: Does open access help? *Research Policy, 40*(10), 1332–1338. http://dx.doi.org/10.1016/j.respol.2011.05.025

6. Burroughs Wellcome Fund & Howard Hughes Medical Institute. (2006). Data management and laboratory notebooks. In *Making the right moves: A practical guide to scientific management for postdocs and new faculty* (2nd ed., pp. 143–152). Chevy Chase, MD: HHMI.

7. DataONE. (n.d.). Education modules. Retrieved from http://www.dataone.org/education-modules

8. University of Dundee & Open Microscopy Environment. (n.d.). About OMERO—OME. Retrieved from http://www.openmicroscopy.org/site/products/omero/omero-platform-v4# analyse

9. Madin, J. S., Bowers, S., Schildhauer, M. P., & Jones, M. B. (2008). Advancing ecological research with ontologies. *Trends in Ecology & Evolution, 23*(3), 159–168. http://dx.doi.org/10.1016/j.tree.2007.11.007

10. Porter, J. H., Hanson, P. C., & Lin, C.-C. (2012). Staying afloat in the sensor data deluge. *Trends in Ecology & Evolution, 27*(2), 121–129. http://dx.doi.org/10.1016/j.tree.2011.11.009

11. Deans, A. R., Yoder, M. J., & Balhoff, J. P. (2012). Time to change how we describe biodiversity. *Trends in Ecology & Evolution, 27*(2), 78–84. http://dx.doi.org/10.1016/j.tree.2011.11.007

12. Lawrence, B., Jones, C., Matthews, B., Pepler, S., & Callaghan, S. (2011). Citation and peer review of data: Moving towards formal data publication. *International Journal of Digital Curation, 6*(2), 4–37. http://dx.doi.org/10.2218/ijdc.v6i2.205

13. Economic & Social Research Council. (n.d.). Data citation: What you need to know. Retrieved from http://www.esrc.ac.uk/_images/Data_citation_booklet_tcm8-21453.pdf

14. Newton, M. P., Mooney, H., & Witt, M. (2010, December). *A description of data citation instructions in style guides.* Poster presented at the International Digital Curation Conference (IDCC), Chicago, IL. Retrieved from http://docs.lib.purdue.edu/lib_research/121

15. Mooney, H., & Newton, M. (2012). The anatomy of a data citation: Discovery, reuse, and credit. *Journal of Librarianship and Scholarly Communication, 1*(1), eP1035. http://dx.doi.org/10.7710/2162-3309.1035

Other Resources

DataONE. (n.d.). Investigator toolkit. Available at http://www.dataone.org/investigator-toolkit. Provides links to tools for searching, citing, data cleanup, R, and more.

Duke, C. S. (2006). Data: Share and share alike. *Frontiers in Ecology and the Environment, 4*(8): 395. http://dx.doi.org/10.1890/1540-9295(2006)4[395:DSASA]2.0.CO;2

ESA. (n.d.). Resources and tools. Retrieved from http://www.esa.org/esa/?page_id=2651

Hook, L. A., Santhana Vannan, S. K., Beaty, T. W., Cook, R. B., & Wilson, B. E. (2010). Best practices for preparing environmental data sets to share and archive. http://dx.doi.org/10.3334/ORNLDAAC/BestPractices-2010

ORNL DAAC. (n.d.). Data management for data providers. Retrieved from http://daac.ornl.gov/PI/pi_info.shtml

Piwowar, H. A., Vision, T. J., & Whitlock, M. C. (2011). Data archiving is a good investment. *Nature, 473,* 285. http://dx.doi.org/10.1038/473285a

Whitlock, M. C. (2011). Data archiving in ecology and evolution: Best practices. *Trends in Ecology & Evolution, 26*(2), 61–65. http://dx.doi.org/10.1016/j.tree.2010.11.006

APPENDIX B: Feedback and Assessment of the Data Information Literacy Session

End-of-Session Quick Feedback Form

1. Please list, in order of priority to you, four or five things from today that were new to you or updated what you had previously known.
2. What are three things that you will do differently in managing your data, based on today's session?

Post-Session Survey

1. *Skip this question if you did not participate in the interviews.* If you participated in an interview with Dean and Brian (spring of 2012), did the interview prompt you to examine your data management practices, and if so, are there any changes you made before the instruction session?

2a. How effective was the following article in describing why data management is important for your discipline?

   Wolkovich, E. M., Regetz, J., & O'Connor, M. I. (2012). Advances in global change research require open science by individual researchers. *Global Change Biology, 18*(7), 2102–2110. http://dx.doi.org/10.1111/j.1365-2486.2012.02693.x

   1 = Ineffective | 2 | 3 = Okay | 4 | 5 = Very effective

2b. Comments:

3a. How effective was the following article in providing you with best practices that you could apply to data management in your current research project(s)?

   Borer, E. T., Seabloom, E. W., Jones, M. B., & Schildhauer, M. (2009). Some simple guidelines for effective data management. *Bulletin of the Ecological Society of America, 90*(2), 205–214. http://dx.doi.org/10.1890/0012-9623-90.2.205

   1 = Ineffective | 2 | 3 = Okay | 4 | 5 = Very effective

3b. Comments:

4a. How useful were the exercises (i.e., spreadsheet and relational database data structures) to improving your understanding of and ability to work with structuring data?

   1 = Not useful at all | 2 | 3 = Okay | 4 | 5 = Very useful

4b. Comments:

5. Are there changes you have made or plan to make in how you manage research data as a result of the training session and readings?

6. Please list any other criticisms or favorable comments and suggestions about the readings, exercises, discussion, or other aspects of the training session.

PART III

Moving Forward

CHAPTER **9**

DEVELOPING DATA INFORMATION LITERACY PROGRAMS

A Guide for Academic Librarians

Sarah J. Wright, Cornell University

Jake Carlson, University of Michigan

Jon Jeffryes, University of Minnesota

Camille Andrews, Cornell University

Marianne Bracke, Purdue University

Michael Fosmire, Purdue University

Lisa R. Johnston, University of Minnesota

Megan Sapp Nelson, Purdue University

Dean Walton, University of Oregon

Brian Westra, University of Oregon

INTRODUCTION

The Data Information Literacy (DIL) project showed that developing educational programs on data for graduate students is a big area of opportunity for librarians. However, developing successful DIL programs can seem daunting, and you may be wondering: How do I get started? Do I have the knowledge to create a DIL program that will have an impact on students? Will I have the resources and support that I need to be successful? The DIL project teams, based in libraries at Purdue University (two teams), Cornell University, the University of Minnesota, and the University of Oregon, learned a great deal from their experiences. This chapter will share what we have learned to help other librarians create and implement DIL programs of their own. The information and guidance presented in this chapter is based on the collective experiences of the five DIL project teams in crafting their programs for graduate students in several science, technology, engineering, and mathematics (STEM) disciplines. We have included discussions of our approaches, pragmatic tips, and references to the resources that we used.

In reviewing the work done by the DIL project teams, we saw a natural progression of activities taken by each team. The stages of developing a DIL program are visualized in Figure 9.1 and are used to structure this chapter. Of course, developing a DIL program is not a totally linear process and we found that the stages built on one another in many interconnected ways. However, the figure and the structure of this chapter are meant to be illustrative of a general approach that could be applied by academic librarians.

Figure 9.1 shows each of the stages of developing a DIL program: planning, developing the program, implementing, and assessing and evaluating. You may find, as we did, a need to

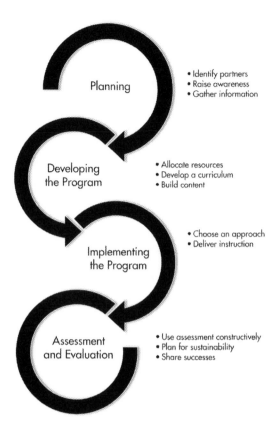

Figure 9.1 Stages of developing a data information literacy program.

move back and forth between the stages: retracing, reconsidering, and cycling through the tasks within a stage several times. In the sections that follow, we outline the activities performed in each of these stages. For the planning stage, we have grouped together the information-gathering and awareness-raising activities that most often occur early in the process. For the development stage, we discuss actions necessary to develop the program, such as building the curriculum and the content in response to the needs identified in the planning stage. For the implementation stage, we pull together information about different approaches and issues that you may encounter in the process of delivering instruction. The approach that you choose may be determined by the needs identified in the planning stage, as well as by the types of content that you have chosen to address. For the final stage, assessment and evaluation, we provide information on using assessment to inform future iterations of your program and tools for planning for sustainability so that your DIL program continues to grow and flourish.

Why Are Librarians Teaching DIL Skills?

The DIL project teams identified a strong desire for support in data management skills. The academic library community identified data curation as a top trend in 2012 (Tenopir, Birch, & Allard, 2012). This area of support provides an opportunity for libraries to gain entry into the research life of students and faculty. Having librarians teach data management skills is advantageous for many reasons. First, many academic librarians have a broad understanding of scholarship in general and an in-depth understanding of disciplinary best practices in scholarly communication. Librarians have the ability to identify and recommend resources, tools, and even skills that researchers need but may not be aware of. Librarians have experience and skills in the organization and dissemination of a variety of materials that may be applied to data management. It takes time, energy, and a fair amount of professional development to take on these roles, but doing so can result in new depths of involvement in the research mission of the academy and new partnerships with faculty and graduate students.

PLANNING

This section contains advice on identifying partners (e.g., faculty, fellow librarians, other campus service providers), raising awareness of the importance of DIL, and gathering information

so that the DIL program is informed by the real needs of constituents.

In times of tight budgets and limited resources, it is important to invest time and energy strategically. As a library begins to develop its DIL program, it must align these activities with other information literacy and research support programs offered locally. For example, it might better serve the students, as well as you and your colleagues, to combine similar instructional approaches or integrate outcomes throughout a curriculum, as opposed to running parallel programs. Integrating and mapping the DIL outcomes into existing frameworks and assessment already taking place will reveal natural affinities between these information skill sets and will help ensure buy-in across library and campus partners.

The integration of programs is also more efficient for teaching and scheduling of library staff. Collaborating with fellow librarians and others who are already teaching related skills is the most efficient way to establish a new DIL program. In fact, in any environment, fellow librarians are one of the most important resources in the development and implementation of a DIL program. Collaboration can take many different forms: some librarians may be interested in co-teaching, others may adjust existing materials to fit their needs independently, while some may want only to be informed about progress. Whatever the form, collaboration with librarians is one of the surest ways to establish and grow your program.

The partnerships forged by the DIL project teams with faculty members generally relied on existing relationships.

How to Identify Collaborators

Although data management and curation are topics that are often systemic to all disciplines, many faculty members may not see it as a pressing need to address or have the time to teach their students about DIL topics. Even if they are aware of the need, they may not be prepared to work with the library to address this topic to due misconceptions regarding library roles. Faculty can have a range of perceptions of the value that library and information science can bring to their laboratory or classroom. Given these and other differences among faculty, it can be challenging to identify potential faculty partners. However, the following strategies assisted the DIL project and may have some value for other institutions.

Low-Hanging Fruit

The "low-hanging fruit" strategy centers on leveraging your existing social capital: the connections that you have made with faculty and students through providing services to them. The people with whom you already have an established working relationship are more likely to be open to hearing your pitch on DIL. The partnerships forged by the DIL project teams with faculty members generally relied on existing relationships. The route to partnerships can vary, but may look like this:

- An existing need is identified by the professor. The partnership can begin with instruction sessions for a specific course or to meet specific educational needs of the professor's students that may or may not include DIL skills.
- A need is identified by the librarian. In the case of the Carlson and Sapp Nelson Purdue team, Megan Sapp Nelson had identified issues in student work from previous contact with students. This team presented these issues to the course faculty members (who concurred) as a part of generating interest in DIL.

Coming to an Understanding

"Coming to an understanding" refers to the progression of these initial opportunities to norming conversations during which the disciplinary faculty member and the librarian come to a consensus that there is an issue that needs to be addressed, define what that issue is, and begin to develop strategies to address it. In the DIL project, this was accomplished primarily through interviewing faculty and students.

Working Relationships

"Working relationships" are developed as work with DIL progresses beyond informal conversations. This process generally happens as the librarian works closely with the disciplinary faculty members, asking questions and making suggestions. Needs identified may shift and potential strategies for addressing needs are not always realistic. Our teams struggled with time constraints as well as other challenges as the DIL project progressed. As with any interdisciplinary project, several meetings are often spent identifying common ground, as well as

DATA INFORMATION LITERACY INTERVIEW TOOL

This project used a standardized tool, the Data Information Literacy Interview Instrument (http://dx.doi.org/10.5703/1288284315510), to have a structured conversation around DIL needs of the students and faculty member partner. Our goal was to understand how data management and curation was practiced by the research team members and to identify areas of need as seen by the students and faculty in the lab. The structured interview encouraged professors to think carefully about issues of data management, and it allowed librarians to introduce the DIL competencies to faculty in order to find out analogous disciplinary terminology. These interviews helped us identify the most serious needs as perceived by the faculty member.

identifying differences and possible roadblocks. Those who identify and develop workarounds for differences or roadblocks early have an advantage with regard to long-term success.

How to Promote Data Information Literacy (Raising Awareness)

For the faculty and others in the lab, commitment to data management and curation within a research team is not without impact on resources. At the very least, time is invested in the learning and practice of new skills. New tools or technologies may be needed, which bring associated hardware, software, and time costs. The faculty and other stakeholders must see a compelling reason to invest scarce resources into developing and engaging in a DIL program.

These are arguments that can be made that may have an impact on a DIL project's disciplinary professors:

> *We can help you improve the data management practices among your current students.* Decreased errors, more efficient use of time, reduced frustration, and easier data sharing between project partners are just a few of the benefits of having graduate students who receive training and are familiar with data management best practices.
>
> *We can help ease the transitions between graduate students who work with the same data.* Better documented and organized data can ease the transition between graduate students and has a direct impact on time spent by the professor searching for or recreating data from work done by a former graduate student. It also enhances professional reputation when students graduating from a particular research group have these skills.

MAINTAINING FLEXIBILITY TO SUSTAIN WORKING RELATIONSHIPS

The goal of the project was to create a tailored solution for each individual faculty member and research group. In the process, disciplinary or situational constraints were identified to provide an educational intervention that met the needs of the students and faculty partners. In the case of the team from the University of Oregon, the research group was completing their work on a grant. Therefore a significant obstacle was the very short time frame available before the project ended. By being flexible, the team was able to create interventions that addressed the faculty researcher's needs and time constraints while meeting the goals of the DIL project.

> *We can improve your project's compliance with [insert funder]'s mandates regarding data management plans.* Funding agencies increasingly expect or require data to be managed and shared. The decrease in available grant funding in recent years makes even slight differences in the quality of proposals extremely important. A thorough and thoughtful data management plan (DMP) helps to support a case for the reliability of the group proposing the research.
>
> *We can help you increase the impact of your research.* Emerging data journals and the use of DOIs to permanently connect articles to data sets mean that professors now have the ability to track citations to their data as well as their articles. Studies have shown that the publication of data sets along with articles increased citations (Piwowar, Day, & Fridsma, 2007). Highly cited data sets may help to support the tenure and promotion of a researcher.
>
> *We can help provide open access to your data via sharing in repositories.* For professors

---

**ARGUMENTS FOR ENGAGING IN
DATA INFORMATION LITERACY**

- We can help you improve the data management practices among your current students
- We can help ease the transitions between
  graduate students who work with the same
  data
- We can improve your project's compliance
  with your funder's mandates regarding data
  management plans
- We can help you increase the impact of your
  research
- We can help provide open access to your data
  via sharing in repositories

---

concerned with the high costs and restricted access to scholarly journals,
providing data through an open source
repository represents another level of
service to the profession and a way for
researchers to enable long-term access
to their data.

Each of these points may be effective for
some faculty members. The level of impact
may be dependent upon rank, professional
obligations, disciplinary expectations, and personal opinions and habits. For an untenured
assistant professor, the highest priority may be
to create a strong case for tenure. Therefore,

WHAT WORKED FOR US

In our case, the actual approach for recruiting
faculty to the DIL project often started from a
reflective conversation during which disciplinary professors considered how well their students
managed data. In nearly every case, the professors
expressed some serious concerns and needs around
the data practices of their students—concerns that
the professor did not have the time or expertise to
address. The goal was then to convert an observed
need(s) into an educational program targeted to
address the need(s).

---

emphasizing the impact that can result from
publishing data could be an effective tool.
For a full professor with a long-established research history, the argument for safeguarding
the knowledge that they gathered throughout
their career and making it available for future
use may be more compelling. Getting to know
the faculty members' priorities before having a
conversation will allow the librarian to select
the approach most likely to succeed.

Understanding the Needs
of Constituencies

A key component to success with the DIL project was developing an understanding of any
disciplinary norms with data and incorporating
these norms into our educational programming
wherever possible. Conducting an environmental scan will provide baseline knowledge that can
help you develop your educational program. We
had success reviewing the scholarly literature of
the discipline along with reports, websites, and
other relevant materials produced by organizations or agencies affiliated with the discipline.
In addition, conducting an environmental scan
of local data management and curation practices will familiarize you with disciplinary attitudes and behaviors. Spend time learning about
practices in the department through identifying
related resources such as courses on research
ethics, training for graduate research assistants,
or more informal manuals of practice available
on department websites.

Our suggestions for performing an environmental scan include the following:

1. Perform a literature review in your discipline. This might reveal published best
   practices for the specific subject area. Literature may come from the disciplines
   themselves or from publications in the
   library science field.

2. Perform an internet search for data management best practices in your discipline. Pay special attention to results from relevant disciplinary societies and institutes.

3. Know the funding agencies and organizations in your discipline and whether data management requirements exist.

4. Search for disciplinary data repositories to learn what types of requirements and guidelines they provide. Some repositories, such as ICPSR (2012) or the UK Data Archive (Corti, Van den Eynden, Bishop, & Wollard, 2014), published guidelines for managing data in ways that support their eventual curation.

5. Find journals in the field that include data supplements and look at examples of archived data sets for ideas for cultivating best practices. Some journals have requirements for open data.

6. Identify professional organizations related to the discipline. This may be useful as more programmatic approaches to data management evolve.

There are many potential places to look for information, and as interest in data management continues to grow, the amount of information will increase. Some fields are further along than others and therefore have a much greater body of literature and online resources associated with data management. In our case, the teams focusing on ecology and related subjects found more information than the teams focusing on engineering.

You may want to increase the scope of the environmental scan beyond disciplinary norms and include resources at your institution. Questions that you may want to ask include

- What are the specific resources relating to data available to researchers at your institution?

ENVIRONMENTAL SCANNING IS THE WAY TO YOUR FACULTY'S HEART

Early in the process, each of the DIL teams set out to increase our understanding of our respective disciplines by conducting an environmental scan of the discipline. Our intention was to identify how each discipline recognized, discussed, and addressed research data management and curation issues. As expected, the quantity and quality of the materials found by each team varied, but every team was better informed in their interactions with faculty and students. For example, as a result of preliminary searching in the library catalog, the Cornell librarian team member brought a book published by The Long Term Ecological Research Network on data management to a meeting with the faculty. The faculty member had worked with one of the authors and was very interested in reading the book. The other DIL teams had similar experiences and found that faculty appreciated the librarians' ability to find pertinent disciplinary information and bring these materials to their attention.

DISCIPLINES AND THE DATA INFORMATION LITERACY COMPETENCIES

We hypothesized from the beginning that researchers from different disciplines would interpret the competencies differently, due to specialized practices or cultural norms. This proved to be true in each of the five DIL case studies. However, we also found different data practices within the subfields of disciplines or even among individual projects. For example, though civil engineering as a discipline is still considering how to respond to challenges in managing and curating data, the University of Minnesota team partnered with a research group that was affiliated with the Network for Earthquake Engineering Simulation (NEES). NEES has an online virtual research platform, NEEShub.org, that includes a data repository. The University of Minnesota team reviewed materials produced by NEEShub and incorporated them into their educational program, and vice versa. NEEShub.org incorporated a version of the team's instructional materials for its online educational offerings.

- What are local practices and attitudes with regard to data management?
- What are the strategic priorities for your institution?
- What potential barriers do you foresee?
- What resources (e.g., people, skills) would you need to consider or include in your program to be successful?

Conversations with additional stakeholders may allow for the identification of additional needs and factors or clarify possible responses to include in your DIL program. The environmental scan may help you to identify potential collaborators as well.

Understanding and Working With Faculty

Collaborating with faculty is often both challenging and very rewarding. Faculty are busy people, so it can be difficult for them to find the time to focus on a collaboration like this. In addition, their attention may be divided among research, teaching, and administrative duties. Ideally, you will work with faculty to identify the needs of the students and to determine the timing and means of delivering the instruction. You will need to work together to determine what skills you can reasonably address. Most likely neither of you will have the expertise to address all of the students' needs, but you will have complementary skills and can bring in outside experts as needed.

The time needed to address all of these issues will vary with the degree of involvement of the faculty and the scope of your program. At minimum, a substantive initial meeting to discuss student needs, timing, and means of delivery will begin the process. If you are offering a one-session workshop, that may be all of the time you require for planning. However, developing a project larger in scope, such as a series of classes or a mini-course, may require much

> ### RECOMMENDATIONS FOR WORKING WITH FACULTY
>
> Based on our experiences working with faculty collaborators on the DIL project, we offer these recommendations:
>
> - Be prepared for faculty attention levels to shift as the project progresses; their focus on the project may ebb and flow depending on other commitments.
> - Have clearly defined expectations and roles going into the project. However, be flexible if those expectations and roles must change over the course of the project.
> - If you need faculty input at a certain time, or require that a certain amount of faculty time be allocated to the project, make those needs clear and make sure that the faculty member can make those commitments. You may even want to specify these needs as a statement of support in writing.
> - Faculty (and students) often don't understand the language used in libraries. For example, the terms *data curation, data management,* and *metadata* may not resonate with them. Be prepared to translate and speak the researcher's language.
> - The faculty member has extensive knowledge of the discipline; use that expertise to provide context and rich examples for the students. This is key in engaging the students in the topic.

more time to discuss and plan course content and delivery.

Understanding and Working With Graduate Students

Graduate students are an important constituency for academic libraries. They are often at the research frontline, not only in data collection, processing, and analysis, but also in managing, describing, and documenting research data. In our experience, graduate students generally receive minimal training to take on these important tasks. Working with graduate students to develop and implement educational programming is a way for librarians to address a critical need of students and faculty, and a way to build or strengthen connections with this important user group.

In planning and developing instruction in DIL competencies for graduate students, you must gain an understanding of their environment and their needs *from their perspective.* Graduate students often engage in multiple roles: student, member of a research project, instructor, and so forth. The nature and intent of the educational programming that you develop will shape your interactions with the graduate students that you intend to target. Plan to spend some time talking and interacting with the graduate students you are targeting. We have found that graduate students' interpretations of their environment, roles, and perceived needs often vary greatly from those expressed by their faculty advisor. Graduate students will likely provide you with a more nuanced and complete understanding of how DIL competencies are acquired and practiced, as well as how you could respond to any gaps.

Although there are likely to be differences in the lives of graduate students according to their discipline, area of research, institution, and so forth, we found the following elements to be true of most of the graduate students we worked with in the DIL project:

- Graduate students are busy people. They are both learning their discipline and taking on professional responsibilities through teaching, research (their own plus supporting other research activities), and engagement. This leaves very little time for things that are interpreted as being something "extra" for them to do.
- Graduate students are under a lot of pressure. Not only do graduate students take on a lot of responsibilities, but they are

---

RECOMMENDATIONS FOR WORKING WITH GRADUATE STUDENTS

Although many factors complicate making connections and working with graduate students on developing data competencies, it can be done. There are several key considerations in planning and developing educational programs for this population:

- In developing your DIL program, don't just focus on the faculty, but take time to connect with the graduate students. Try to get a sense of what they already know and what they perceive as important in working with data.
- Be prepared to articulate how your program will address their needs, both in the future and in their current situations.
- Recognize that they are busy people and try to meet them where they are. This could mean getting time in an existing meeting or embedding yourself in existing structures. It may also mean that you work with them outside of a regular workday.
- Set realistic expectations, both for graduate students and for your program. You may not be able to do everything that you would like to do right away. Give your program a chance to develop over time and give yourself room to be successful.

---

under pressure to produce results quickly. As one faculty member told us, graduate students have to do three things: find a research project to join, produce results that they can claim credit for, and graduate. Anything else may be seen as detracting from what graduate students must accomplish as students.

- Graduate students are expected to be "independent learners." They have reached a stage in their educational career where they are expected to be able to formulate and conduct their own research, develop and teach their own courses, and to produce presentations and publications that favorably compare to those of veteran researchers. Although they are certainly willing to help when needed, faculty mentors generally expect graduate students to be able to address questions and problems on their own, without detailed instruction.

- Graduate students are presumed to have already learned DIL skills. When asked how graduate students acquire knowledge and skills with data generally, the faculty we interviewed believed that students had acquired them through previous course work or other experiences as undergraduates. For many graduate students this was not the case. They lacked previous experience in working with data and acknowledged to us that they were acquiring their skills as they went along.

- Graduate students may have a "short-term mentality." One sentiment from faculty that we heard frequently in our interviews was that graduate students did not have a sense of the lasting value of the data that they were producing and therefore did not always recognize the need to treat their data as an institutional asset. Because graduate students lack the experience of using data beyond what was originally envisioned, faculty found it tough to convince them to take better care of the data that stay behind long after they graduate.

DEVELOPING THE PROGRAM

Once you've established partners and determined needs, it's time to develop your program. This section contains advice on allocating resources (time, money, expertise, and so forth), developing a curriculum in response to local interest and needs, and crafting the materials that you'll teach.

Available Resources

When looking toward implementation, you should consider the resources available to you. What time, money, and expertise will you need to carry out the program, and how well do those match the resources available at your institution? What technology do you need? Do you need additional training? Where will you teach? At what scale should you be planning your DIL program? The answers to these and other questions should be derived from the information you gathered during the planning stage. For example, online educational resources are often the most scalable, but there is a substantial upfront cost in developing modules, such as gaining expertise (or hiring others) in using online learning technologies. On the other hand, in-person instruction demands can rapidly outstrip the available time of instructors. The services or resources that you previously identified that address similar needs may help you to make decisions. It may be easier to use the same technology others are using and substantially decrease the cost of developing online resources to the point that it becomes more sustainable than doing in-person instruction. If your organization has a centralized information literacy program, coordinating with it may be part of your plan, particularly if your program extends across subject liaison areas. As you are working to flesh out the framework of your DIL program, it is essential to determine whether collaborators are on board and what times would work best for them. What are they able to commit to? Recruiting other librarians to collaborate on creating programmatic instruction will help spread the work around as well, but again, influencing others to be a part of the program will likely be necessary. Do you have enough buy-in from collaborators to develop the DIL program at the scale you would like, or do you need to adjust your expectations to better match the available resources? Available resources will have a large effect on the scale and scope of the program that you are able to develop.

Developing a Curriculum

Developing an effective and successful curriculum starts with learning the needs of your constituencies to determine which learning goals and outcomes will most resonate with, and benefit, your students. Whether using a structured interview tool, such as the Data Information Literacy Interview Tool), or a tool developed in house, such as a quick survey sent to students to identify pain points and areas of interest, this feedback will help guide curriculum development.

Upon completion of the needs assessment, the DIL instructor(s) will want to look through the identified topics of interest and begin to prioritize which topics to include in the curriculum. Some factors to consider include the length of instruction, the mode of instruction (e.g., online videos, in-person workshop), and whether any prerequisites should exist (i.e., do students need to have some baseline skills?). You should also consider your own areas of knowledge and expertise; certain skills may fall outside the instructors' skill sets. Will you not include these skills, or will you recruit outside experts? For example, the University of Minnesota team found a user need in skills related to data visualization and analysis. Not confident in teaching these discipline-specific areas, the team incorporated campus resources where students could get more expert assistance in these areas, such as training on statistical tools and advanced Excel techniques.

At this point in the process it can be valuable to bring stakeholders (faculty, research

> **DEVELOPING THE CURRICULUM**
>
> With the information gained from interviews with faculty and graduate students, each DIL team set out to identify instructional interventions to address the gaps that we found in the graduate curriculum covering data management skills. However, each team found that students and faculty expressed a potential interest in receiving training around almost every one of the DIL competencies. The Cornell team, for example, used the following questions to help them narrow down which of the competencies to focus on:
>
> - Does the competency address a gap we found in the curriculum?
> - Do we have the expertise to address the need? If not, could we bring someone else in who does have the expertise?
> - Where could we add the most value?
>
> After answering these questions in concert with the disciplinary faculty, the team decided to focus on these four DIL areas: *data management and organization, data analysis and visualization, data sharing,* and *data quality and documentation.*

advisors) into the instructional planning to act as sounding boards for the proposed goals and outcomes of your instructional intervention. These conversations can act as reality checks to make sure that that information gathered and decisions made regarding which skills to cover align with faculty goals. These conversations also assist with managing stakeholder expectations, providing these key players with a sneak preview (and opportunity to provide feedback) before the instruction is implemented.

Instructors also need to be realistic in their expectations of student comprehension when determining the scope of information that can be effectively conveyed and successfully transmitted in the time allotted. For many students, this curriculum will be their first instruction in DIL, so they will need time to orient themselves.

Developing Outcomes

After determining which DIL competencies are most critical to the target audience, the next step is developing learning outcomes for instruction. "Learning outcomes are statements of what a successful learner is expected to be able to do at the end of the process of a learning experience such as the course unit or the course model" (Gogus, 2012b, p. 1950). Although the terms are often used interchangeably, learning outcomes are distinguished from learning objectives as they tend to go beyond the general aims or goals of the instruction to the resulting expectations and evidence of what a student knows or can do after instruction (Gogus, 2012a). Without a clear idea of exactly what students need to learn or accomplish, it is difficult, if not impossible, to design effective instruction or assess whether or not it is successful; therefore, specifying learning outcomes is an essential first step.

Good learning outcomes are specific, measurable or observable, clear, aligned with activities and assessments, and student centered rather than instructor centered. They also specify the criteria for and the level of student performance and begin with action verbs. Bloom's taxonomy is an excellent source for action verbs and is widely used as an educational tool for classifying goals and outcomes (Gogus, 2012a).

Planning for Assessment

Assessment should be considered early in the DIL program planning process, even before designing your instruction. However, many librarians are not assessment experts (including most of us in the DIL project), which may make the idea of assessment somewhat daunting. Fortunately, we found that by keeping a

> ### TRANSLATING DIL COMPETENCIES INTO LEARNING OUTCOMES
>
> The DIL competencies identified by Carlson, Fosmire, Miller, and Sapp Nelson (see Chapter 1 of this book) were a useful starting place for generating and refining the specific learning outcomes for our educational programs. In order to turn a DIL competency into a learning outcome, we replaced the more vague terms such as familiarize or understand with more action-oriented verbs such as locate or define. We described each learning objective as follows: learning area, preliminary outcomes/objectives/learning goals, and possible pedagogy. For example, from the broad competency theme of discovery and acquisition of data, the following learning outcomes are possible:
>
> - Evaluate disciplinary data repositories (from a given list according to particular criteria) in order to determine requirements and suitability for data deposit.
> - Find and evaluate the quality of a data set in order to decide whether it would be of use.
>
> Note that these learning outcomes are more specific, measurable or observable, and clear than the more generic and unmeasurable "become familiar with data repositories in the discipline." Also note that many different learning outcomes could be developed to address the broad competency.

few basic principles in mind, assessment was not so foreign. Plus, specifying learning outcomes is the first step in planning for assessment, so if you are following along, you have already started defining your assessment without realizing it.

Assessment of student learning is the process of understanding what participants know and can do in relation to the outcomes that you are trying to achieve. It is not enough to say we have covered certain DIL topics and now our work is done. Without getting feedback from our students and seeing if it measures up to our criteria for success, it is impossible to know whether students have learned DIL skills and are able to apply their knowledge or transfer it to other situations.

There are two types of assessment—formative and summative—each with several levels of assessment: institutional, program-level, and instruction-session level. Formative assessment occurs during the instructional process and provides feedback for the students on how they are doing. This lets instructors know how well students are receiving the instruction early on and allows for course corrections and clarifications. Summative assessment occurs after the instruction concludes and provides measures of how well the instructional outcomes have been achieved and the efficacy of the instruction. Classroom (or instruction session) assessment of student learning is outcomes based and focuses on what students demonstrably know and can do after instruction. This may include measures such as examination of final assignments or projects using a rubric (a defined standard of performance) as well as pre- and post-tests. Program-level assessment is discussed in the final section of this chapter, "Assessment and Evaluation."

The more opportunities that students have to practice and receive direct and timely feedback on their skills, in accordance with specific criteria and in situations they will encounter in the real world (or as close as possible), the more likely that learning will be achieved (Radcliff, 2007). This can happen in a number of ways. One of the most effective is course-integrated, outcomes-based assessment that uses learning outcomes as the goals to measure student accomplishment. Planning activities that allow students to practice their newly learned skills and to get or give feedback can help you as the instructor gauge whether students are grasping the concepts taught.

Assessment, particularly outcomes-based assessment, can be one of the most challenging parts of developing an educational program. However, you may already have resources available at your campus (such as research and assessment units, survey centers and tools, and so forth) to assist you in crafting a workable approach for assessing your DIL program. If you are just getting started in crafting your DIL program, you may want to begin by employing lightweight methods, like the 1-minute paper, to make the process of assessment less onerous. The 1-minute paper exercise is a way to quickly check for students' self-reported understanding or confusion. The method is simply a very short in-class writing activity that can be completed in 1 minute or less, by asking students to respond to a question designed to provide the instructor with feedback about their learning. For example, a popular set of questions to ask

---

THERE ARE MANY PATHS TO STUDENT ASSESSMENT

The DIL teams used several student assessment methods. The following examples show that success can be achieved using a mix of both formal and informal, and formative and summative, methods when measuring student success.

Formative: Several teams (both Purdue teams and the University of Oregon team) conducted formative assessments that included informal examinations of student-created materials, feedback on in-class exercises, or "1-minute paper" reflections to gauge students' learning in order to give feedback and make course corrections.

Summative: The Carlson and Sapp Nelson team from Purdue created a rubric to allow themselves and the TAs to judge the quality of students' code. They also examined students' final design notebooks and attended the students' final design reviews to give feedback.

Combination of formative and summative: Two teams, Cornell and the University of Minnesota, had students complete data management plans (DMPs) in successive sections to provide formative assessment and then used the final DMPs for summative assessment. They both assessed the DMPs according to the criteria on a rubric, which can be found in the team chapters.

at the end of a session for a 1-minute paper is (1) What have you learned? and (2) What do you still have questions about? Although it is common to use open-ended and reflective questions, 1-minute papers are very adaptable and can be used for a variety of purposes depending on the questions asked. As you become more comfortable with your DIL program, you can add in more advanced approaches to ascertain its impact on student knowledge and behaviors with DIL topics.

Building Course Content

Once you've determined what to teach, developing your teaching materials is the next step. It is critically important to capture the attention of the students early and often, and you should build your instructional content with this in mind. Successful engagement of students can be accomplished by tailoring your instruction specifically to their needs and situations. One approach would be to solicit real-world stories of data loss or error as a result of less than ideal data management. Sharing these stories early on in your DIL program may capture students' attention. Ideally these stories come from faculty (or fellow students), which makes the impact these losses have on work real. These stories are unfortunately all too common, so finding them should not be difficult. Drawing students into the topic at the outset and facilitating their buy-in will pave the way for a successful instructional session.

The content of your session can be delivered in a variety of ways. Two common approaches are the instructor-led lecture on specific topics, and implementing active learning–based activities that allow students to get hands-on experience with some specific data practices. (More information on active learning can be found on the University of Minnesota's Center for

Teaching and Learning website: http://www1 .umn.edu/ohr/teachlearn/tutorials/active /what/.) Strategies for approaching instruction are discussed more fully in the next section, "Implementing the Program," but the content will need to align with the instructional approach (e.g., it might be hard to incorporate active learning into an online video tutorial), the learning styles of the intended audience, and the comfort level of the instructor. Generally it is a good idea to have your students use the data sets that they themselves are responsible for developing or managing in your lessons and activities. This reinforces the learning objectives as the students have a real investment in the results of the lesson. However, it's important to recognize that not all students will come to your training with their own data sets, or they may be working on data sets that are at different stages of development. In these cases, you may need to provide fictional scenarios to give students something with which to work. Care should be taken in developing fictional data so that it reflects the attributes and characteristics of data that would normally be found in the student's field of study.

The resources that you are teaching students to use may also drive your instructional content creation. For example, if teaching about a particular data repository (either institutional or subject-based), you will want to make sure that the content you create matches the requirements of that repository. In fact, looking at relevant data repositories may be a good way to determine which pieces of content are the most important to cover for a particular audience—for example, metadata standards used by the repository, policies for preservation, and perhaps even licensing concerns.

As more librarians and faculty develop educational programs and materials for teaching DIL competencies, more ready-made

---

LEARNING OUTCOMES AND THE INSTRUCTIONAL DESIGN PROCESS

In the DIL project, the use of learning outcomes helped us design a clear picture of the intended results and therefore helped to guide the development of our instruction activities. For example, for the learning outcome "evaluate disciplinary data repositories in order to determine requirements and suitability for data deposit," the Cornell team knew they would need to provide students with a list of potential repositories in their field (using Databib to identify them: http://databib.org/) as well as a list of potential evaluative criteria for data deposit. They then designed an in-class exercise that had students examine at least one repository in their subject area according to the evaluative criteria to see if they would recommend depositing their data (an activity that is grounded in their real-world practice) and then report back to the whole group with their findings (allowing the instructor to assess their evaluation and give feedback).

---

instructional content is becoming available. Not all resources may be appropriate to use when developing and implementing your own DIL program, but they might be worth investigating as they could spark some ideas for your specific context and audience. See the end of this chapter for a list of resources that may help you design your own DIL program.

IMPLEMENTING THE PROGRAM

Finally! You've worked so hard to get to this point, which is perhaps the most exciting stage of the process, and you're ready to teach. This section contains advice on choosing and delivering an instructional approach, whether it is in-person instruction for small groups, instruction aimed at a large online audience, or somewhere in between.

Choosing an Approach

Once goals and outcomes of the course are determined you will need to develop instructional approaches or pedagogies (lectures, learning activities, online videos, and so forth) that lead students to successfully acquire the knowledge and skills that you have identified as your learning outcomes. There are many possible instructional approaches that one can choose. The DIL teams each chose a different approach to fit the needs of their communities. Each of these approaches had associated pros and cons, listed in Table 9.1.

- The Cornell team offered a one-credit mini-course on data management with sponsorship from the natural resources department.
- The Carlson and Sapp Nelson team from Purdue took an embedded librarian approach with their project partner, a service-learning center based in electrical and computer engineering. They offered a skills session to introduce concepts and good practices, designed tools and resources to support their application, and attended design reviews and team meetings as consultants to help encourage and reinforce their adoption.
- The Bracke and Fosmire team from Purdue developed a checklist of practices for students in an agricultural and biological engineering group and then offered a series of workshops to teach the skills needed to carry out these practices.
- With assistance from an instructional designer, the University of Minnesota team developed an online training module that they used in conjunction with an in-person session for a civil engineering research section.

TABLE 9.1   *The Pros and Cons of the DIL Instructional Approaches*

Approach: mini-course (Cornell)	**Pros**
	Co-teaching the course with faculty from the department increased faculty engagement
	Course format provided opportunities to practice application of best practices, and the ability to build on prior sessions
	Cons
	Time investment is substantial, both for librarian and faculty collaborator
	Must have buy-in from university department to offer course, and from library administration to spend librarian time teaching. (Many libraries consider teaching a university course a high achievement for a librarian, so this may not be a con but should still be considered)
Approach: online course (Minnesota)	**Pros**
	Very scalable. While initial time investment may be high, modules can be reused, repurposed, and recombined, increasing the potential impact of the training
	Online format provides the opportunity for students to reference the materials at the time of need, potentially resulting in improved data practices
	Cons
	May require assistance from an instructional designer, or someone with experience building online content
	Impact is increased by combining with an in-person session, due date, or some other kind of encouragement. Students tended to forget or put off completing the module until the last minute
Approach: one-shot session (Oregon)	**Pros**
	Small group setting allows materials to be closely targeted to their specific needs, increasing student awareness of tools, resources, and best practices
	Because the time investment is small, increased likelihood of getting buy-in from reluctant or busy faculty and graduate students
	Cons
	Not very scalable if you have lots of research groups interested in such targeted training.
	Limited time with students may mean that material covered is not retained as well as it would be if there were more opportunities for activities and repetition
Approach: embedded librarianship (Carlson and Sapp Nelson team from Purdue)	**Pros**
	Group setting allows materials to be closely targeted to their specific needs, increasing student awareness of tools, resources, and best practices
	Ongoing relationship with students and faculty provides multiple opportunities for evaluating student work and providing feedback
	Cons
	Not very scalable as interest increases
	Time investment is large, since the librarian participates in group meetings and is closely involved in development of tools and resources
Approach: series of workshops (Bracke and Fosmire team from Purdue)	**Pros**
	Workshops allow materials to be closely targeted to developing specific skills and best practices
	Clear expectations such as a checklist make it easier for students to see what is required, resulting in increased student compliance
	Cons
	Very specific outcomes (checklist of practices) may result in the students not realizing that the same best practices could apply in other situations
	Time investment is large, since librarian must develop specific checklist and accompanying instruction. May not be easily scaled if other groups want such targeted instruction

- The University of Oregon team partnered with a group conducting research in ecology whose funding for the project was winding down. They offered a seminar to connect students to data management and curation resources developed by their disciplinary community.

For a more in-depth discussion of each team's DIL program, please refer to Chapters 4 through 8.

Delivering Instruction

If you've taught other classes and workshops then you may be completely comfortable with being in front of a classroom delivering instruction. If, however, you're new to teaching or are delving into new territory, perhaps developing online modules for the first time, then you may be feeling pretty nervous. The best solution for nervousness is preparation and practice. Once you've planned everything out, the next step may be practicing with colleagues, significant others, or even your dog (probably not helpful if you're developing online modules). To help you prepare, in this section we'll discuss some things you'll need to consider while you're delivering instruction.

Scheduling Sessions

As discussed in the previous section, there are a wide variety of implementation possibilities, from online courses to embedded librarians and beyond. In the case of workshops or other training sessions, it's important to schedule them to coincide with research team availability. Ideally, DIL training would be integrated and coincide with a relevant part of the data life cycle, but this is not always possible. A research team may have individuals working with data from multiple stages of the data life cycle. In general, it is

best to avoid conflicts with research field trips or conferences, and to target instructional interventions so that they are timed as closely as possible with real research workflows and events. As with any type of instruction, just-in-time instruction that students can apply immediately will be more effective than instruction not tied to a recent or upcoming activity. If students have no opportunity to apply what is being taught (for example, they are new graduate students without data of their own), then you may want to incorporate more activities and opportunities for practice with fictitious data to help reinforce what is being taught. Note that schedules that work for research teams may not coincide with typical academic schedules. You may find that weekend workshops or winter sessions timed to avoid summer field research will work better than semester-based scheduling.

Feedback for Students

In the midst of planning the curriculum and collecting the content that you'll teach, it can be easy to forget to plan how you'll communicate with your students. Again, in our experience, different teams used different methods. For the online modules developed by the University of Minnesota team, communication was mostly via e-mail, some of it automated. For the mini-course taught by the Cornell team, the Blackboard course management system's discussion board was used for collecting and providing feedback on assignments. The University of Oregon's team as well as both of Purdue's teams included plenty of time for direct student contact to provide feedback on their work. The method you choose should fit your comfort level and work for what you're trying to accomplish. Formal feedback will require different methods than will informal feedback, so if you're assigning grades you will need a more formal system in place than if you're collecting notebooks and writing a note or giving verbal feedback in a one-shot workshop. Regardless of the method you choose, feedback is an important step toward maintaining the students' interest and engagement and should not be overlooked.

Maintaining Interest (Theirs and Yours)

In the "Building Course Content" section, we suggested that you build instructional content with the goal of capturing the attention of the students early and often. Strategies for maintaining their interest include tailoring instruction specifically to their needs and situations, and using active learning techniques when you're in a face-to-face environment. However, no matter how well you prepare, there will probably be a moment when you notice a student yawning, multitasking on e-mail, or not completing the online modules you worked so hard on. Remind yourself that graduate students are busy people, don't take it personally, and then see if there's anything that you can do to improve their experience. Note that if you're bored, your students are definitely bored. You cannot be an engaging teacher if you're not excited, so make sure you plan content that's exciting to you too. The more excited or passionate that you are, the easier it will be to draw students into the topic, and facilitating their buy-in will ensure a more successful program.

Responding to Formative Assessment

Formative assessment happens during the instructional process and provides feedback for students on how they are doing, lets instructors know how students are receiving the instruction, and allows for course corrections and clarifications. Assessment while you're teaching can help reveal whether or not students are learning, whether you're covering too much or too little, and when it may be necessary to

make adjustments. Adjustments can be substantial, such as adding a new class session or online module to provide additional information. They can also be small, like changing a due date to accommodate students' schedules, providing additional help, or reviewing a topic at the beginning of the next class or meeting. Avoid asking for feedback about something that you are unwilling to change. So for example, if you or your faculty stakeholders require that a certain topic be covered, don't ask students if they would rather skip it. If you do ask for feedback, let the students know how you'll be using it and why it's important so that they can be properly engaged in the process. Most importantly, follow up to let the students know how you used their feedback to make improvements to the instruction. If assessment is handled this way, students are much more likely to continue to be active participants since they can see that they have a real effect on the way instruction is delivered.

ASSESSMENT AND EVALUATION

After completing your instruction, it is important to assess and evaluate what worked and what didn't. This section contains advice on using program assessment constructively, planning for sustainability, and sharing your successes in order to continue to grow your program.

Making Good Use of Program Assessment

Program-level assessment focuses on the effectiveness and reach of an instructional program as a whole. A sustainable program does not end once instruction has been delivered. Getting feedback from students and stakeholders helps you to determine what improvements and changes should be made. Program-level assessment can include measures of student satisfaction, self-reported skill attainment, teacher effectiveness, and program design (usefulness of activities, readings, and so forth).

How Our Teams Used Program Assessment to Inform Next Steps

Once the DIL teams offered their instruction, each team conducted a summative program assessment. Here again the specific metrics and approaches varied according to the team's programmatic goals and objectives. Some of the teams distributed an evaluation survey for students to complete and return. Other teams conducted brief follow-up interviews with faculty and graduate students to learn how their efforts impacted them and others. Still others collected student work from the class and analyzed it for evidence that the students understood and were able to apply the concepts that they had learned in the program. The feedback we gathered helped us to plan the next steps in developing a sustainable program that would continue to fill the needs of our communities.

The Cornell team's final evaluation survey showed marked differences between students' self-assessments of their knowledge, skills, and abilities with regard to the learning outcomes before and after taking the class, and nearly all students indicated that they would recommend the class to other graduate students. This assessment helped the Cornell team to successfully propose that the class become a regular offering of the Department of Natural Resources. Responses concerning the usefulness of certain topics also helped the team refine the course framework for the 2014 semester.

The Carlson and Sapp Nelson team from Purdue interviewed the electrical and computer engineering faculty they worked with

to assess their perceptions of their work at the end of the program. As a result, conversations ensued about scaffolding DIL further into the curriculum. The Carlson and Sapp Nelson team from Purdue also reviewed and analyzed the lab notebooks students produced to gain a better understanding of how students did or did not incorporate what was taught in the DIL program into their work. The results of this analysis led to a more student-driven approach to incorporating DIL into the student teams in Engineering Projects in Community Service (EPICS).

The feedback that the Bracke and Fosmire team from Purdue received helped them to determine what the agricultural and biological engineering students had learned from the experience and to define areas for further exploration. They presented their work in DIL to the associate dean of research in the College of Agriculture and received her support for additional offerings. In the spring of 2014, librarians at Purdue taught a semester-long pilot program in data management and curation for graduate students in the College of Agriculture. The program was structured in ways that allowed for student interests and needs to drive the content to be covered. In addition to being responsive to student needs, adopting a flexible structure will allow librarians to better understand questions on scope, pace, and delivery of the material.

Evaluative assessment feedback collected from students at the end of the online course helped the University of Minnesota team make some adjustments to improve the civil engineering students' experience with the online modules they developed. Students were so new to the concepts of data management that even an introductory video was confusing to them. Delivering instruction online limited contact between students and instructors, making it hard for students to ask questions or discuss difficult concepts. The Minnesota team has started offering more in-person workshops, which are very popular. Online content that was easy to procrastinate completing has now been repurposed for a hybrid online/in-person approach: video lessons are sent to students the day before the hands-on workshop in this flipped classroom approach. The online class is still available as a standalone, self-paced tutorial for those that can't come to the workshops.

After completing the training session, the Oregon team surveyed the ecology and landscape architecture faculty and students about the session to gauge overall usefulness and investigate changes in data management practices of students as an outcome. These conversations resulted in several opportunities to grow the program, including a request to teach more advanced topics to another research group, a request for a guest course lecture, and new collaborations with faculty in the chemistry department who want instruction for their research teams. Finally, the original participating faculty are now proponents of DIL instruction for incoming graduate students. With all of these opportunities, the University of Oregon team is especially interested in assessing the proper balance between making things very specific for a particular group and creating content that can be used more broadly.

Developing a Sustainable DIL Program

Building a sustainable DIL program in your library will require continued investment of time and resources. However, the skills and knowledge sets needed to teach data management are not unfamiliar to academic librarians, particularly those who have been involved with information literacy efforts previously.

We have found that the key components to grow your initial efforts into sustainable programs include the following:

- Identifying what worked well with your initial efforts
- Engaging with and obtaining the commitment of the library (particularly library liaisons) to those areas to sustain and advance your program
- Investing in scalable educational tools that can be repurposed and easily updated to meet the needs of a broad user audience

Above all, communication is essential. A campus with hundreds or even thousands of researchers presents a unique challenge for promotion and awareness of new services offered by libraries. Within academic institutions, we commonly face communication silos of collegiate, departmental, research group, and even individual, proportions. The successful DIL program requires a communications strategy that brings together the various research services offered by the libraries and promotes them in a systematic way.

Identify What Worked (and Share Successes!)

As you evaluate and reflect on your DIL program, think about what really captured people's attention and which aspects of your training were the most engaging. In some cases, there might be an academic department on campus that is already engaged in data management topics and will uniquely benefit from your DIL training program. A good example of success will help build momentum for your program, and this will become a jumping-off point for your campuswide program. Once you have an advocate or two, interview them to find out what incentives worked for them. Did they appreciate the training of their graduate students? Did they like the integration of the DIL principles in their curricula? What impact did your program have on student practices? Then use this as your "case study" when talking with other departments on campus. Tell the story of what worked with your initial cohort of students in order to demonstrate how these same principles can be expanded to the new department or discipline. Better yet, see if you can get your faculty partners or students that you taught to tell the story of your DIL program and its impact on others. Your work is likely to resonate with other faculty and students if it is conveyed by their peers.

Library Staff Engagement

To take the DIL program to a new discipline, you will likely need the buy-in and commitment of the library subject liaisons to that department. Rather than viewing the librarian liaison as the gatekeeper to that discipline, remember that he or she is your biggest resource! You cannot teach every student DIL competencies and expect to develop specialized subject knowledge in each area as well.

There are several elements to consider when engaging with your library's liaisons. First, invest in training for library staff on DIL skills. Training sessions (perhaps adapting the same DIL program that was developed for your students) should result in the library liaison obtaining a better understanding of DIL skills and, hopefully, a stronger commitment to the sharing of this knowledge. Librarians should be familiar with the DIL competencies in order for them to fully understand the benefits to their user populations.

Next, empower subject liaisons to lead the DIL efforts in their area. Library staff, particu-

larly those who are subject librarians, will be essential to reaching new user populations as information gatherers, instructors, and promotion experts. Have your library liaisons start with interviewing one or two faculty in their departments on DIL-related needs using the DIL interview protocol or other instruments, or by leading a focus group of graduate students. This information-gathering exercise will highlight the disciplinary needs for the group and empower the liaisons to take control of their users' needs.

Finally, remind staff that they don't have to start from scratch. Once their population's DIL needs are better understood, you can work with them to evaluate your existing programming and adapt the DIL training to meet the needs of their disciplines. With their subject expertise and your DIL experience, your combined efforts will enable you to scale a DIL program to a variety of disciplines on campus.

Scalable Delivery Tools

To most effectively expand your DIL program, consider educational delivery that is well documented and/or easily captured for reuse. For example, if you are teaching a workshop session, consider creating a written script and a detailed session outline that includes "stage cues" indicating any actions on the part of the instructor. This documentation, along with your presentation slides and other handouts, will allow for another individual to replicate and adapt your session more easily. For example, the University of Minnesota team created an instructor's guide to their hybrid course (available at http://z.umn.edu/teachdatamgmt) to better allow for other library liaisons, at their institution and beyond, to adapt and reuse their materials. Alternatively, your training might be captured in a digital format to scale beyond the in-person format and reach a variety of users. Recording a training session using Camtasia Relay, Jing, or a more sophisticated video recording tool will allow you to post the video to the Web or share it via e-mail. Finally, any training tools that you use should follow the same principles of data management that you are teaching. Your files should be available using open standards to allow for the broadest possible reuse. Consider including open licenses, such as Creative Commons (https://creativecommons.org/licenses/), to indicate how others (including non-librarians!) can adapt and reuse your effective training materials.

Aim High

Establish ambitious long-term goals for your program—for example, working with your institution's graduate school to have data management modules integrated into the overall orientation activities for incoming students to ensure that all students are exposed to at least the core principles. To do this, identify partners who can assist with developing resources or who can champion your cause. Locating partners such as your graduate school or your vice president for research and understanding their mission, goals, and the venues they work in, as well as the training they already provide, can help you reach beyond the libraries and truly provide institutional-level support for DIL.

CONCLUSION

We have shared our work from the DIL project with the hope that it will inspire and encourage librarians and others to take the next step in developing and implementing DIL programs of their own. We have presented this information in ways that allow for flexibility in adaptation and further development, since we know that others will continue to innovate beyond what we've talked about here. We have also included both what we did in our programs and what we would recommend based on our experiences, sharing honestly when things did not go as hoped or expected, since we want to enable people to learn from our work. Above all, we hope that this chapter is useful to you in considering how you might go about launching a successful DIL program of your own.

As DIL is still an emerging area, we encourage you to share the DIL instruction work that you do with your colleagues and peers. We need to develop a community of practice in this area and to learn from each other. Only by connecting and communicating with other initiatives—within our libraries, within our institutions, or with the broader community—can we continue to grow and build DIL in order to help prepare and educate the next generation of researchers for their professional careers. We look forward to the amazing work that you will do to help prepare the next generation by teaching them the skills they need for effective data management and curation.

REFERENCES

Corti, L., Van den Eynden, V., Bishop, L., & Wollard, M. (2014). *Managing and sharing research data: A guide to good practice*. London: Sage Publications Ltd.

Gogus, A. (2012a). Bloom's taxonomy of learning objectives. In N. M. Seel (Ed.), *Encyclopedia of the sciences of learning* (pp. 469–473) [SpringerLink version]. http://dx.doi.org/10.1007/978-1-4419-1428-6

Gogus, A. (2012b). Learning objectives. In N. M. Seel (Ed.), *Encyclopedia of the sciences of learning* (pp. 1950–1954) [SpringerLink version]. http://dx.doi.org/10.1007/978-1-4419-1428-6

Inter-University Consortium for Political and Social Research (ICPSR). (2012). *Guide to social science data preparation and archiving: Best practices throughout the data lifecycle* (5th ed.). Retrieved from http://www.icpsr.umich.edu/files/deposit /dataprep.pdf

Piwowar, H. A., Day, R. S., & Fridsma, D. B. (2007). Sharing detailed research data is associated with increased citation rate. *PLoS ONE, 2*(3), e308. http://dx.doi.org/10.1371/journal.pone .0000308

Radcliff, C. J., Jensen, M. L., Salem, J. A. Jr., Burhanna, K. J., & Gedeon, J. A. (2007). *A practical guide to information literacy assessment for academic librarians.* Westport, CT: Libraries Unlimited

Tenopir, C., Birch, B., & Allard, S. (2012). *Academic libraries and research data services: Current practices and plans for the future.* Chicago, IL: Association of College and Research Libraries.

APPENDIX: Links to Useful Resources

Because links quickly become out of date, we've chosen to provide only a small sampling of the wide range of resources that exist, particularly resources that our teams relied most heavily upon. In addition to the DIL project website, we recommend the e-Science Portal for New England Librarians (http://esciencelibrary.umassmed.edu/), particularly the DIL section (http://esciencelibrary .umassmed.edu/DIL_Home).

Resources for Learning About Faculty Needs

Interview instruments used to discuss data management needs and expectations with faculty collaborators as part of our DIL project: http://dx.doi.org/10.5703/1288284315510

Career profiles, including description of the profession, key roles and responsibilities, and how research data management figures in responsibilities; created as part of Data Management Skills Support Initiative (DaMSSI) with a focus on higher education institutions in the UK: http:// www.dcc.ac.uk/training/data-management-courses-and-training/career-profiles

Data curation profiles provide information about data management requirements as articulated by the researchers themselves; authors from universities across the United States. Data Curation Profiles Directory: http://docs.lib.purdue.edu/dcp/

Resources for Learning About Graduate Student Needs

Interview instruments used to discuss data management needs and expectations with graduate students as part of a DIL project: http://dx.doi.org/10.5703/1288284315510

Although they are more general in scope, the following reports discuss developing and offering library services for graduate students:

Lewis, V., & Moulder, C. (2008). *SPEC Kit 308: Graduate student and faculty spaces and services.* Retrieved from http://publications.arl.org/Graduate-Faculty-Spaces-Services -SPEC-Kit-308/

Covert-Vail, L., & Collard, C. (2012). *New roles for new times: Research library services for graduate students.* Retrieved from http://www.arl.org/storage/documents/publications /nrnt-grad-roles-20dec12.pdf

Resources for Exploring Assessment
General Assessment Resources

Cornell University Center for Teaching Excellence's Setting Learning Outcomes (http://cte.cornell .edu/teaching-ideas/designing-your-course/settting-learning-outcomes.html) and Assessing Student Learning (http://cte.cornell.edu/teaching-ideas/assessing-student-learning/index.html) are good introductions to developing learning outcomes for instruction and to general course and program-level assessment. You may have similar guidance at your institution.

University of Illinois at Urbana-Champaign University Library's Tips on Writing Learning Outcomes (http://www.library.illinois.edu/infolit/learningoutcomes.html) provides a quick guide to the definition and creation of learning outcomes for information literacy assessment.

Assessment and evaluation site from Purdue University's Center for Instructional Excellence (http://www.purdue.edu/cie/teachingtips/assessment_evaluation/index.html) differentiates between assessment and evaluation and provides useful resources and tips.

This book is an excellent introduction to and reference on general information literacy assessment: Radcliff, C. J., Jensen, M. L., Salem, J. A. Jr., Burhanna, K. J., & Gedeon, J. A. (2007). *A practical guide to information literacy assessment for academic librarians.* Westport, CT: Libraries Unlimited.

Classroom Assessment Test Resources

(Including the 1-minute paper exercise many of the teams used, and many more.)

The following is a classic resource on assessing student learning in the higher education classroom.
Angelo, T. A., & Cross, K. P. (1993). *Classroom assessment techniques: A handbook for college teachers.* San Francisco: Jossey-Bass.

The following article details three approaches to information literacy assessment (fixed-choice tests, performance assessments, and rubrics) and their theoretical backgrounds, benefits, and drawbacks.
Oakleaf, M. (2008). Dangers and opportunities: A conceptual map of information literacy assessment approaches. *portal: Libraries and the Academy, 8*(3), 233–253.

The following online sources provide a quick definition and several generally applicable classroom assessment techniques (CATs) for evaluating course outcomes, attitudes, values, self-awareness and instruction:
George Washington University's Teaching & Learning Collaborative: http://tlc.provost.gwu.edu/classroom-assessment-techniques

Virginia Commonwealth University's Center for Teaching Excellence: http://www.vcu.edu/cte/resources/cat/index.htm

Iowa State University's Center for Excellence in Learning and Teaching: http://www.celt.iastate.edu/teaching/cat.html

Field-tested learning assessment guide (FLAG) for science, math, engineering, and technology instructors' Classroom assessment techniques (CATs)—overview provides peer-reviewed classroom assessment techniques as well as tips on their use by faculty members in the STEM disciplines: http://www.flaguide.org/cat/cat.php

Resources for Building Course Content

The University of Minnesota's online and hybrid course content is available for reuse and adaptation. There is also an instructor's guide that walks through the pacing of the course, plus links to handouts and activities used in the in-person session. http://z.umn.edu/teachdatamgmt

The New England Collaborative Data Management Curriculum (NECDMC) was put together by the Lamar Soutter Library at the University of Massachusetts Medical School in collaboration with libraries from several other institutions. The curriculum can be used to teach data management best practices to undergraduates, graduate students, and researchers in STEM disciplines. http://library.umassmed.edu/necdmc/index

Education Modules developed by DataONE (Data Observation Network for Earth). Education modules are CC0—No rights reserved, but DataONE asks that users cite DataONE and appreciates feedback. http://www.dataone.org/education-modules

ICPSR (Inter-university Consortium for Political and Social Research) published *Guide to Social Science Data Preparation and Archiving,* which is a thorough introduction to data management best practices in the social sciences. http://www.icpsr.umich.edu/icpsrweb/content/deposit/guide/index.html

MANTRA research data management has online training designed by the University of Edinburgh for "PhD students and others who are planning a research project using digital data." http://datalib.edina.ac.uk/mantra/index.html

CHAPTER **10**

WHERE DO WE GO FROM HERE?

Further Developing the the Data Information Literacy Competencies

Megan Sapp Nelson, Purdue University

INTRODUCTION

Chapter 1 provided a description of the DIL competencies as they were initially conceived (Carlson, Fosmire, Miller, & Sapp Nelson, 2011). Chapter 3 discussed how the competencies were modified and used as a means of gathering information for the DIL project. A primary objective of the DIL project was to create instructional interventions based on these competencies and to explore data-related educational needs within the lab environment. Faculty partners informed this process through in-depth interviews and by responding to the instruction proposed.

As we were conducting the DIL project we recognized a need for continued development of the DIL competencies. Through the interviews, faculty responded to the competencies in light of their own experiences of data management. For each specific competency faculty interviewees were asked, "Are there any skills that are not listed in this competency that you think should be included?" The responses provided guidance for how the DIL competencies might be enhanced, altered, or removed altogether in future versions.

This chapter explores the faculty-proposed changes to the DIL competencies, which are listed here in an order that follows an approximate relationship to the data life cycle.

- Discovery and acquisition of data
- Databases and data formats
- Data conversion and interoperability
- Data processing and analysis
- Data visualization and representation
- Data management and organization
- Data quality and documentation
- Metadata and data description
- Cultures of practice

- Ethics and attribution
- Data curation and reuse
- Data preservation

Following the suggested changes and a discussion on their implications, this chapter will describe future research areas that would enhance understanding of disciplinary practices and curriculum design for these competencies.

DISCOVERY AND ACQUISITION OF DATA

Skills in this competency include the following:

- Locates and utilizes disciplinary data repositories
- Evaluates the quality of the data available from external sources
- Not only identifies appropriate external data sources, but also imports data and converts it when necessary so it can be used locally

Students need critical thinking skills and techniques to retrieve data from a source external to the research laboratory or classroom. Generally, interviewees agreed with the content of the skills list presented in the interview, with a few exceptions. One faculty member focused on using critical thinking to evaluate the contents of an externally produced data set for quality. The faculty member did not describe the actual metrics by which an individual evaluates data quality. However, the need for metrics was implied.

> I think also, the skill to evaluate the quality of data. It's very easy for anyone to publish data

online and very often when we get it, it's not very useful. So we need to look at this and make a decision and say, "Okay. It's helpful for us," or "It's not useful."

—ELECTRICAL AND COMPUTER ENGINEERING
FACULTY MEMBER

Another interviewee agreed that an "appropriate level of skepticism of outside data sources" was important. He explained:

Know your source; know your quality, particularly when we're working with remote sensing GIS data sets. Just understand that they're inaccurate, there's no way around it.

—AGRICULTURAL AND BIOLOGICAL
ENGINEERING FACULTY MEMBER

This revealed the need for analytical thinking around quality for a specific type of data: GIS (geographic information system). And it raised the question of whether different data types require different metrics of quality and whether they already exist within disciplines. If so, knowledge of the existence of disciplinary measures of data set quality may be an appropriate addition to the *discovery and acquisition of data* competency.

Faculty also raised a concern about negotiating access to externally acquired data sets.

To evaluate a hypothesis, you need to find data. Data sets like this are not going to be available, so really what you need to be able to do is to understand how to create this data and then to figure out who has the ability to create this data and then who has the authority to allow you access to the data. This is the kind of thing that I would be involved in. My students would figure out how to create the data,

and then I would be figuring out who has the ability to collect it and who has the authority to give us the data. And then talking with . . . [the data producers] about how to generate this data, whether they're open to it, and how to generate this data in a way that doesn't impact their business and doesn't expose the privacy of anything that they care about.

—ELECTRICAL AND COMPUTER ENGINEERING
FACULTY MEMBER

This faculty member identified that needed data may not be publicly accessible. To intuit who might create data, to make inquiries into the existence of the data, and to negotiate access to the data is a complex access process. Extensive knowledge of the literature, the discipline, and institutional structures to identify those who may be collecting data and an introduction to basic usage agreement terms may be appropriate additions to the *discovery and acquisition of data* competency.

DATABASES AND DATA FORMATS

Skills in this competency may include the following:

- Understands the concept of relational databases and how to query those databases
- Becomes familiar with standard data formats and types for the discipline
- Understands which formats and data types are appropriate for different research questions

The critique of the *databases and data formats* competency included a related skills list for this area. The comments focused on decision making in the design of databases.

The thing that I don't really see included here is an understanding of some of the implications of the different types of databases. . . . There are several different database products, and within those database products there are usually multiple database engines. So, for example, in MySQL you have a choice between the ISAM engine and an[. . .]other one. But one has higher data integrity and is sort of more enterprise ready but requires more memory. So the other one is the default installed engine for MySQL, because it is a lower resource usage.

—ELECTRICAL AND COMPUTER ENGINEERING
FACULTY MEMBER

This reflection implies the need for nuanced understanding of the strengths and weaknesses of database products and programming languages. It appears that graduate students and faculty researchers use disciplinary expertise, technical information, and research planning and vision to create criteria by which to judge the most appropriate database products and features that will contribute to an efficient, successful research project. The "development of criteria for decision making" may be an overarching competency in DIL, related to the need for critical thinking throughout the research life cycle. Another issue was the time students have to develop these skills.

Capabilities for statistical analysis are a little weak. And there are courses they can take on campus for the statistical and the relational databases, so maybe it's something that we should be requiring. The problem is that if they're going to do a Master's thesis, they take only seven courses. Two of them have to be outside of the department, so I guess . . . we could ask to make sure that one of those is either a database course or a statistical analysis course.

—CIVIL ENGINEERING FACULTY MEMBER

"Critical thinking about the development of building a database" was also reported as a needed enhancement of the DIL competencies.

For my discipline at least, understanding those concepts of how to build a good database would be important in addition to simply knowing how to create tables and querying. And maybe that's implied by "concept of relational databases," but to me it wasn't there.

—ELECTRICAL AND COMPUTER ENGINEERING
FACULTY MEMBER

In this case, critical thinking applies to the design of the database. This faculty interviewee called for the addition of "best practices of database design" to the *databases and data formats* competency. This may result in knowledge of the most appropriate, efficient ways to program a database.

Enhanced decision making and critical thinking skills were a necessary addition when choosing appropriate file formats for a given research project.

I would add to this the skill of understanding the advantages of different types of formats of files. This issue of knowing text files are human readable but not necessarily computer readable; XML files on the other hand are computer readable but bloated and inefficient; binary files are [at risk for having] insufficient documentation of their format, but are generally most efficient. If you're going to work with text files, you have choices. You can do delimiting between fields; you can have things in front that tell you how long fields are. Students must understand the trad-eoffs in using files in these ways and how it makes them easier or harder to work with.

—ELECTRICAL AND COMPUTER ENGINEERING
FACULTY MEMBER

Again, the necessity of picking the best tool for the job—this time for choosing file formats—is an important addition. This faculty interviewee considered critically analyzing strengths and weaknesses of available formats and understanding and predicting the consequences of the choice of file format for the long-term management of the research project to be a foundational skill. This choice represents a key decision in the research process that can have impact throughout the research life cycle. Helping students to identify those key decisions and make wise choices for their research can be addressed through the DIL competencies by including "the development of standard operating procedures or decision matrixes."

DATA CONVERSION AND INTEROPERABILITY

Skills in this competency include the following:

- Is proficient in migrating data from one format to another.
- Understands the risks and potential loss or corruption of information caused by changing data formats.
- Understands the benefits of making data available in standard formats to facilitate downstream use.

For the faculty interviewees, this was an area that was crucial but not as explicit as they would have liked. Faculty interviewees focused on the regular replacement of versions of software that leads to problems for future use of data.

[Students need an] understanding that formats like Microsoft Word .doc files are specific and proprietary to Microsoft and that there is a need to store those in some format which you can be certain that you can open again later. The problem with .doc files is that the only reliable way to open them is to use the version of Word that created them. If that version of Word becomes outdated or runs on machines that are too old, then you never know what you're going to get.

—ELECTRICAL AND COMPUTER ENGINEERING
FACULTY MEMBER

The concepts of "format obsolescence" and "changes to software over time" need to be addressed in the DIL competency skills list.

There was concern that students do not think critically about the impact data conversion has on the contents of the data. While the competency did address this, faculty interviewees specifically identified student data as potentially problematic because students tended to made conversions without fully understanding the ramifications. One interviewee went so far as to say:

I don't know that students are aware that they tend to have more faith in their data than I do.

—AGRICULTURAL AND BIOLOGICAL
ENGINEERING FACULTY MEMBER

The revelation that data conversion may call into question the quality of data ties to the need for students to "think critically throughout the data management process" and "recognize the implications of their decisions."

DATA PROCESSING AND ANALYSIS

Skills in this competency include the following:

- Is familiar with the basic data processing and analysis tools and techniques of the discipline or research area
- Understands the effect that these tools may have on the data
- Uses appropriate workflow management tools to automate repetitive analysis of data

The DIL competencies as originally proposed did not mention *programming* explicitly. In the eyes of faculty interviewees, this was an area that needed to be included.

> [I would add] . . . these quantitative tools that I mentioned about using programming languages and knowing how to automate. Scripts in R, for instance. We're doing a lot of that in my lab now.
> —Ecology/landscape architecture faculty member

For the faculty interviewees, the success of a student relies on efficient and proficient use of scripting and programming to process data. One of the faculty members we interviewed highlighted one student who was an excellent data manager because of excellent programming abilities, which allowed him to process data quickly and efficiently through the use of scripting.

A major aspect of being an excellent programmer is the ability to learn new languages and techniques for the processing of data and then implement those techniques in an appropriate way.

> So the other piece is learning how to learn new techniques, right? How to go to the lit-

erature, how to go to the web, how to pick up and teach yourself new tools.
> —Ecology/landscape architecture faculty member

This "lifelong learning ability" (to understand and add tools to a personal research repertoire) facilitates the graduate student's ability to manage research data. The need for lifelong learning skills is imperative for all disciplines in scientific research, but it is rarely explicit. The need for making this long-term acquisition of skills apparent and built into the research experience and courses emerged consistently across the interviews.

> Certainly most . . . basic use of the tools [is learned] in a statistics class or a methodology class or something like that. But to me what happens is that . . . [students] tend to learn fairly basic application in those classes and then the transference of learning those tools to applying them toward a specific research project, critically, are very different skills. And they get that mostly in one-on-one mentorship. . . . I mean any faculty member working with a graduate student on their thesis. To me, that's the mentorship.
> —Ecology/landscape architecture faculty member

Some faculty expressed concern that analysis tools changed the data. A faculty interviewee was adamant that students understand that raw data should be kept in an unaltered state.

> I mean, we don't change the data. Once the data is there, I don't want them changing the data. . . . This is very important.
> —Natural resources faculty member

The researchers alter and analyze data sets, but the raw data should be preserved. "Keeping the raw data" should be added to this competency to underpin conversion and interoperability.

DATA VISUALIZATION AND REPRESENTATION

Skills in this competency include the following:

- Proficiently uses basic visualization tools of discipline
- Avoids misleading or ambiguous representations when presenting data in tables, charts, diagrams, and so forth
- Chooses the appropriate type of visualization, such as maps, graphs, animations, or videos, based on an understanding of the reason/purpose for visualizing or displaying data

Data visualization and representation received the most feedback by far. Faculty agreed that this was a fundamental competency for which the vast majority of graduate students needed to develop advanced skill sets.

> I'd say it's essential because it's communication. If we don't communicate, we haven't done much in the long run.
>
> —ECOLOGY/LANDSCAPE ARCHITECTURE
> FACULTY MEMBER

The suggestions fell into a broad spectrum of interests and concerns. A frequent refrain was the need to identify data that tell a story.

> "Avoids misleading or ambiguous representations when presenting data," I'd also put in there saying what data not to show.
>
> —ELECTRICAL AND COMPUTER ENGINEERING
> FACULTY MEMBER

> I would say the thing that I don't see here that's most important is being able to evaluate, "Does this graph show what I expected it to show?"
>
> —ELECTRICAL AND COMPUTER ENGINEERING
> FACULTY MEMBER

For a graduate student to gain this competency, he or she must have a clear understanding of what to communicate, and then, what the visualization is actually communicating. Critical analysis identifies which data fields heighten understanding or increase explication of the findings. This necessitates a higher level of understanding about the content of the data set and the research project as a whole.

Faculty interviewees took that need for critical thinking further, to address the use of data visualizations to make conclusions that are valid.

> I think some of these ideas are introduced in courses and probably they see it in practice. I think it is something—at a basic level—used within the discipline. But I don't think that the part of understanding how these [visualizations] can be used to support the decision making process [is present]. And that may be a skill—you know—of connecting it to that. So if they understand the reason or purpose for visualizing, then [they can] utilize . . . [visualizations] in support of making decisions.
>
> —ELECTRICAL AND COMPUTER ENGINEERING
> FACULTY MEMBER

The need for informed decision making based upon visualization and representation again ties to the need for critical thinking across the data life cycle. In this case, critical thinking extends to asking questions of the data for the purpose of understanding it and making informed decisions.

Finally, the concept of students "learning multiple representation tools and choosing the most appropriate tool for the story they wish to tell" was a necessary addition to the DIL competency.

> I wish my graduate students had much more background in a broader array of representational tools[,] . . . [like] the students I teach in landscape architecture. We teach them those skills explicitly in our coursework; we spend huge amounts of time. We teach them representation. We have courses where they learn that it's not just a media skill, but . . . [they] are representing information and data, and how to do that compellingly. The science students get very little of that.
>
> —Ecology/landscape architecture faculty member

The idea that successful future scientists need new media skills is an area in which there is a need for additional research before proposing revisions to the competencies. The DIL project has just scratched the surface of the needs in visualization.

DATA MANAGEMENT AND ORGANIZATION

Skills in this competency include the following:

- Understands the life cycle of data, develops data management plans, and keeps track of the relation of subsets or processed data to the original data sets
- Creates standard operating procedures for data management and documentation

This competency was generally supported by the faculty interviewees.

> I'd say part of the standard operating procedures are to have very high levels of annotation, whether it be in your programming files or in your data sets themselves about what the data is, what the units are, when it was collected, where there might be errors. I mean I keep extensive records of my own notes so that at the end, I look back and I've crossed off every single thing I've needed to do for every single line of data. I don't think most students are that thorough.
>
> —Ecology/landscape architecture faculty member

However, establishing best practices and using them presented a difficulty arising from the lack of consensus regarding what the best practices entail.

> When you say "utilizes best practices and understands the importance of frequently updating their understanding of what best practices are," in order to do that, one has to have readily available sources that tell you what they are.
>
> —Ecology/landscape architecture faculty member

Standard operating procedures vary across disciplinary practice and research methodology. Designing and consistently using a standard operating procedure requires in-depth knowledge of how the different types of equipment and techniques used within the laboratory impact the collection of data. This systems thinking may be intuitive to the faculty interviewees. However, it is unclear how graduate students design research methodologies that may be based on an entire laboratory of methodologies and equipment without documentation about those environments. This need for specifying not only what skills the graduate students need, but also at what point in their research careers they are likely to learn these skills, points to a larger issue—namely that not all data competencies may be needed or learned during the graduate research phase of a scientific researcher's career.

DATA QUALITY AND DOCUMENTATION

Skills in this competency include the following:

- Recognizes, documents, and resolves any apparent artifacts, incompletion, or corruption of data
- Utilizes metadata to facilitate an understanding of potential problems with data sets
- Documents data sufficiently to enable reproduction of research results and data by others
- Tracks data provenance and clearly delineates and denotes versions of a data set

Few faculty interviewees wanted to augment or change this area. In one case, however, the faculty member sought to clarify a type of documentation that he felt was important but was not referenced in the DIL competencies. The need for a "story" of the changes that a data set goes through was the primary concern.

> *Interviewer:* So you're saying that the amount of documentation and description is good for your purposes—you can get a sense of what they're doing—but it wouldn't be enough for someone else outside of your lab to make sense of it. What is the gap there? What would be needed for somebody else to understand?
>
> *Faculty:* I think in my lab we have a cumulative knowledge. So from the beginning,

we know . . . for example, that we have a research proposal. So we know the basic idea of what we want to do. And then we do some experiments and then the next experiment, we write the difference from the previous one. Then, so if you accumulate knowledge, then you understand the difference. Then you look at something and say, "Okay, I understand where it comes from." But for somebody else, just by looking at the difference, it does not make enough sense. . . . To understand what this means. Unless you understand the history.

> —Exchange with electrical and computer engineering faculty member

A major concern of professors was that individuals outside their laboratory may misunderstand, misrepresent, or misuse their data, if shared. The importance of providing not simply the context for an individual data set but also the context for the data set in relation to the entire project is a nuanced change that needs to be included in the competencies.

Another nuance regarding data quality and documentation is the use of externally written documentation (such as documentation for a software programming language) when creating new data products. Particularly with the reuse of software code, faculty found that the successful use of outside documentation is a necessary skill for students. The use of outside documentation reflects the need to establish the context of the production of a new data object, regardless of the origin of those context documents.

> Maybe include outside documentation. This seems to imply that it's all about organizing the data itself, putting things in the data. But I've found oftentimes outside documentation

is actually . . . more helpful than just looking at code.

—Electrical and computer engineering
faculty member

"Knowledge of tools to assist with the creation of documentation" was brought up as a necessary addition, particularly in the context of software developers. For specific software programming languages, there are software tools that collate and/or create documentation from the software as it is written.

METADATA AND DATA DESCRIPTION

Skills in this competency include the following:

- Understands the rationale for metadata and proficiently annotates and describes data so it can be understood and used by self and others
- Develops the ability to read and interpret metadata from external disciplinary sources
- Understands the structure and purpose of ontologies in facilitating better sharing of data

Metadata and data description were generally accepted as necessary, but not very well understood, aspects of data management by the faculty interviewees. While the competencies as written were generally held to be accurate by the faculty, one interviewee felt that an even more basic need existed.

Almost maybe even a basic level of understanding the rationale for metadata, but even just . . . a basic understanding, basic knowledge of [the concept of] metadata. And examples.

—Electrical and computer engineering
faculty member

The authors of the competencies assumed that there was a need for all graduate students to understand that such a thing as metadata exists, that it provides some basic level of function to a data set, and that it can be useful during research projects. However, this assumption may have been unrealistic.

In the GIS world, you're at the mercy of other people's data. You're the beneficiary and at their mercy. I don't know how many students go into metadata. I mean certainly when I was learning it until probably like four or five years ago, I didn't go into the metadata that much. But I now use it as the source to describe what I think about this data, what are the caveats to it.

—Ecology/landscape architecture
faculty member

This concept may be outside of graduate students' previous experiences with data management. A missing step might be to explain what metadata is and why it is useful.

CULTURES OF PRACTICE

Skills in this competency include the following:

- Recognizes the practices, values, and norms of his or her chosen field, discipline, or subdiscipline as they relate to managing, sharing, curating, and preserving data
- Recognizes relevant data standards of his or her field (e.g., metadata, quality, formatting) and understands how these standards are applied

There were mixed responses to this competency. No one rejected or augmented any of the skills listed. However, many of the respondents focused on the idea that cultures of practice remained unformed within their discipline. Even so, some thought that it was important.

> This is really important, and I think that it's such a changing target right now. I think it's the journal requirements and the funding requirements that are making it important and making it essential. . . . They're absolutely right to do so.
> —Ecology/landscape architecture
> faculty member

But respondents were unclear as to what comprised *cultures of practice*. The ecology/landscape architecture faculty member went on to say: "But it's something that most of us are ill-prepared for. We're just sort of like, 'Oh, okay. What do we do?' And we ourselves have had very little training in this."

On the other hand, one faculty member described this as not being critical for the students to do their work.

> It's probably . . . you know, they can do their work without understanding this. It's not essential that they have this. It's best if they do, but they don't. I convey it to them just simply through our discussions of what we're doing, why we're doing it, and so on. I guess I could be doing more, but we don't talk about all of these functions. I mean we talk about some of them, but not all of them.
> —Civil engineering faculty member

Given this lack of clarity with a simultaneous indication of importance, this competency needs to be investigated further. It is unclear that the definition of *cultures of practice* proposed is reflective of current scientific research practice.

> I don't even know if there are practices, values, and norms. I would love . . . guidance.

So the question is, do our graduate students know these things? I mean, I'm between "I don't know" to "I guess," because we've sort of ignored it. . . . So I'm not sure which is the right way to frame that. But no, we're clueless about this. How's that?
> —Natural resources faculty member

ETHICS AND ATTRIBUTION

Skills in this competency include the following:

- Develops an understanding of intellectual property, privacy and confidentiality issues, and the ethos of the discipline when it comes to sharing and administering data
- Acknowledges data from external sources appropriately
- Avoids misleading or ambiguous representations when presenting data

The *ethics and attribution* competency briefly mentions intellectual property. This emerged as a problem. Given the complex nature of intellectual property in the research software field, a faculty interviewee spelled out what a graduate student who creates software should know about intellectual property.

> *Interviewer:* What do you think your graduate students should know regarding intellectual property and these sorts of issues?
> *Faculty:* There are two answers to that. My first answer is that he shouldn't worry about it. As a Ph.D. student, he should focus on doing the research and publishing that research and graduating. Now, clearly that answer is not complete, because it ignores all of the problems that come with ignoring intellectual property and it got us to where we are today. But that is probably what's best for him

in the short-term. Second, what is best for the lawyers especially who will have to help us deal with it if we ever had to deal with it, is for him to understand that when he's working on something he needs to be cognizant of whose resources is he using, who is paying for his time, and who currently owns what he is doing. Right, so he should be aware of Purdue's policies on work that he's doing and who owns the work that he's doing.
—ELECTRICAL AND COMPUTER ENGINEERING
FACULTY MEMBER

The faculty interviewee was ambivalent about the utility of this type of knowledge to a student while explicitly listing this as a skill that the student needed to successfully manage data. There was an acknowledgment that lack of knowledge of intellectual property issues can lead to problems of data management. However, this took time that in the professor's viewpoint needed to be spent on primary research and the development of a dissertation project. This ambivalence is representative of how faculty members felt about a number of DIL competencies. They listed many as very important or essential while simultaneously agonizing about how little time was available to teach students the competencies while meeting research deadlines.

The same faculty interviewee clarified the reference to patents in the *ethics and attribution* list.

They should probably be taught the pros and cons of patents on hardware and software and inventions and what that means. And given the concept of what it means to invent something. They should understand something about this issue of "first to invent" versus "first to file" and therefore the importance of documenting everything that you think

of. Although, did the system change? It used be first to invent, and I think it may have switched to first to file?
—ELECTRICAL AND COMPUTER ENGINEERING
FACULTY MEMBER

It is clear that the proposed competency is important but that more detail would reflect a nuanced understanding of the needs of graduate students as they transition to researchers. Disciplinary researchers are sometimes unclear themselves on the terms and conditions under which it is important to file for patents. This is a clear opportunity in which libraries may contribute to the DIL of graduate students. Patent librarians and copyright librarians both have expertise to teach developing researchers in these areas.

DATA CURATION AND REUSE

Skills in this competency include the following:

- Recognizes that data may have value beyond the original purpose, to validate research, or for use by others
- Is able to distinguish which elements of a data set are likely to have future value for self and for others
- Understands that curating data is a complex, often costly endeavor that is nonetheless vital to community-driven e-research
- Recognizes that data must be prepared for its eventual curation at its creation and throughout its life cycle
- Articulates the planning and activities needed to enable data curation, both generally and within his or her local practice

- Understands how to cite data as well as how to make his or her data citable

Interviewees commented that they were satisfied with the list as it was given; however, faculty might perceive this topic to be outside of their domain. One faculty member commented: "So, what is data curation?" This needs to be explored with a broader group of disciplinary faculty members.

DATA PRESERVATION

Skills in this competency include the following:

- Recognizes the benefits and costs of data preservation
- Understands the technology, resources, and organizational components of preserving data
- Utilizes best practices in preparing data for its eventual preservation during its active life cycle
- Articulates the potential long-term value of his or her data for self or others and is able to determine an appropriate preservation time frame
- Understands the need to develop preservation policies and is able to identify the core elements of such policies

Interviewees rarely augmented the topic of data preservation. Faculty were less experienced with it. The few critiques elucidate possible ways of describing the competency that researchers may respond to more readily.

The only thing I'd add to this, when you say "utilizes best practices and understands the importance of frequently updating their understanding of what best practices are . . ."

well, in order to do that, one has to have readily available sources that tell you what they are.

—ECOLOGY/LANDSCAPE ARCHITECTURE
FACULTY MEMBER

Another faculty member focused in on the long-term, local reuse of the data by

making sure that any data that you care about is accessible, is replicated, and is in a format that you can still read.

—ELECTRICAL AND COMPUTER ENGINEERING
FACULTY MEMBER

This response covered several DIL competencies. However, it shows the crucial interconnectedness of data curation, reuse, and preservation in the mind of this faculty member. The roughly linear format in which we presented the competencies did not show their actual roles and interplays. Presenting them in a format that shows their interconnectedness may encourage researchers to perceive them differently.

FURTHER DEVELOPING THE DATA INFORMATION LITERACY COMPETENCIES

The need for critical thinking as a necessary precursor to decision making about research projects and for the design of new research projects emerged as a strong theme. Critical thinking is a fundamental trait of an information literate individual (ACRL, 2014). The heavy focus by the faculty interviewees on this higher order thinking ability implies a need that is not present consistently among graduate students. There is a need for studies on how to instill critical thinking around data management. This would provide welcome insight into a crucial facet of data management that builds a well-rounded scientist, as well as an information literate individual.

Further investigation is needed into whether critical thinking about data management is necessary in disciplines outside of science, technology, engineering, and mathematics (STEM), or if this emphasis is a manifestation of the scientific method that underpins research in the STEM disciplines. Extending DIL to include social scientists and humanities researchers would elucidate whether the need for critical thinking skills with regard to data is truly universal.

The primary addition identified for specific competencies was that of visualization skills. A variety of questions arose as fruitful areas of future study:

- Do all graduate students in the sciences need data visualization skills, or only students in selected disciplines?
- Are there visualization skills or tools that are most appropriate in specific disciplines?
- Do scientific disciplines now prize visualization to the point that credit courses in visualization are logical additions to scientific graduate curricula?
- What role can visualization training play in creating a successful scientist in the long term?

These are areas of investigation that could have long-term impact on professional success for scientists.

The developers of the DIL competencies explored the broad range of competencies STEM researchers need to be successful in working with data. There is a need for investigation regarding how these competencies may be strategically embedded across higher education, from undergraduate programs, into graduate school, and even into postdoctoral programs. Identifying those skills that are appropriate at all stages of the developing researcher's career would help in planning to introduce skills "just in time" and in personally meaningful ways to students.

The next step for this research is curriculum mapping: to identify, within an undergraduate or a graduate curriculum, the courses that are logical places to introduce basic concepts of data management into the curriculum (Harden, 2001). The DIL competencies presume a basic understanding of data management concepts. However, the current curricula in most disciplines do not introduce these basic concepts systematically and progressively. Using educational techniques such as scaffolding, which would incorporate elements of data management bit by bit (Dennen, 2004), from the beginning of undergraduate curricula could help graduate students have stronger preparation for their research responsibilities.

The limitation of the research was the narrow scope of interviews and disciplines asked to respond to the competencies. Intended to be an initial foray into faculty reactions to the competencies and a few ways to teach them to graduate students, the project included only a small number of STEM disciplines. A necessary next step will be to get feedback from many more faculty on their perception of the relevance, utility, and accuracy of the competency list.

REFERENCES

Association of College and Research Libraries (ACRL). (2014). Information literacy competency standards for higher education. Retrieved from http://www.ala.org/acrl/standards/information literacycompetency

Dennen, V. P. (2004). Cognitive apprenticeship in educational practice: Research on scaffolding, modeling, mentoring, and coaching as instructional strategies. *Handbook of Research on Educational Communications and Technology,* 813–828. Retrieved from http://www.aect.org /edtech/ed1/31.pdf

Carlson, J., Fosmire, M., Miller, C. C., & Sapp Nelson, M. (2011). Determining data information literacy needs: A study of students and research faculty. *portal: Libraries & the Academy, 11*(2), 629–657. http://dx.doi.org/10.1353/pla .2011.0022

Harden, R. M. (2001). AMEE guide no. 21: Curriculum mapping: a tool for transparent and authentic teaching and learning. *Medical Teacher, 23*(2), 123–137.

CHAPTER 11

FUTURE DIRECTIONS FOR DATA INFORMATION LITERACY

Growing Programs and Communities of Practice

Jake Carlson, University of Michigan

INTRODUCTION

This chapter articulates future directions in advancing the practice of data information literacy (DIL). Beyond further defining the 12 DIL competencies, which is the subject of the previous chapter, I focus on the development of a strong community of practice in this area. Here I examine two sources of information in determining what these next steps could be: the established information literacy community of practice and the emerging community engaged in DIL. Librarians interested in furthering DIL could learn a lot from information literacy, particularly in the questions and challenges that they have addressed over the years. In the first part of this chapter, I examine the recently released draft of the Association of College and Research Libraries' (ACRL's) framework for information literacy and some of the literature produced by information literacy experts for insight. Next, I turn to transcripts from the discussions that took place at the DIL Symposium held in 2013 at Purdue University. The symposium was attended by more than 80 librarians, holding positions mostly in data services or information literacy, to explore roles, responsibilities, and approaches for librarians in teaching data competencies. Many insights for future directions came out of the symposium that could provide an agenda for growth.

EXPLORING DATA INFORMATION LITERACY THROUGH THE LENS OF INFORMATION LITERACY

One of the central strategies of the DIL project was to leverage the investments made by the library community in understanding and responding to information literacy. The DIL case studies illustrated how we informed our work through the lens of information literacy. However, there are many additional avenues for exploring potential linkages between information literacy and DIL.

This is an interesting time to examine how information literacy might inform and propel DIL forward as information literacy itself is undergoing a transition. In the year 2000, the Association of College and Research Libraries (ACRL) released *Information Literacy Competency Standards for Higher Education,* which has largely defined how information literacy has been understood and practiced in academic libraries in the 21st century (Bell, 2013). In 2011 ACRL launched a task force to review the standards to explore whether a revision was needed to better reflect current thinking on information literacy. The changes recommended by the task force included broadening the definition to include other types of literacies and creating a framework to connect these literacies, acknowledging affective and emotion-based learning outcomes rather than focusing exclusively on cognitive outcomes, and recognizing students as content creators and curators (ACRL Information Literacy Competency Standards Review Task Force, 2012). ACRL formed the Information Literacy Competency Standards for Higher Education Taskforce (http://www.ala.org/acrl/aboutacrl/directoryofleadership/taskforces/acr-tfilcshe) and charged them with updating these standards. This taskforce has released multiple drafts over the course of 2014. The new framework for information literacy is still in a period of review as of this writing. The quotes and observations made in this chapter are based on the June 2014 iteration and may not be reflective of the final document (http://acrl.ala.org/ilstandards/wp-content/uploads/2014/02/Framework-for-IL-for-HE-Draft-2.pdf).

A major shift in the "Framework for Information Literacy for Higher Education" document is how it approaches information literacy. Rather than prescribing a set of expected outcomes, the framework focuses on identifying and connecting core concepts as well as encouraging flexible implementations. This new framework for information literacy rests on threshold concepts. The June 2014 iteration of the framework document describes threshold concepts as "those ideas in any discipline that are passageways or portals to enlarged understanding or ways of thinking and practicing within that discipline" (ACRL, 2014, p. 1 of Draft 2). From this perspective, information literacy becomes much more nuanced in implementation rather than teaching broadly defined skills to students through a one-size-fits-all approach.

Using informed learning as its foundation, the ACRL (2014) framework document defines information literacy as

> a repertoire of understandings, practices, and dispositions focused on flexible engagement with the information ecosystem, underpinned by critical self-reflection. The repertoire involves finding, evaluating, interpreting, managing, and using information to answer questions and develop new ones; and creating new knowledge through ethical participation in communities of learning, scholarship, and practice. (p. 2 of Draft 2)

Another approach to information literacy that has gained attention is that of informed learning. Informed learning, as articulated by Bruce (2008), recognizes that "teaching and learning must bring about new ways of experiencing and using information and engage students with information practices that are relevant to their discipline or profession" (pp. viii–ix). A central component of informed learning is looking at not only what people learn, but also, how they learn it.

Data Information Literacy and Information Ecosystems

There are strong alignments between informed learning, ACRL's proposed framework for information literacy, and the DIL project. The DIL project was predicated on our developing an understanding of the contexts and environments in which the faculty and graduate students worked. This included the environmental scans and literature reviews conducted by each of the five DIL project teams to identify how and to what extent selected fields of study discuss issues relating to the 12 DIL competencies. It included gathering information about the structure and operation of the research lab in which the data were generated, and how the students we intended to teach used data. Through engaging in these activities, we constructed a preliminary understanding of the "information ecosystem" of our students and were able to align our educational programs with disciplinary and local cultures of practice.

However, there are many additional avenues for further exploration in understanding the information ecosystems as they pertain to students' work and experiences with research data. Our interviews revealed that the educational experiences of students on data management and curation were often informal, uneven, and experiential. Therefore, a student's information ecosystem, as it pertained to data, was likely to be ill-defined at best. Our exploration into disciplinary and local information ecosystems of research data was primarily intended to inform the development of our educational programs. More research into information ecosystems as a foundation for generating, processing, analyzing, applying and disseminating research—and how these ecosystems are understood and practiced from the point of view of students and faculty—would help librarians respond effectively to opportunities and needs.

Data Information Literacy and the Challenge of Context

Some research on information literacy postulates that an individual's approach to information literacy is informed by his or her views of teaching, learning, and information literacy generally, which are adopted implicitly or explicitly in different contexts (Bruce, Edwards, & Lupton, 2006). This finding on the importance of how learning is experienced and the effect of context on the efficacy of information literacy has implications for DIL.

Each of the five DIL teams operated in a different context and, as a result, each crafted different approaches for planning and implementing programs. Two case studies operated in a classroom setting. The Cornell University team created a stand-alone mini-course for credit, and the University of Minnesota team developed a hybrid program with an initial in-person session and then online learning modules. The three other case studies took place "in context," either within the laboratory or in the field. The Carlson and Sapp Nelson team from Purdue University worked on-site as embedded librarians in a lab. The Bracke and Fosmire team from Purdue offered a series of workshops in the lab space of the faculty partner. The team from the University of Oregon offered their program during a regular meeting of the faculty's research team. Each team assessed the impact that their program had on student learning, but larger questions on context remain. For instance, to what extent did the setting for DIL education programs (e.g., classroom, online, lab) have an effect

on student learning? Will DIL programs have a greater impact on student learning if their focus is on data that students are responsible for themselves, as opposed to data sets external from their lab and used in a classroom environment?

There are additional opportunities for research on the contextual aspects of data skills that would aid our collective understanding and action on DIL. First, we need to develop a better understanding of students' relationships to the data that they are generating or working with. How do they perceive their role as a producer of data, especially given that they typically have varying degrees of authority over the data that they are working on? Do they view data as merely a means to an end (a recognized scholarly product such as a journal article or a graduate thesis), or do the data hold value for them as a unique information resource in its own right?

Data Information Literacy in the Presence of Standards and Cultural Norms

Ethical participation in communities of learning and scholarship is a key component of ACRL's draft "Framework for Information Literacy for Higher Education." This represents the importance of cultural connectedness in information literacy, an acknowledgment that an individual's perceptions and actions as a producer and consumer of information is informed by, and in turn informs, the larger cultures of practice. This recognition of larger connections was inherent to the DIL project as well, and we incorporated *cultures of practice* into the DIL competencies so that we could both understand connections and impart them to a larger community.

One of the challenges that we encountered was a lack of widely accepted standards or norms in the disciplines of our faculty partners for handling, managing, sharing, and curating research data. Many research communities are becoming more aware of the need to consider research data as an asset that has value outside of the lab in which they were generated. This recognition may be due to the mandates of funding agencies and increasing attention to data validity and access by high-impact journals. Even when a community has launched discussions and is taking action to build knowledge and resources around making data accessible, these efforts may not be widely known beyond those few individuals or institutions taking the initiative. For example, DataONE is an initiative to build infrastructure and develop practices around sharing data sets about "life on earth and the environment that sustains it" that has received a great deal of support from the National Science Foundation (DataONE, n.d., "DataONE vision"). However, the University of Oregon team discovered that the ecology faculty partner had only a minimal awareness of DataONE. The Oregon team took this as an opportunity to introduce students and faculty in the lab group to DataONE. They used materials generated by DataONE to discuss considerations and requirements for sharing data outside of the lab.

This absence of widely adopted norms and practices for data management and curation presents both opportunities and challenges to developing and teaching DIL programs. Librarians can play an important role in connecting researchers to the efforts of communities that are addressing these issues. They can help these efforts take root through DIL education both on home campuses and through the professional associations within disciplines. In instances where community efforts have yet to catch on, librarians can act as a catalyst through education of issues and considerations

for research data. Ultimately, it is up to the discipline to take ownership and action regarding norms and practices surrounding research data. As DIL initiates change and spurs action, we need a better understanding of how best to foster change within communities and how librarians might be effective agents of change.

Data Information Literacy and Preparing Students for the Workplace

Many in the library community realize that information literacy considerations should extend beyond the classroom, into the workplace. This is acknowledged, in part, within ACRL's new draft "Framework for Information Literacy for Higher Education," which advocates for a more contextualized understanding of the information ecologies in which students are immersed. Embedded within this document are statements on preparing students for professional work through developing their ability to work in teams and the need to better understand the information literacy needs of students enrolled in professional degree programs.

The drafts of the new information literacy framework reflect findings from library science research on how and to what extent information literacy is applied in the workplace. A recent report from Project Information Literacy described its findings on how information literacy skills are put to use by students who have joined the workforce (Head, 2012). Researchers sought perspectives from both employers and employees regarding the information-seeking behaviors of recently hired college graduates. Among their findings was the recognition that employers valued information literacy proficiencies in new hires, but that new hires did not always apply these skills effectively. New hires often defaulted to using information that could be found quickly using a search engine rather than using other sources of information or demonstrating persistence in seeking information that would address their needs more effectively. In addition, new hires formed adaptive strategies for addressing their information needs, which were typically trial-and-error. Disconnections between information literacy as taught in academic settings and the information literacies applied or needed in the workplace are found in other studies as well. Weiner (2011) noted that the complex, unstructured, and open-ended nature of the workplace contrasts with the more prescribed and directed atmosphere of education. Lloyd and Williamson (2008) took this observation a step further by noting that the generalizations of research done in educational environments do not necessarily reflect the realities of information needs in the workplace. They found that there is a multitude of possible workplaces, each with its own set of contextualized practices, norms, and expectations that make it difficult for information literacy (as typically defined by librarians) to translate effectively outside of a text-based research environment. Instead of viewing information literacy as a set of skills to master, they argued that educators must see it as a holistic practice that considers environmental context as well as the social and physical experiences of the person with information.

Research into information behaviors and needs in the workplace continues to be an important area for informing information literacy theories and programs. Similar explorations are needed to inform the development of DIL, as many students go into jobs outside of academia. As companies become more and more data driven, new employees need to be equipped to work in data-intensive environments and excel as responsible data stewards. We were not able to address this with much depth in the DIL project; however, we recognized the large impact that the environment, expectations, and needs of employers will play in shaping educational programming surrounding data management and curation. For example, the Carlson and Sapp Nelson team from Purdue worked with students developing software code as a component of their participation in the Engineering Projects in Community Service (EPICS) program. The literature review revealed concerns regarding how code was managed and organized within software companies. This team spoke with a few managers at software firms and heard concerns about similar issues that arose in their needs assessment with the faculty and students in the EPICS program: insufficient documentation, difficulties in handing off code to other teams, and quality assurance challenges. Looking forward, we need to be able to move beyond anecdotes to an objective understanding of how to respond to data management and curation needs in the workplace. Just as the information literacy community has begun to investigate the needs of the workplace to inform program development, the DIL community needs to conduct research into the practices and needs of the workplace with regard to working with data.

FURTHER DEVELOPING DATA INFORMATION LITERACY: A COMMUNITY PERSPECTIVE

The DIL project team held a symposium at Purdue University on September 23 and 24, 2013. The intent of the symposium was to foster a community of practice in research libraries centered on developing and implementing sustainable institutional DIL programs. Although the symposium included presentations from the DIL project teams about the work that they had done, the primary focus was on synthesizing what we learned. This was so that we could provide practical guidance for others to create DIL programs as well as articulate potential roles and responsibilities for librarians in DIL. The symposium included presentations, discussions, exercises, and other activities to engage participants on these topics. The schedule, videos, and materials used at the symposium are openly available at http://docs.lib.purdue .edu/dilsymposium/.

Throughout the symposium, participants were encouraged to consider areas for further development in DIL, both within their own institution and for a broader community of practice. The final session of the symposium was a group discussion on this topic. The themes that emerged from this discussion are presented here.

Raising Awareness

The idea that librarians should provide research data services is taking root in many academic libraries; however, librarians teaching competencies for working with research data is a relatively new development. Teaching DIL skills is a natural fit for librarians as information literacy is a central component of libraries. It is a logical step then to look to what we have learned about how librarians have developed information literacy programs to inform our efforts with data.

It is important to recognize that information literacy was not universally accepted as a role by librarians even after the release of the landmark ACRL's *Presidential Committee on Information Literacy: Final Report* in 1989, which codified the term (ACRL, 1989). Questions arose on the actual meaning of the term *information literacy* and how it was fundamentally different

from other roles such as bibliographic instruction (Snavely & Cooper, 1997). Others pushed back against information literacy, dismissing it as a public relations exercise and a social problem that librarians invented to solve and reclaim relevancy (Foster, 1993). Getting the library community to embrace information literacy required an investment of time and effort on the part of those who saw its potential for libraries and for organizations, such as ACRL, which fostered dialogue at national and international levels. DIL is going through a similar gestation period where definitions, roles, and responsibilities are being discussed and debated in the library community. This will require advocates who can speak passionately and articulate paths toward advancing an awareness of DIL and how librarians could contribute.

Raising awareness of DIL will also require investment and activism at the local level. Our ability to develop DIL programs will depend on our ability to present compelling arguments to colleagues in libraries and on campus. Crafting these arguments will be challenging since time and resources are issues for academic libraries. Librarians may be reluctant to take on this responsibility, especially if it is not an administrative priority for the library.

Most importantly we must raise awareness of DIL among the faculty, students, and administrators at our institutions. We must articulate clear messages that speak to the needs of stakeholders with regard to data. A central tenant of the DIL project was taking the time to know our partners' environments, practices, and challenges in working with data. We believe that this investment enabled us to forge meaningful connections with the faculty and students. Most of the DIL teams are continuing to work with their faculty partners to refine the programs that they developed through this project.

Forming Communities of Practice

As interest and capacity for DIL take root, we need to find ways to come together as practitioners in this emerging field to form a community of practice. Communities of practice facilitate the communication of information, strategies, and experiences, thereby enabling members to learn from each other in ways that foster professional development. They are important for defining common terminologies and concepts, forging standards and best practices, and identifying potential areas of growth.

By design, DIL straddles two existing communities of practice: information literacy and data services. Information literacy communities are well established, having developed multiple communication venues, publications, and other support structures within the library profession and beyond. ACRL's information literacy standards have been widely accepted and adopted. On the other hand, data services is a less established field, though there are some professional conferences and other venues for discussion, such as the International Digital Curation Conference (http://www.dcc.ac.uk/events/interna tional-digital-curation-conference-idcc), IASSIST (http://iassistdata.org/), and the Research Data Access and Preservation Summit (http://www.asis .org/rdap/). We are also seeing an increasing number of publications and initiatives that address data services provided by libraries, such as the *Journal of eScience Librarianship* (http://escholarship.umass med.edu/jeslib/).

The community of practice for data librarians is different from the community supporting information literacy. Although librarians comprise a sizable block of the membership of professional organizations and attendees at conferences, they are joined by information technologists, research faculty, data scientists, and others whose work centers on managing and curating data. Within the larger data community there is much discussion regarding roles and responsibilities and the knowledge and skill sets needed to assume them. Roles in supporting data work that have been discussed include data creators (researchers), data scientists, data managers, data librarians, data stewards, and data publishers (Lyon, 2013; Pryor & Donnelly, 2009; Swan & Brown, 2008). Although roles and responsibilities are in flux, including multiple perspectives in the discussion encourages the inclusion of a wider range of issues and viewpoints.

A foundational goal for those involved in information literacy is to connect with other communities with complementary interests and aims (ACRL, 1989). An example is the 2013 ACRL report, which explored strategic alignments between information literacy and scholarly communication, noting that they have multiple areas of mutual interest and that opportunities exist for collaboration to address these areas (ACRL, 2013). This report also included data literacy as one of the points of intersection.

Today we are in the process of defining DIL. How communities of practice will form around DIL remains to be seen. Will DIL find a home as a component of a larger established community, such as data services or information literacy, or will it develop its own distinct community? Participants at the DIL Symposium expressed an interest in creating a means of communicating and sharing information about resources and developments in DIL with one another through discussion lists or other channels. We did not want to create an additional silo, but rather to grow and sustain connections with the communities from whom we could model and learn. As DIL becomes more recognized and accepted as a role for librarians, those engaged in DIL activities will have to consider what their needs are as a community and if satisfying those needs would mandate a distinct community of practice, a presence within larger communities, or some combination of both.

Developing and Sharing Materials

A component of forming and maintaining communities of practice will be developing a means to share approaches, methods, and materials in ways that those within (and outside of) the community can apply them. At the DIL Symposium, attendees referenced the different types of materials they would like to have to support their work. They spoke about the power of sharing real-life "data horror stories" to raise the interest of faculty and students and motivate them to attend educational programming. Several attendees stated that they would like to have illustrations of how good practices in data management and curation resulted in positive changes for researchers, such as an increased impact for researchers who made their data sets openly available, or specific benefits to a lab. Relevant stories have not been easy to find, but this is changing. For example, figshare.com is posting success stories through social media; Dorothea Salo, a faculty associate at the University of Wisconsin–Madison's School of Library and Information Studies, created a listing of "data horror stories" (https://pinboard.in/u:dsalo/t:horrorstories/); and DataONE collects and posts real-world data issues and challenges (https://notebooks.dataone.org/data-stories/).

Participants in the DIL Symposium mentioned their desire for a clearinghouse of educational materials that could be used to generate ideas or repurposed for use in a different program or environment. We are starting to see organizations create educational materials that support librarians and others in teaching data competencies. The University of Massachusetts

Medical Center, with support from the National Library of Medicine and others, has invested considerable effort in developing data literacy curricula and learning modules that can be adapted (http://library.umassmed.edu/necdmc/index). DataONE has also developed education modules that can be augmented and reused to meet local needs (http://www.dataone.org/education-modules). What is missing is a centralized repository for collecting materials that address a particular need in the DIL community, along with narratives that would provide the context for how these materials were used and the impact they made. Although locally created materials may be less adaptable than materials created with the specific intent of repurposing, they provide insight into the development process, the approaches taken, and lessons learned. This was a primary goal in creating this book: to share the materials that we developed and our experiences in using them.

Professional Development

In this evolving environment we are seeing interest in DIL grow and opportunities for librarians to take initiative expand. It is important for librarians to educate themselves in these new skills so that they can take on DIL education in effective ways. However, the lack of models and curricula can make it difficult for librarians to prepare or respond to the opportunities on their own. The capacity and capabilities of librarians and others involved in teaching DIL or in developing programs will need to advance. Therefore, we must explore what professional development opportunities librarians need to develop their own competencies in data management and curation theories and practices, as well as how to best teach these competencies to students. One possible approach comes from the Society of American Archives (SAA). The SAA offers a certification program to educate its professional workforce on curating born-digital archival materials. Their Digital Archives Specialization (DAS) program (http://www2.archivists.org/prof-education /das) requires participants to complete at least 9 continuing education courses and pass a comprehensive 3-hour examination to receive the 5-year renewable certification.

The DIL competencies were developed with an assumption that they would likely extend beyond the knowledge of a typical librarian, faculty member, or information technology (IT) professional. Launching a comprehensive DIL program requires multiple experts from a variety of units within the institution. One of the topics of conversation at the DIL Symposium was the need to be able to connect with the faculty to understand their needs and to convey what the library community has to offer. Since librarians with subject liaison responsibilities connect with the faculty in the departments they serve, they can be paired with data and/or information literacy librarians to develop and implement DIL programs. However, library liaisons may be uncomfortable with or unable to take on additional responsibilities in an unfamiliar area. Other librarians with specialized expertise such as metadata, managing digital repositories, or in intellectual property can participate in the program. A community of practice in the library (and the larger institution) will likely be needed. Developing such a community that spans the library organization would help reduce the barriers to participation in DIL programs and help ensure that community members' knowledge, skills, and connections are applied appropriately.

A critical component of the success of an internal community of practice is the support received from the library's administration.

Carlson (2013) identified lack of organizational support as one of the barriers to increased engagement of librarians in working with research data. In addition to securing needed approval and resources, library administrators have contacts within the university administration and with others on campus to which other librarians may not have ready access. They may be able to help raise awareness about the DIL activities underway in our libraries to larger audiences to help extend our reach. An important consideration in developing sustainable DIL initiatives is what professional development in DIL might mean for a library as an organization, in addition to individual librarians.

Scoping Data Information Literacy

A set of questions that arose at the DIL Symposium was about the balance between general best practices in working with data and disciplinary standards. Many disciplines do not have accepted standards surrounding the management, publication, and curation of research data. This makes it difficult to develop DIL programs that align with a student's professional identity. Some of the DIL teams relied on established standards, using them as a foundation and adapting them to local practices. Other teams focused on developing solutions based on best practices relating to the DIL competencies generally and then tying them to existing local practices. Furthermore, some of the teams decided to incorporate several of the DIL competencies into their programs, while others chose to focus on just one or two of them. Other factors, such as specific issues and learning objectives to be addressed in the program, weighed heavily in the team's determination of the scope of their program. However, the driving factor in decisions of scope was the amount of student time and access available to each of the teams.

It is not yet clear what, if any, the universal competencies for managing, sharing, and curating data are and how they could be taught to an audience from different research fields. A symposium participant suggested that the 12 DIL competencies could serve as a standard in the same way as ACRL's (2000) *Information Literacy Competency Standards for Higher Education* has. There is some appeal to this idea as the DIL competencies are meant to be widely applicable across multiple fields of study. However, as noted in Chapter 10, the DIL competencies have not been fully vetted beyond the DIL project, so it is premature to anoint them as a standard. It is also worth noting that since *Information Literacy Competency Standards for Higher Education* was published in 2000, several discipline-specific information literacy standards have been created, including standards in science and engineering/technology (ALA/ACRL/STS Task Force, n.d.), anthropology and sociology (ALA/ACRL/ANSS Task Force on IL Standards, 2008), and nursing (Health Sciences Interest Group, 2013).

We found that the DIL competencies were a useful framework for gathering information from faculty and students, for informing the DIL programs that we developed, and for facilitating conversation and comparisons between the five case studies. However, we recognize that as more DIL programs take root there will likely be a need for librarians and others to craft specific or targeted variants of the DIL competencies. These variants may be based on disciplinary practices and needs, but they could also be based on a particular research method, data type, or context—for example, a set of competencies primarily focusing on sharing data outside of the lab. There is certainly plenty of opportunity for exploration

beyond the foundational set of DIL competencies that we employed in the DIL project, provided that we keep the focal point of DIL on addressing the real-world needs of researchers through acquiring a solid understanding of their environments.

Audiences for Data Information Literacy Programs

The DIL Symposium participants raised questions about expanding the target audience for DIL beyond graduate students in the science, technology, engineering, and mathematics (STEM) disciplines and expressed interest in developing DIL programs for undergraduate students. One of the recurring themes from the interviews with faculty was the assumption that graduate students had already had some exposure and experience in working with data prior to their coming to work in the lab—an assumption that was not always correct. DIL programs developed for undergraduate students would prepare them for a data-intensive workplace or facilitate their transition to graduate school, where they may be expected to assume responsibilities for developing, managing, and working with data sets. A particular challenge in developing DIL programs for undergraduates will be tailoring these programs to the undergraduate environment. Unlike graduate students, undergraduates do not typically have responsibilities that pertain to the production of data sets outside of a specialized undergraduate research opportunity program (UROP). Therefore it may be difficult to connect them in meaningful ways to the issues that arise when working with data. However, undergraduates are often consumers of data sets, and developing a DIL program from that perspective may serve as a useful introduction. In addition, many colleges and universities have programs that provide undergraduates with opportunities to engage in research projects, such as Michigan's UROP (http://www.lsa.umich.edu/urop/) or the National Science Foundation's Sponsored Research Experiences for Undergraduates (REU) programs (http://www.nsf.gov/crssprgm/reu/). These programs can serve as potential points of entry for DIL. We expect the interest in undergraduate education on data topics to increase as more attention is given to the value of well-managed data sets and the need for an educated workforce to steward them.

There may be other audiences for DIL programs beyond students. Faculty may benefit from instruction on data management and curation, but that would pose multiple challenges. As busy as graduate students are, faculty are even busier. Faculty are also experts in their fields and may require a much different approach in instruction than students. Furthermore, faculty may have developed familiar routines, even if they acknowledge that these routines are less than ideal. Faculty may be reluctant to commit to changes in working with data if learning curves are deemed too high or the immediate benefit is not clear and does not outweigh the perceived costs of investment. Lab or IT staff who are tasked with administering and stewarding data sets may be motivated to participate in a DIL program.

CONCLUSION

The time is ripe to develop the role of librarians and other information science professionals in delivering DIL programs and to form communities of practice to support these endeavors. The information literacy community can serve as a useful point of reference. In addition, the intersections between data, information literacy, and other communities within the library

field should be recognized and cultivated. Providing DIL programming requires the involvement of individuals with different skill sets and perspectives within (and outside of) libraries.

This chapter identified growth areas for educational programming for graduate students in working with research data. The response that the DIL project has received from faculty, students, administrators, and others at our respective institutions has been phenomenal, and we expect a high level of interest to continue. The DIL project itself ended, but the work that the five DIL teams did at four academic institutions continues to pay dividends as we pursue our individual efforts. This is truly an emerging area of need and one in which librarians can play a significant leadership and teaching role. We look forward to seeing DIL and supporting communities of practice take root in the coming years.

REFERENCES

ACRL Information Literacy Competency Standards Review Task Force (2012, June 2). *Task force recommendations.* Retrieved from http://www.ala.org/acrl/sites/ala.org.acrl/files/content/standards/ils_recomm.pdf

Association of College and Research Libraries (ACRL). (1989). *Presidential Committee on Information Literacy: Final report.* Retrieved from: http://www.ala.org/acrl/publications/white papers/presidential.

Association of College and Research Libraries (ACRL). (2000). *Information literacy competency standards for higher education.* Retrieved from http://www.ala.org/acrl/files/standards/standards.pdf

Association of College and Research Libraries (ACRL). (2013). *Intersections of scholarly communication and information literacy: Creating strategic collaborations for a changing academic environment*. Chicago, IL: Association of College and Research Libraries.

Association of College and Research Libraries (ACRL). (2014). *Information literacy competency standards for higher education* [Draft report]. Retrieved from http://acrl.ala.org/ilstandards/wp-content/uploads/2014/02/Framework-for-IL-for-HE-Draft-2.pdf

ALA/ACRL/Anthropology and Sociology Section Instruction and Information Literacy Committee Task Force on IL Standards. (2008). Information literacy standards for anthropology and sociology students. Retrieved from http://www.ala.org/acrl/standards/anthro_soc_standards

ALA/ACRL/STS Task Force on Information Literacy for Science and Technology. (n.d.). *Information literacy standards for science and engineering/technology*. Retrieved from http://www.ala.org/acrl/standards/infolitscitech

Bell, S. (2013, June 13). Rethinking ACRL's information literacy standards: The process begins [ACRL InsiderBlog]. Retrieved from http://www.acrl.ala.org/acrlinsider/archives/7329

Bruce, C. (2008). *Informed learning*. Chicago, IL: Association of College and Research Libraries.

Bruce, C., Edwards, S., & Lupton, M. (2006). Six frames for information literacy education: A conceptual framework for interpreting the relationships between theory and practice. *ITALICS, 5*(1), 1–18. http://dx.doi.org/10.11120/ital.2006.05010002

Carlson, J. (2013). Opportunities and barriers for librarians in exploring data: Observations from the Data Curation Profile workshops. *Journal of eScience Librarianship, 2*(2): Article 2. http://dx.doi.org/10.7191/jeslib.2013.1042

DataONE (n.d.). What is DataONE? Retrieved from http://www.dataone.org/what-dataone

Foster, S. (1993). Information literacy: Some misgivings. *American Libraries, 24*(4), 344, 346.

Head, A. J. (2012). *Learning curve: How college graduates solve information problems once they join the workplace* [Report]. Retrieved from Project Information Literacy website: http://projectinfolit.org/images/pdfs/pil_fall2012_workplacestudy_fullreport_revised.pdf

Health Sciences Interest Group—Information Literacy Standards for Nursing Task Force. (2013). Information literacy competency standards for nursing. Retrieved from American Libraries Association website: http://www.ala.org/acrl/standards/nursing

Lloyd, A., & Williamson, K. (2008). Towards an understanding of information literacy in context: Implications for research. *Journal of Librarianship and Information Science, 40*(1), 3–12. http://dx.doi.org/10.1177/0961000607086616

Lyon, L. (2013, January). *What is a data scientist?* Presented at the IDCC Symposium, Amsterdam, The Netherlands. Retrieved from http://www.dcc.ac.uk/webfm_send/1128.

Pryor, G., & Donnelly, M. (2009). Skilling up to do data: Whose role, whose responsibility, whose career? *International Journal of Digital Curation, 4*(2), 158–170. http://dx.doi.org/10.2218/ijdc.v4i2.105

Snavely, L., & Cooper, N. (1997). The information literacy debate. *Journal of Academic Librarianship, 23*(1), 9–14. http://dx.doi.org/10.1016/S0099-1333(97)90066-5

Swan, A., & Brown, S. (2008). *The skills, role and career structure of data scientists and curators: An assessment of current practice and future needs* [Technical report to the JISC, University of Southampton]. Retrieved from http://eprints.ecs.soton.ac.uk/16675/

Weiner, S. (2011). Information literacy and the workforce: A review. *Education Libraries, 34*(2), 7–14. Retrieved from http://education.sla.org/wp-content/uploads/2012/12/34-2-7.pdf

CONTRIBUTORS

Camille Andrews is a learning technologies and assessment librarian at Albert R. Mann Library, Cornell University. She is involved in instruction and information literacy–related initiatives as well as assessment for learning outcomes, technologies, and spaces.

Marianne Bracke is an agricultural information sciences specialist and an associate professor at Purdue University. Her research focuses on the changing roles for librarians working with disciplinary faculty in the age of e-science, data curation, and information literacy issues.

Jake Carlson is the research data services manager at the University of Michigan Library. In this role, he explores the application of the theories, principles, and practices of library science beyond the domain of traditional library work. In particular, Carlson seeks to increase the Library's capabilities and opportunities to provide services supporting data-related research. Much of his work is done through direct collaborations and partnerships with research faculty. Carlson is one of the architects of the Data Curation Profiles Toolkit (available at http://datacurationprofiles.org) developed by Purdue University and the University of Illinois at Urbana-Champaign and is the principal investigator of the Data Information Literacy project (http://datainfolit.org), a collaboration between Purdue University, Cornell University, the University of Minnesota, and the University of Oregon.

Michael Fosmire is the head of the Physical Sciences, Engineering, and Technology Division of the Purdue Libraries. He has written and presented extensively on information literacy topics and codeveloped a three-credit graduate/advanced undergraduate–level course in geoinformatics.

Jon Jeffryes is an engineering librarian at the University of Minnesota–Twin Cities. He is the liaison to the biomedical, civil, and mechanical engineering departments and acts as the standards librarian. His research focus is on information literacy integration and the specific information needs and practices of engineering students.

Lisa R. Johnston is an associate librarian at the University of Minnesota–Twin Cities. She leads the libraries' data management and curation initiative and is the codirector of the University Digital Conservancy, the University of Minnesota's institutional repository. Her research areas of focus are scientific data curation, open access models for research publications and data, and educational approaches to training faculty, staff, and students in data information literacy skills and best practices. She has an MLS and a BS in astrophysics, both from Indiana University.

C. C. Miller is the GIS specialist at MIT Lincoln Laboratory. While at Purdue University, he codeveloped and taught a three-credit graduate/advanced undergraduate–level course in geoinformatics, and at MIT he continues to build infrastructure that expands, clarifies, and fosters researcher access to spatial data.

Mason Nichols earned a master's degree from the Brian Lamb School of Communication at Purdue University in 2013. His responsibilities for the DIL project included maintaining the project's Web presence via the wiki and social media channels as well as assisting with transcription, environmental scans, and publications pertaining to the project.

Megan Sapp Nelson is an engineering librarian at Purdue University. She is the liaison to the civil and electrical engineering departments. Her research centers on data management practices of small-scale research projects, particularly those that are multidisciplinary and international in scope.

Dean Walton is a science librarian for biology, geology, and environmental studies and an associate professor at the University of Oregon. He has extensive experience as a field ecologist doing data collection and analysis. This background serves as a foundation for the faculty research support, reference services, and information literacy classes he provides UO clientele.

Brian Westra is the Lorry I. Lokey science data services librarian at the University of Oregon. He works with research faculty and graduate students in the natural sciences to develop sustainable research data management solutions. His research is focused on technology and skill development in support of user-friendly curation activities that can be applied early in the data life cycle.

Sarah J. Wright is the life sciences librarian for research at Cornell University's Albert R. Mann Library. Her interests include data curation and scholarly communication and information trends in the molecular and life sciences disciplines. In addition to serving as liaison for the life sciences community at Cornell, she also participates in Cornell University Library research support service initiatives, including data curation, as a Research Data Management Service Group (RDMSG) consultant.

INDEX

Page numbers in italics refer to tables, boxes, and figures.

Page numbers in italics refer to tables, boxes, and figures.

Page numbers in italics refer to tables, boxes, and figures.

Page numbers in italics refer to tables, boxes, and figures.

Page numbers in italics refer to tables, boxes, and figures.